TRAGEDY ON TRIAL

TRAGEDY ON TRIAL

The Story of the Infamous Emmett Till Murder Trial

RONALD K.L. COLLINS

Foreword
by Congressman Bobby L. Rush

For the Record
by Lonnie G. Bunch, III
Secretary of the Smithsonian Institution

CAROLINA ACADEMIC PRESS

Durham, North Carolina

Library of Congress Cataloging-in-Publication Data

Names: Collins, Ronald K. L., author.
Title: Tragedy on trial : the story of the infamous Emmett Till
    murder trial / Ronald K.L. Collins.
Description: Durham, North Carolina : Carolina Academic Press,
    LLC, [2023] | Includes bibliographical references and index.
Identifiers: LCCN 2023045356 | ISBN 9781531027490 (paperback) |
    ISBN 9781531027506 (ebook)
Subjects: LCSH: Till, Emmett, 1941–1955. | Lynching—
    Mississippi—History—20th century. | African Americans—
    Crimes against—Mississippi. | Racism—Mississippi—History—
    20th century | Trials (Murder)—Mississippi—Sumner.
Classification: LCC HV6465.M7 C65 2023 | DDC 364.1/34—dc23/
    eng/20231003
LC record available at https://lccn.loc.gov/2023045356

CAROLINA ACADEMIC PRESS
700 Kent Street
Durham, North Carolina 27701
(919) 489-7486
www.cap-press.com
Printed in the United States of America

to

KEITH SIPE

a fearless publisher who values the importance of truth in
the marketplace and without whom this account of the evils
of murderous men, the perversion of our legal system,
and the perpetuation of widely accepted falsehoods
might never have been revealed.

and to

JAMIE RASKIN

who passionately supported this project even when he was
busy striving to save our constitutional Republic.

CONTENTS

PART II
Summary of Closing Arguments

PART III
The Verdict

PART IV
Tragedy on Trial

PART V

Justice (Still) Delayed—The Unending and Tortured Story of Emmett Till

Appendix

About the Author

Acknowledgments

Index

Image gallery appears following page 194

The past refuses to lie down quietly.

—DESMOND TUTU (1998)

* * * *

Truth-telling...is...a critical form
of reparation.

—SHERRILYN A. IFILL (2007)

* * * *

The story of Emmett Till refuses to fade
into the background.

—REVEREND WHEELER PARKER (2023)

* * * *

If we're going to continue to move forward as
a nation we cannot allow concerns about discomfort
to displace knowledge, truth or history.

—JUSTICE KETANJI BROWN JACKSON (2023)

* * * *

I cannot imagine our nation did not have
any federal law against lynching when so many
African Americans have been lynched.

—CONGRESSMAN BOBBY RUSH (2020)

* * * *

As our nation strives to become a more
perfect union, we must reckon with America's past,
including the history of racialized violence
that has permeated our nation.

—SENATOR CORY BOOKER (2022)

FOREWORD

BOBBY L. RUSH[†]
Elder & Congressman

Rage. Relived rage! Reinvigorated rage! An omnipresent rage.

Ronald Collins's mind-opening book *Tragedy on Trial: The Infamous Story of the Emmett Till Murder Trial* is a long-overdue and indispensable account. This amazing book throws yet more logs on the raging fire of judicial injustice that still permeates America's legal system. We who have inherited America's racial inequalities and violence in every quarter, especially in its courts, still cling to a very basic yet radical expectation: that justice will "run down like waters, and righteousness like a mighty stream."

Professor Collins, through the powerful imagery of the Mississippi racial madness in a small, rural town courtroom, has shed an illuminating light on the campaign that ruthlessly tried, and almost succeeded, to legitimize inhumanity. With skill and vigor, he has done so by examining the long-lost trial transcript of the two brutish white bastards who murdered Emmett Louis "BoBo" Till, a fourteen-year-old black-skinned, God-gifted, energetic boy. His precious and promising life was stolen and savaged in ways that stunned the world when his courageous mother, Mamie Till-Mobley, proclaimed, "Let the world see what they did to my boy." The world then saw Emmett there in an

---

† Congressman Rush (D-IL, 1992–2022) of Chicago is an African American contemporary of Emmett Till and was the lead House sponsor of the Emmett Till Anti-Lynching Act (discussed in this book), which was signed by President Biden in 2022. He also sponsored the Emmett Till and Mamie Till-Mobley Congressional Gold Medal Act of 2021. The act provides for the posthumous presentation of a Congressional Gold Medal in commemoration of Emmett Till and Mamie Till-Mobley. After it was awarded, the medal was given to the National Museum of African American History and Culture.

open casket, first at the A.A. Rayner & Sons Funeral Home and then at the Roberts Temple Church of God in Christ on Chicago's South Side.

Like so many others, I thought I knew pretty much all there was to know about the Till murder trial and the hasty not-guilty verdict by an all-white male jury. Then I read *Tragedy on Trial* and learned of so many other evils lurking in the transcript. To think that this shocking story might have been lost to time reveals how the story of prejudice must be retold to new generations in truthful and unapologetic ways. Tenacity in the cause of truth is no sin.

In a real sense, America was on trial when the twin evils of white racial superiority and its violence-based racism were put on center stage for the world to see. I have long been mesmerized by the finality of Emmett's death—just imagine the "testimony" of his lifeless body floating in a Mississippi river with only his young black feet protruding above the waters in the hot Mississippi sun. The orchestrated malice of it all is painful to comprehend. The plan was for a watery grave: a 70-pound metal fan tied with barbed wire was fixed around the boy's neck. His body was grossly disfigured and macabre. And yet, in time, an undeniable truth miraculously arose—a truth first sensed by Black people who saw the gruesome photos in *Jet* magazine and other Black-owned publications.

The evil intentions of Emmett's murderers and their accomplices were no match for his lifeless body rising mightily from the dark river. That immortal image has ignited a generation of victims around our nation and throughout the world to stand tall and speak out. My martyred friend and courageous comrade Fred Hampton (Emmett's contemporary generationally and by residence) often said, "You can kill a revolutionary, but you can't kill a revolution."

Emmett Till, that precious underaged and unintentional revolutionary, stirred a civil rights revolution in America and human rights revolutions in Africa, Asia, and South America. His tragedy helped to inspire an ethos that was part and parcel of the Viet Nam anti-war movement and thereafter the women's rights movement. Even today, when we think of heroic and courageous women wed to social justice, we can never overlook the bravery of Mamie Till-Mobley, to whom much indebtedness and tremendous gratitude are owed.

In our human condition, rage cannot and must not exist in a vacuum. Martyrs must not be robbed of the catalytic power of their martyrdom. Martyrs, even the innocent and young like Emmett, are God's instruments for His purposes and His Shalom . . . and our collective well-being.

The racist barbarians who killed Emmett, along with their justice-denying conspiratorial courtroom cohorts, could never have anticipated the immortal outcomes of their dastardly deeds. "But as for you, you meant evil against me; but God meant it for good, in order to bring it about as it is today, to save many people alive." So it is written in Genesis.

We, all freedom-loving people, owe Professor Collins a big, boisterous "Thank You." His book reminds us all of the unfinished work of faithful truth-seekers. And thank God for this book, even as infuriating as it is to read the story of judicial justice gone woefully wrong. The powerful account of *Tragedy on Trial* awakens in us a rapacious rage that has long been the common cause of America's second-class citizens. That same rage is the tributary channel into the river of righteous resistance and our unyielding fight for freedom, justice, and equality.

America is still on trial. Its moral purpose and promise remain unfulfilled. Let us march with justice, step by step into the light of a more moral world. Let us vow to "resist the devil[,] and he will flee from you." This reality is today even more poignant because Emmett's accuser, Carolyn Bryant, recently died without telling the truth in her memoir about Emmett Till's murder. The book you are about to read, however, provides a powerful antidote to that lie and so many others related to the trial and its aftermath—lies that have echoed too long in the halls of time.

Suppressed truth is like a planted seed; it will grow! Thankfully, *Tragedy on Trial* has done its part in helping to uproot the weed of racial injustice.

FOR THE RECORD
TELLING THE UNVARNISHED TRUTH

LONNIE G. BUNCH, III

Secretary of the Smithsonian Institution

One of the core principles at the heart of the Smithsonian's National Museum of African American History and Culture is to tell the "unvarnished truth," a phrase often used by the late Dr. John Hope Franklin, the dean of African American historians. I had first learned about him from my father, who used every meal as a teaching opportunity and once told us about a brilliant historian whose writing had resonated with him in his history course at Shaw College. I am not sure how old I was at the time, but I know it was the only historian my scientist dad ever discussed at the dinner table.

Years later, when I became the museum's founding director, I enlisted John Hope to help me make scholarship a robust, integral part of the museum by chairing its Scholarly Advisory Committee. I felt like my dad was with us as we discussed how the museum should take shape and what it should prioritize. John Hope would always remind me that it must tell the unvarnished truth about our history, to help the nation confront its tortured racial past. He passed away in 2009, but his words continue to live on, engraved in the museum's entrance hall, inspiring anyone who aspires to help the nation live up to its founding ideals. And they continue to embody my desire to use history as a weapon in the fight for justice and equality.

When I found out that legal scholar and educator Ronald K.L. Collins was working on a book to tell a more complete narrative about the trial of Emmett Till's killers, I was excited to learn the unvarnished truth about what really happened. It is a story that had been lost to time, and as is often the case with historical examples of racial terror and injustice, it was also buried by people determined to obscure their own roles in maintaining a system that allowed it to happen.

So much of a historian's job is to uncover truths in the past, no matter how complicated or painful. We do it through intensive scholarship and meticulous research that leads to new evidence, new insights, and new interpretations. James Baldwin wrote in *The Fire Next Time*: "Time reveals the foundations on which any kingdom rests and eats at those foundations, and it destroys doctrines by proving them to be untrue." I would argue that more than time is necessary to destroy doctrines; it also takes a willingness to challenge conventional wisdom and the fortitude to uncover the unvarnished truth.

With *Tragedy on Trial*, Professor Collins does that vital work, shedding valuable light on one of the most consequential moments of the past century. This interrogation of our nation's complicated past examines how the historical record gets obfuscated, how myths are fixed into the public consciousness, and how justice has often been denied by the very institutions meant to secure it.

Although the murder of Emmett Till is one of the most pivotal events in American history, it was also sadly unremarkable, typifying the casual destruction of Black bodies in the Jim Crow South. In the crucible of racial terror in 1950s Mississippi (a state so tethered to its slaveholding past that it did not ratify the Thirteenth Amendment until 1995), Emmett's lynching could have been just another Black boy killed. Another false accusation of sexual impropriety used as a pretext for racist violence. Another statistic. Were it not for Emmett's mother, Mamie Till-Mobley (Bradley at the time), those in power may have been able to act as so many others had before, protected by a racist system and shrouded in obscurity.

Mrs. Till-Mobley's refusal to allow the nation to look away, despite the incomparable pain of the death of her child, changed the country forever. When she chose to have an open-casket funeral at Chicago's Roberts Temple Church of God in Christ and allowed pictures to be taken of Emmett's disfigured body, it became the catalyst that reignited the civil rights movement.

To that point, much of the work done in the fight for civil rights had been legal, involving taking arguments all the way to the Supreme

Court. But milestone victories like *Brown v. Board of Education*, although vital, were not enough to counteract the entrenched racism of the South. Indeed, they only served to spur violent backlash—including Emmett Till's murder.

When Black World War II veterans returned home, they attempted to change things to reflect the freer and fairer lives they had experienced overseas, but these efforts were carried out largely at a local level. Emmett's murder was the first event to really serve as a national wakeup call and galvanize people. It demonstrated that people on the ground must confront the evils of segregation head-on and that all people of conscience must be active participants in changing the country.

A generation of civil rights activists pointed to it as the clarion call to act, including Rosa Parks, who later told Mrs. Till-Mobley she was thinking of Emmett when she refused to relinquish her seat on a Montgomery bus; the Greensboro Four, who sat to demand service at a segregated North Carolina Woolworth's; the Freedom Riders of the Student Nonviolent Coordinating Committee, including a young John Lewis; and Martin Luther King, Jr., who delivered his "I Have a Dream" speech on the anniversary of Emmett's death.

Emmett Till resonates with me personally on many levels: as a Black man, as a father, and as a historian. When I was contemplating the content of the National Museum of African American History and Culture, I knew Emmett's story must be central to it, not just because it was a tragedy that became a historic movement, but also because I had an important promise to keep.

During my time at the Chicago Historical Society, I had the great fortune to meet Mrs. Till-Mobley. She was gracious in spending time with me, allowing me to hear firsthand what she had gone through and recounting the memories of her son. Just before her death in 2003, she spoke to me about how she had carried the burden of Emmett's death and the meaning of his loss for nearly fifty years. She was tired. She wondered who would carry that burden of history and the weight of his memory when she was gone. I knew it was a direct appeal to me and to the entire historical community to ensure that Emmett and countless other victims of racial terror would never be forgotten.

Her words echoed in my mind during the creation of the National Museum of African American History and Culture. The challenge before me was how to carry out Mrs. Till-Mobley's wishes in a way that not only respected Emmett's life but also spoke to the broader importance of what he meant to the nation.

The potential for a profound tribute to the lives and legacies of Emmett and Mrs. Till-Mobley came in 2005, when the Department of Justice reopened the murder case and disinterred Emmett's body, later reburying him in a new casket. The original was to be placed in storage, but unfortunately it was improperly stored in a shed and fell into disrepair.

When I found out about it, I reached out to Emmett's cousin, Simeon Wright. The family asked me if we would like to take the casket into the museum's collections to preserve it and help tell Emmett's story. I was unsure whether it was appropriate to do so. The last thing I wanted to do was create a ghoulish spectacle that stripped Emmett of his humanity. Ultimately, in conversations with senior staff, we decided the artifact was too important to leave out of the first national museum devoted to viewing America through an African American lens.

Emmett's casket has proven to be one of the museum's most powerful and profound exhibits. Soon after the museum opened, I witnessed its effect in action. A young Black woman was overcome with emotion as she stood next to the exhibit, absorbing the magnitude of this simple casket with a glass top that had revealed racism's ugly truth for the world to see.

An older white man approached and asked if he could cry with her. She hesitated but agreed, and they locked arms and stood in silence, two strangers crying together for the unthinkable murder of a child decades before. It was a moment of unguarded, shared humanity unlike any I had experienced. I think Mrs. Till-Mobley would have appreciated her son's ability to help visitors learn, heal, and grow together.

That is the power and promise of an honest telling of history. It allows us to look at our past in a richer and more meaningful way. It allows us to bring people together to understand the human impact of moments in time. And it allows us to gain a better perspective on our present by contextualizing where we have been and how we got where we are today. In so doing, we gain the tools of understanding to build a better-shared future.

I have always felt museums have an important role to play in addressing social and racial injustice by defining reality and giving hope. By seeking the unvarnished truth. But that duty does not belong only to cultural institutions or historians; it is the responsibility of all institutions dedicated to the truth.

Black newspapers have always been an important voice in the chorus calling for equal rights. Pioneering editors like Robert Abbot of the *Chicago Defender*, William Monroe Trotter of the *Boston Guardian*, Charlotta Bass of the *California Eagle*, and Jefferson Lewis Edmonds of the Los Angeles *Liberator* realized that as journalists, as guardians of a community seeking the equality central to the American promise, they had a sacred responsibility to act. The Black press continues to provide its readers with information often ignored by mainstream papers, confronting the systems that help perpetuate racism.

As *Tragedy on Trial* demonstrates, the Black press was a vital witness to history during the trial of Emmett Till's murderers. The most obvious contribution is the horrific photograph David Jackson of *Jet* magazine took of Emmett in his casket, battered beyond recognition, a surrealistic approximation of a face that would haunt any person of conscience.

Although no mainstream newspaper would carry the gruesome picture, *Jet's* editor John Johnson made the courageous decision to do so, and other African American publications followed suit.

Tragedy on Trial shows how vital the Black press was in keeping an accurate record of the events of the trial, pointing out other witnesses who were not called to testify and may have been connected to Emmett's kidnapping and murder, and debunking the myriad lies and half-truths in William Bradford Huie's popular accounts of the event that have stubbornly persisted for decades. With their contemporaneous reporting on the trial, the Black press also allowed Professor Collins to piece together the closing arguments that were inexplicably omitted from the trial transcript.

In the prologue below, Professor Collins asks, "Where do we turn to for the truth?" Where, indeed? We live in an age of increasingly brazen efforts to rewrite history, to pretend slavery was beneficial to the enslaved, to ban curricula that discuss race, and to remove books from libraries. It is nothing new, of course, this effort to maintain a founding myth sanitized and stripped of its ugliest parts.

Challenges to the entrenched power structure from the disenfranchised have always been met with a reactionary backlash; the greatest pushes to rewrite history books and build statues to venerate the Confederacy came not directly after the Civil War but in eras where Black people were asserting their rights as human beings—during the post-Reconstruction Jim Crow era and during the civil rights movement.

Now, as a backlash to the grassroots movement and political campaigns in the wake of George Floyd's murder, we see the same kinds of reactionary efforts that aim to whitewash American history.

So, to answer Professor Collins's question, the truth must come from historians and educators, legislators and corporate leaders, artists and writers, parents and students—in short, it must be a collective effort by all who recognize that an educated citizenry is vital to our democracy and that we cannot simply erase the distasteful parts of our history.

When reading about the concerted attempts to change the narrative of the trial, I think of the oft-quoted line from the Jimmy Stewart western *The Man Who Shot Liberty Valance*: "When the legend becomes fact, print the legend." We owe it to ourselves as a nation not to simply accept what we have been told about the past. In fact, I would argue that we do a disservice to our children and grandchildren if we gloss over the reality of our history in favor of a comforting fiction.

The Emmett Till story is an example of how history changes depending on the narrator, how perception can become reality, and how only through an honest appraisal of the evidence can we piece together what truly happened.

One of my life's great privileges was getting to know John Lewis, the civil rights icon and long-time congressman who was instrumental in getting the National Museum of African American History and Culture built. I attended some of his bipartisan pilgrimages to milestones of the civil rights movement, including one to Mississippi, where we stood at the site of Emmett Till's murder. It was a poignant and emotional moment, but Congressman Lewis helped ease the pain by reminding us how Emmett had been a powerful rallying cry for justice.

As we rode the buses back to Alabama where the tour had originated, we stopped in a rest area, and Congressman Lewis, Congressman Steny Hoyer, and I went into the restroom. Sadly but unsurprisingly, racist comments were scrawled on the walls, a reminder that the hate residing in people's hearts is not as easily changed as laws.

That reality was also evident in the bullet-riddled sign that marked the site where Emmett's body was pulled out of the Tallahatchie River. In 2021, the Smithsonian's National Museum of American History displayed one of several historical riverside markers made and replaced by the Emmett Till Memorial Commission. Due to repeated acts of vandalism, the latest version had to be constructed with bulletproof steel. But no matter how hard those with a vested interest in erasing Emmett Till and Mamie Till-Mobley try, whether with bullets or laws, they will never be able to do so. Their memory and legacy belong to the world.

This year, 2023, is indicative of the dichotomy inherent in the Emmett Till case. In one respect, Carolyn Bryant's death closed out one of the most infamous chapters in American history, though it offered no satisfying resolution. She made the accusation that set the deadly chain of events in motion, and despite the discovery of a 1955 arrest warrant for kidnapping, she was never charged. Neither she; her husband, Roy; his half-brother, J. W. Milam; nor anyone else involved in the conspiracy and connected to the crime ever faced true justice.

In many respects, though, Emmett's legacy is more secure than ever. A year after the release of a wonderful film about Emmett and Mamie and the passage and signing of the Emmett Till Anti-Lynching Act, President Biden declared three historic sites to be protected memorials: the Roberts Temple Church where Emmett's body was displayed (now the Emmett Till and Mamie Till-Mobley and Roberts Temple National Monument); Graball Landing, where his body was discovered; and the Tallahatchie County Second District Courthouse, the setting of *Tragedy on Trial*.

What were places of pain, of desperate attempts to thwart justice and rewrite history, will now forever stand as testaments to the resilience of a mother who demanded justice for her son and helped the nation leap forward in its long search for redemption.

Meanwhile, the names Roy Bryant and J. W. Milam and Carolyn Bryant will be mere footnotes in history and share in the ignominy and anonymity of other racists shunned by decent people who recognize the corrosive effects of hatred and strive for a better nation.

As *Tragedy on Trial* proves, there is a long list of heroes who deserve our attention, not just Mamie and Emmett but all who, like Professor Collins, are dedicated to revealing the unvarnished truth and perfecting our union. My deepest gratitude to them all.

PROLOGUE

THE UNJUST TRIAL AND ITS DECEPTIVE AFTERMATH

Time does not turn backward, but memory does. When memory is erased, however, the past dies with it. The evil of murder ends a life and thus ends the prospect of its future, while the evil of the suppression of truth destroys the memorial record of that life. That is why history is so important. Properly understood, it can serve as a moral yardstick when it comes to acts wrongfully committed and unjustly perpetuated.

No moral imperative can, however, be grounded in a lie, especially when that lie uproots the very possibility of understanding the past. Of course, past wrongs do not easily invite present reconciliations. That all-too-human failing helps to explain why there has been deep-seated resistance to fully and openly acknowledge the troubling truths of racial injustice in America. That mindset closets the evils of the past; sometimes it even condemns those who expose such evils as being "un-American." Yet if the *true* past remains concealed or denied, then the very idea of equal justice rings hollow, if only because so much of the past determines the future.

Only that which has had life can have a history. There is no history of nothing. By that logic, when life ceases, its history often ceases with it. What remains is memory. Hence, to move forward, we must first look backward.

* * * *

Memory cuts deep but in different ways depending on who is on the receiving end of its blade. On the one hand, "the memory of lynching," as Sherrilyn Ifill has stressed, "is indelibly engraved on the collective psyche of blacks."[1] On the other hand, as Roy Bryant complained, "Emmett Till is dead. I don't know why he just can't stay dead."[2] Till's afterlife tormented Bryant, one of the two men charged with the boy's murder. It was thirty years later, he emphasized, and people were still hounding him about the case. By his mindset, he had reason to be surprised. After all, a jury of his white male peers had found Bryant and his half-brother accomplice, J. W. Milam, "not guilty."

Of course, everyone in that Tallahatchie courtroom knew otherwise, even though the five defense lawyers did their devil's-advocate best to legitimatize the murderous malice in the minds of the two men who took Emmett Till's life. That evil, that "crime so unjust" as Bob Dylan tagged it in song,[3] could not, and did not, die. The poet Langston Hughes did not let it pass in 1955[4] nor did Congressman John Lewis let it pass in 2020. His words: "Emmett Till was my George Floyd. He was my Rayshard Brooks, Sandra Bland, and Breonna Taylor."[5] The evil of the Till tragedy persists for at least two reasons: because justice was first denied in the courtroom in 1955, and because even now, sixty-nine years later as of the time of this writing, the full truth of what occurred remains either undisclosed or unclear.

The popular account of the Till murder trial largely begins and ends with the statement that "an all-white male jury" rendered a predictable verdict after a brief deliberation. While there is surely truth there, such snap judgments leave out much that is both significant and revealing. For example:

---

1. Sherrilyn Ifill, *Confronting the Legacy of Lynching in the 21st Century: On the Courthouse Lawn*, Boston: Beacon Press (2018), p. 143. See also *ibid.*, p. xvi ("Perhaps it is the gruesome nature of the lynching ritual act itself that becomes indelibly etched onto the collective psyche of a black community for generations. . . .").

2. Quoted in Mamie Till-Mobley & Christopher Benson, *Death of Innocence: The Story of the Hate Crime that Changed America*, New York: One World/Random House (2004), p. 261. The irony, of course, is that the "perpetrators of this violence [have long taken] pride in their terrorism." Sherrilyn Ifill, *Confronting the Legacy of Lynching*, p. x (foreword by Bryan Stevenson).

3. Bob Dylan, "The Death of Emmett Till," Warner Bros. Inc. (1963).

4. Langston Hughes, "Langston Hughes Wonders Why No Lynching Probes," *Chicago Defender*, October 1, 1955, reproduced in *The Lynching of Emmett Till*, ed. Christopher Metress, Charlottesville, VA: University of Virginia Press (2002), pp. 124–27.

5. John Lewis, "Together, You Can Redeem the Soul of Our Nation," *New York Times*, July 30, 2020 (posthumous op-ed).

- What of the efforts of the African American press to ferret out the full truth of the crimes?
- And what of the courageous efforts of an African American doctor to locate and then safeguard witnesses?

Then there were those directly involved with the trial:

- What of the two sheriffs who played key roles in the case?
- How was the jury selected and by whom?
- Who were the lawyers, and what role did they play?
- What of the judge, and how important was his role?
- Who were the witnesses, and how credible were they?
- And what of the role played by Emmett Till's mother as a witness for the prosecution?

And then there is the matter of what never became part of the evidentiary record of the trial:

- What of the missing witnesses and their stories?
- What of the evidence excluded from the trial and what the jury knew of that evidence?
- And just how important was the procedural posture of the case—the fact that the defendants, though originally charged with kidnapping and murder, were tried *only* for murder?

Though the answers to those questions are central to any meaningful account of the Till tragedy, they have too long remained largely outside of the popular purview.

It is appalling but true: the Till story is layered with lies, some of which have gained staying power by virtue of their repetitiveness over decades. Which raises the question: Where does one turn to for the truth? From newspaper, magazine, and television accounts from before the trial? From accounts of the murder trial itself? From press accounts that appeared shortly after the trial? From interviews with some of those then involved in the matter? From books? From government investigations and reports? From documentaries? How do we best approach the full truth?

* * * *

The Emmett Till murder trial revealed much about what occurred when a young boy from Chicago visited his cousins in Mississippi to pick cotton by day and play in the evening. Even so, the *whole* truth about what occurred on August 28, 1955, was not on display for all to hear and remember. Since the trial was for *murder* and that crime alone, the *kidnapping* charge fell to the wayside until after the trial when a second grand jury would consider that matter. Still, evidence was tendered in the murder trial that bore directly on the question of kidnapping. That kidnapping was prompted by what had been told to the defendants about Till's alleged exchanges with the spouse of one of the defendants along with what came to be known as his "wolf whistle."[6] When word got out, it sparked fires of white male rage fueled by a culture of racism. Men with combustible tempers, men with guns, and men with no consciences sped into homicidal action of a most foul kind. Two were arrested, tried for murder, and then acquitted. The first official account of those historic moments of race and law in America was recorded by James T. O'Day, the trial court reporter.

To many, the trial transcript of *State of Mississippi v. J. W. Milam and Roy Bryant* is unknown. For them, it is one of those dead documents weighed down by 62,551 words of legalese. After the trial, the transcript seemed to vanish, a crucial document lost to history. A copy, however, did remain in the possession of J. J. Breland, one of the defense lawyers. Around 1962, a graduate student named Hugh Stephen Whitaker "obtained his copy of the transcript, a thick sheaf of onionskin with a binder clip, from Breland, after interviewing him for hours."[7]

As fate would have it, however, even that rare copy was destroyed in a "basement flood in the 1970s."[8] For decades thereafter, no complete

---

6. See Devery Anderson, *Emmett Till: The Murder That Shocked the World and Propelled the Civil Rights Movement*, Jackson, MS: University Press of Mississippi (2015), pp. xvi, 363; Alexis Rogers, "The Living Truth: The Emmett Till Story Special," WishTV.Com, Indianapolis, December 27, 2022, (Wheeler Parker: "It was a wolf whistle. . . . It was [the sort of thing that was] way, way out of line. . . . We knew he had violated a serious law—I mean a death-threatening law."), https://www.wishtv.com/news/local-news/the-living-truth-the-emmett-till-story-special/.

7. Shaila Dewan & Ariel Hart, "FBI Discovers Trial Transcript in Emmett Till Case," *New York Times*, May 18, 2005, sect. A, p. 14.

8. Anderson, *Emmett Till*, pp. 325, 338, 353.

copy of the transcript was available, though various portions of it had been quoted in newspaper articles from the time. Very few people even noticed its public absence for nearly a half-century.

Finally, the transcript resurfaced in September 2004 when FBI agents, serving under the direction of Dale Killinger, discovered a badly faded copy owned by a man who lived in Biloxi, Mississippi—his father, Lee McGarrh Sr., testified as a character witness for J. W. Milam, one of the defendants. The copy, described as "faint and barely legible, [was then] the only publicly known record of the trial. . . . [At the time], Robert J. Garrity, Jr., the FBI's special agent in charge in Mississippi, said . . . that the newly found transcript would allow investigators to review the testimony of witnesses who are now dead and also compare living witnesses' accounts today with what they said in court 50 years ago. . . . The newfound copy was first reported . . . by the *Clarion-Ledger,* the Jackson daily newspaper. Mr. Garrity described it as a 'copy of a copy of a copy.' 'It was in pretty poor shape,' he said, 'so we had to go through it line by line, word by word, and retype it.' . . . It took two weeks for two clerks to transcribe the entire document, except for [two] missing pages."[9] Though a copy of the transcript was available in the archives at Ohio State University before 2007, it did not receive real public notice until 2007. Incredibly, the court reporter did not transcribe the closing arguments of the prosecution and defense lawyers (recreated in Chapters 9, 10, and 11). Despite its limitations, the trial transcript is the longest primary document from the time.

In the three hundred fifty or so pages of this transcript[10]—the apparent last of the surviving primary documents—lives the most extensive in-real-time historical record of the murder, replete with truths, half-truths, untruths, and unfinished facts waiting to be explored. Some have mined the transcript for a few facts, others plucked it for attention-grabbing quotes, and biographers have referred to it to explain or refute this or that claim. But no one has ever published and analyzed the

---

9. Dewan & Hart, "FBI Discovers Trial Transcript"; Anderson, *Emmett Till,* pp. 324–26; Timothy B. Tyson, *The Blood of Emmett Till*, New York: Simon & Schuster (2017), p. 4. Lee McGarrh Sr.'s name was "redacted from the FBI report for privacy purposes." Anderson, *Emmett Till,* p. 471 n. 42. See also Chapter 2 note 14, *infra*.

10. There were also several items reproduced in Clenora Hudson Weems's *Plagiarism—Physical & Intellectual Lynchings: An Emmett Till Continuum* (2007) and also preserved in the William Huie papers at Ohio State University Libraries.

transcript *in toto*. What was true? What was false? What was omitted? Who and what were left out of the story? What do we know about the lawyers for the prosecution? What of the defense lawyers and the arguments they advanced? What did the evidence offered during the trial reveal about the true culprits of this miscarriage of justice, the ones who preordained the result that a bigoted jury desired? What was reported after the trial that either supported or refuted what was set out in the trial transcript? And how does all of this fit into the story of the murder that helped launch a movement?[11]

Over time, people with often essentially the same motive attempted to erase much of the Emmett Till tragedy and murder trial from the memory of recorded history—for example, the attempted quick burial in Mississippi (to prevent national notice), the cotton gin wheel wrapped with barbed wire around Emmett's neck (which remains lost), the missing witnesses (some of whom never spoke fully and truthfully), the long-lost trial transcript (with its curiously missing closing arguments and exhibits), the initial renovation of the courtroom (which changed its appearance considerably), the mutilation or destruction of Till landmark signs (which continues to this day), and more. Thankfully, however, enough has been preserved to reconstruct what happened.

* * * *

What of the *safety* of the witnesses for the prosecution, including Mamie Till-Bradley (Mamie's legal name before her remarriage to Gene Mobley in 1957), and the African American press covering the trial? Before, during, and after the murder trial, their safety had to be guaranteed. For the most part, that was in the hands of one man: Dr. Theodore R. Mason "T.R.M." Howard, a well-to-do medical doctor, noted civil rights leader, and a major figure in the Black community in Mississippi.[12] They found needed shelter and safety at his Mound Bayou

---

11. See Davis W. Houck & Matthew W. Grindy, *Emmett Till and the Mississippi Press*, Jackson, MS: University of Mississippi Press (2008), pp. 154–55 (noting how the civil rights movement evolved); Dave Tell, *Remembering Emmett Till*, Chicago: University of Chicago Press (2019), pp. 121–25 (noting the need to also recognize prior events such as the Montgomery bus boycott and the *Brown v. Board* ruling).

12. See David T. Beito & Linda Royster Beito, *T.R.M. Howard: Doctor, Engineer, Civil Rights Pioneer*, Oakland, CA: Independent Institute (2018), pp. 129–88; David T. Beito &

estate, which was guarded by men with guns. His home was also the command center for gathering information about what happened and planning how to proceed.[13]

Well before the court trial, Mamie had already seen enough to suppose that the evil that seized her son ("Bobo") would be compounded by attempts for a quick and invisible burial in Mississippi.[14] So she had her son's body collected and then shipped from Greenwood, Mississippi, to Chicago; it cost $2,300! Once *The City of New Orleans* train arrived at Central Station at Twelfth Street, Mamie was there to meet it, as was *Jet* reporter Simeon Booker and photographer David Jackson, among others. They "unloaded the box that [carried Emmett's body] and placed it on a flatbed truck, a simple train yard wagon. . . ." As the cameras kept clicking, Mamie kept screaming. When the casket was opened, it emitted a "most terrible odor." "Oh, God. Oh, God. My only boy," she cried.[15] They all proceeded to A. A. Rayner's funeral home. There, with a combination of resilience and determination, Mamie's eyes bore witness to the badly mangled body that was her son: "I stood a long time looking at that body," she recalled.[16] What Mamie saw was mirrored in the chilling close-up photos Jackson took of the boy's dis-

---

Linda Royster Beito, *Black Maverick: T.R.M. Howard's Fight for Civil Rights and Economic Power*, Champaign, IL: University of Illinois Press (2009), pp. 115–69.

13. Till-Mobley & Benson, *Death of Innocence,* pp. 152–53, 156, 167, 168, 170, 172; James L. Hicks, "White Reporters Double-crossed Probers Seeking Lost Witnesses," *Cleveland Call & Post*, October 15, 1955 (rediscovering witnesses and how to release the story).

14. Till-Mobley & Benson, *Death of Innocence,* pp. 129–32. "Sheriff Strider ordered Moses [Wright] to bury Emmett in Mississippi without delay." Simeon Booker with Carol McCabe Booker, *Shocking the Conscience: A Reporter's Account of the Civil Rights Movement*, Jackson, MS: University of Mississippi Press (2013), p. 59. Sheriff Strider had also seen to it that there would be no autopsy. Thanks to Crosby Smith's alerting Sheriff George Smith and to the latter's insistence, Mamie was alerted and the body was transported to Chicago. See Simeon Wright with Herb Boyd, *Simeon's Story: An Eyewitness Account of the Kidnapping of Emmett Till*, Chicago: Lawrence Hill Books (2011), p. 65; Crosby Smith, "Forgotten Witness to a Mississippi Nightmare," *Negro History Bulletin*, vol. 38, no. 1 (December 1972–January 1975), pp. 320, 323.

15. Till-Mobley & Benson, *Death of Innocence,* p. 132. See also Mattie Smith Colin, "Mother's Tears Greet Son Who Died Martyr," *Chicago Defender*, September 10, 1955, p. 1 (providing a detailed account of Mamie Bradley's receiving Emmett's body at the Illinois Central Station).

16. Mattie Smith Colin & Robert Elliott, "Grieving Mother Meets Body of Lynched Son," *Chicago Defender* September 10, 1955, p. 5.

figured face. Those iconic images[17] came into sharper focus when she arranged for an open-casket memorial service, in clear contravention of release orders by Mississippi officials that the casket not be opened.[18]

Meanwhile, on September 5, while Till's body lay in repose, an eighteen-member, all-white, male grand jury heard testimony in the Till murder case. District Attorney Gerald Chatman presented his evidence for the prosecution. The witnesses included Tallahatchie County Sheriff Henry Clarence "H.C." Strider, Tallahatchie County Deputy Sheriff Garland Melton, Sheriff George Smith, and Leflore County Deputy Sheriff John Cothran. Moses Wright and his son, Simeon, were on hand but did not testify. Among other things, there was conflicting testimony about the identity of the body. The testimony concluded at 4:00 p.m.[19]

The next day, a service was held at the Roberts Temple Church of God in Christ in Chicago. "Let the people see what they did to my boy,"[20] Mamie Till-Bradley proclaimed to the world. Thousands in Chicago peered into the open coffin revealing Emmett's grotesquely disfigured face. As Reverend Jesse Jackson put it so well nearly a half-century later, "Mamie turned a crucifixion into a resurrection."[21] Emmett Till was buried at the Burr Oak Cemetery in Alsip, Illinois, on September 6, 1955.

---

17. See Noah Adams, "Emmett Till and the Impact of Images: Photos of Murdered Youth Spurred Civil Rights Activism," National Public Radio, *Morning Edition*, June 23, 2004, http://www.npr.org/templates/story/story.php?storyId=1969702.

18. This was a condition of the release of the body to Emmett's mother. The casket was locked and had a State of Mississippi seal on it. "Promises had been made just to get the body out of Mississippi," said the Chicago funeral home director, A.A. Rayner. He added, "'I had to sign papers, the undertaker had to sign papers, your relatives had to sign papers." Booker & Booker, *Shocking the Conscience,* pp. 59–60.

19. Anderson, *Emmett Till,* p. 61; Elliott J. Gorn, *Let the People See: The Story of Emmett Till,* New York: Oxford University Press (2018), pp. 72–73, 316 n. 6.

20. Houck & Grindy, *Emmett Till and the Mississippi Press,* p. 36 (citing *Biloxi Daily Herald*). Despite the Chicago funeral home director's "promise not to touch up the body, the mortician stitched the eyelids shut, removed the tongue, closed the mouth and refastened the back of the skull using some coarse thread." Booker & Booker, *Shocking the Conscience,* p. 62.

21. Jesse L. Jackson Sr., foreword to Till-Mobley & Benson, *Death of Innocence,* p. xiii. In 2023, the church was designated as a national monument.

That same day, Roy Bryant and J. W. Milam were indicted by a Tallahatchie County grand jury on charges of kidnapping and murder.[22]
When arraigned, they pleaded not guilty and remained in jail until the
trial began. "Judge Curtis M. Swango would preside, having insisted
that the trial be held during the court's current session, due to expire
shortly, rather than in the next session in the spring." What that meant,
and as Simeon Booker of *Jet* magazine realized early on, was that the
prosecution would be without "either the opportunity or resources . . .
to establish an adequate case."[23] Consequently, both time and the ob-
structive actions of Sheriff Strider made the prosecution's task a Sisy-
phean one.

* * * *

The murder trial[24] of the two defendants commenced at the Second
District Tallahatchie County Courthouse in Sumner. Scores of white
men lingered in front of the courthouse with only a few people of color
watching on, but at a safe distance. Compared with what was being reported in the Black press, the trial was in many respects a sanitized
version of what actually happened.

If you take a civil rights history tour through the South, you will
likely come upon the courthouse where the Till murder trial occurred
between September 19th and the 23rd of 1955. The courthouse is located on North Court Street in Sumner, Mississippi, next to a towering
Confederate statue with a chiseled tribute to "our heroes," in memory

---

22. See "Grand Jury Indicts Men with Kidnapping, Murder," *Greenwood Commonwealth*, September 6, 1955, p. 1; "Wolf Whistle Pair Indicted on Murder Count," *Memphis
Press-Scimitar*, September 6, 1955, p. 7. According to one report, "Bryant was implicated
in the death of a Negro who was beaten and left in a ditch last year [1954]." Mattie S. Colin
& Robert Elliott, "Mother Waits in Vain for Her 'Bo,'" *Chicago Defender*, September 3,
1955, 1.

23. Booker & Booker, *Shocking the Conscience*, pp. 62, 63 ("All the parties concerned—the judge, the jury, and the accused—knew that a verdict of not guilty was certain."). Hugh Stephen Whitaker, "A Case Study in Southern Justice: The Emmett Till
Case" (MA thesis, Graduate School of Florida State University, August 1963), p. 147
(statement based on "interviews with all concerned").

24. As discussed later, the defendants were originally charged with both kidnapping
and murder, but they were only tried for murder; after the trial they were brought before
a grand jury in another jurisdiction for kidnapping.

of "the cause that never failed." If the trial were ever to be re-enacted,[25] and on some regular basis, in the original courtroom and based on the trial transcript, one could see in the mind's eye Judge Curtis M. Swango Jr. presiding in the front center of a wildly overcrowded courtroom. The judge banged his gavel as the two defendants—J. W. Milam (six feet, two inches tall, and 235 pounds) and Roy Bryant (five feet, four inches tall, and 160 pounds)—were each joined by their young sons and accompanied by their wives. Many Black Americans came to watch the trial, though only fifty were admitted into the sweltering, humid courtroom with temperatures rising above one hundred degrees. The open windows did little to clear the haze of cigarette smoke. Fans swirled to offer only a modicum of relief. Playing to the crowd, vendors hawked soda pops and lunch boxes during court recesses, but only to whites. Meanwhile, the Milam and Bryant boys were rowdy as they chased one another while playing with their toy guns. Thus did the judicial case begin.

From that same conceptual perch, one can imagine seeing Judge Swango drinking Coca-Cola as the lawyers selected jurors and the three prosecutors and five defense lawyers huddled at nearby desks. The proceeding drew national attention; the national mainstream media and press correspondents included the likes of John Chancellor, Murry Kempton, and David Halberstam. As the trial proceeded, Mississippi and Louisiana radio reporters scurried around to phone in their on-the-spot stories—"Stay tuned to hear the latest from Sumner on the trial."[26] Off to the side, the far side, a small card table marked the segregated spot for the Black reporters.

Moses Wright (Till's great-uncle) was the first witness called by the prosecution. He sat in a chair to the judge's right. It was from there, in what proved to be a historic moment captured by a camera, that Wright

---

25. In February 2022, the DuSable Museum of African American History hosted "Trial in the Delta: The Murder of Emmett Till," a ninety-minute dramatic rendition of the trial. The live event was also video-recorded. Then in October of the same year, the Mosaic Theater Company in Washington, D.C., presented the premier of "The Till Trilogy" by Ifa Bayeza and directed by Talvin Wilks. One of three plays was on the Till murder trial: "That Summer in Sumner."

26. John N. Herbers with Anne Farris Rosen, *Deep South Dispatch: Memoir of a Civil Rights Journalist*, Jackson, MS: University of Mississippi Press (2018), p. 58.

stood and pointed an accusatory finger at the defendant Roy Bryant. When the "new witnesses were ushered in, verbal clashes broke out between civil rights advocates and the locals. The judge could barely keep order, and Sheriff Strider barked commands at the crowd."[27] The tension grew as Willie Reed, one of the surprise witnesses, testified that he heard screaming and whipping coming from the shed where Emmett was being held.

And then there are the images of the time when Carolyn Bryant rested her head on her husband Roy's shoulder after she testified (outside the presence of the jury) about allegedly being touched and later whistled at by Till. Sheriff H. C. Strider added to the fabricated tale when he rendered his perjured and all-too-defendant-friendly testimony. The testimony of the twenty-two witnesses (twelve for the prosecution, ten for the defense) along with closing arguments lasted two-and-a-half days.

* * * *

In the shocking course of it all, there was also the testimony of Mamie Till-Bradley (Emmett's mother). Born in Webb, Mississippi, she had lived in a world in which race determined one's destiny in daily life. That was apparent once she entered the courtroom where seats were segregated by race.[28] Likewise, while whites were addressed by their surnames, people of color were addressed solely by their first names. Though it surely shocked many, it did not surprise the Black press that some of the key witnesses for the State, like Levi Collins (a twenty-year-old Black man who worked for one of the defendants[29]), were nowhere

---

27. *Ibid.*, p. 60.

28. See Metress, *The Lynching of Emmett Till,* pp. 44, 48, 58, 64, 176–77.

29. See James L. Hicks, "They Stand Accused by C-C Reporter: Jimmy Hicks Charges Miss. Officials Aided Lynchers," *Cleveland Call and Post*, October 8, 1955 (per Sheriff Strider's order, "Leroy Collins was in the Charleston jail on Friday at the very hour that the case went to the jury. . . . I charge further that Prosecutors Gerald Chatham and Robert B. Smith were told about this but that they decided that since the sheriff had given his word that Collins was not in the jail, they proceeded to close out the trial without this man whom everyone believes could have positively hung the crime on the two white men and seriously implicated at least one other white man.").

to be found.[30] So, too, with the paucity of evidence available to the prosecutors, thanks in no small part to the pre-trial maneuverings of Sheriff H. C. Strider. The tenor of the trial only compounded such evils as even the most obvious of facts tendered by the State's twelve witnesses were discounted one by one by the five lawyers for the defense. One of those lawyers, J. J. Breland, went so far as to suggest that Mamie had staged her son's death to collect "life insurance" on him—thus was the drift of his questioning when she took the stand. The defense lawyers, aided by Sheriff Strider, even argued that the body was so badly disfigured that no one could identify it as that of Emmett Till. Ironically, on the one hand, the photos taken by David Jackson of *Jet* were neither part of the trial record nor part of any real discussion of the utter savagery of the murder. On the other hand, the very barbarity that produced the horrific figure of the murdered boy was used as a defense to refute Emmett's true identity. In his summation, defense lawyer John Whitten told the jury that he had full confidence that "every last Anglo-Saxon one of you has the courage" to render the right decision, echoing what his colleague J. J. Breland had said earlier. As for the jury, they deliberated for sixty-seven minutes, which included a soda break, before returning a "not guilty" verdict.

There was more, including the basement of the court where the seventy-four-pound cotton gin that had been tied around Till's neck with barbed wire and introduced into evidence was stored before being "tossed out when the building underwent renovations in 1973," only to be retrieved by a local man who sometime thereafter "got rid of it."[31]

Thus it was that Till's murderers, aided by the sheriff and the defense lawyers, transformed a fourteen-year-old living boy into inert matter—a lifeless thing with no name. The *psychology of their evil* thus became manifest: they never viewed Emmett Till as a human being. Bigotry and intoxicating rage followed by official wrongdoing directed their psyches, which in the process denied Emmett his dignity and then his life.

---

30. "One of Milam and Bryant's defense attorneys, J. J. Breland, told graduate student Hugh Stephen Whitaker in 1962 that Collins and [Henry Lee] Loggins had [secretly] been kept in jail [in another county] during the trial" at the behest of Sheriff H. C. Strider. Anderson, *Emmett Till,* p. 379.

31. Anderson, *Emmett Till,* pp. 337–38, 475 n. 86.

* * * *

Mississippi's Governor, Hugh White, "wired the NAACP in New York that he 'had every reason to believe that the courts will do their duty in prosecution.'"

—HUGH STEVEN WHITAKER[32]

[A]fter the jury had been chosen, any first-year law student could have won the case.

—J. J. BRELAND, lead defense counsel[33]

Around 3:48 p.m. on Friday, September 23, 1955, Charlie Cox, the clerk of the court, announced the "not guilty" verdict, this after reports that witnesses had heard "laughter inside the jury room during deliberations."[34] Once announced, the verdict won the excited approval of the white audience. When this phase of the criminal "justice" process was done, black-and-white photographs of the smiling defendants and their wives were captured and then circulated widely. Predictably, protests and rallies were mounted across the nation. "Four thousand church and United Auto Workers packed Detroit's Bethel AME Zion, designed to accommodate 2,500; fifty thousand more lined an eight-block radius around nearby Scott Methodist Church.Representative Charles Diggs [who sat in on the trial] addressed between six and ten thousand people in that city, describing the 'sheer perjury and fantastic twisting of facts' at the trial. . . ."[35] At another protest that occurred on October 16, 1955, Mamie spoke to ten thousand or so people at a rally in Washington, D.C., organized by the Bible Way Church.[36] There was a unified front; this horrific injustice must not stand. That same year, in a letter to a friend, Rosa Parks wrote, "I'm sure you read of the lynch-murder of Emmett Till of Chicago. This case could be multiplied many times in the South. . . ."[37] Soon enough she, too, would respond to the racial injustice that was murdering her people.

---

32. Whitaker, MA thesis, pp. 119–20.

33. Quoted in Stephen Whitfield, *A Death in the Delta: The Story of Emmett Till*, Baltimore, MD: Johns Hopkins University Press (1991), p. 44.

34. Booker & Booker, *Shocking the Conscience*, p. 79 ("but at other times cameramen roamed the courtroom taking pictures").

35. Tyson, *The Blood of Emmett Till*, p. 190.

36. Anderson, *Emmett Till*, p. 198.

37. Tyson, *The Blood of Emmett Till*, p. 210.

One of the more disturbing things about the twists of *State of Mississippi v. J. W. Milam and Roy Bryant* is this: though the defendants were both initially charged with kidnapping and murder, they were only tried on the *latter* charge (at the time, both offenses could be tried as capital crimes under Mississippi law). Proceeding by way of a single criminal charge was due to a jurisdictional issue: though Till was kidnapped in Leflore County, his body was found in Tallahatchie County, where it was *asserted* that the murder occurred. That meant that the kidnapping case had to be prosecuted in one jurisdiction (Leflore) and the murder in another (Tallahatchie). Of course, though Sheriff Strider of Tallahatchie County boldly asserted jurisdiction, there was considerable doubt among local Blacks that the murder happened there.[38] The bifurcation of the crimes made it harder for the prosecution to make its case since the two crimes were unquestionably linked.

Once the verdict was rendered in the murder trial, Judge Swango announced that the prosecution had requested that the kidnapping charges be dropped as far as Tallahatchie County was concerned since those charges fell within the jurisdiction of Leflore County where the kidnapping occurred.[39] When another grand jury was thereafter convened there in early November 1955, it took all of seventy-two minutes for the all-white, all-male panel to refuse to indict the defendants even though there was ample evidence, including evidence in the trial record, of their guilt as to this kidnapping count. "I don't know what to say. I don't see how they could fail to indict those men,"[40] is how Mamie Till-Bradley judged it.

The entire affair—from the barbaric murder to the acquittal to the grand jury's refusal to indict the defendants for kidnapping—was akin

---

38. According to Dr. T.R.M. Howard, "Sunday night a Negro came to me with information that the killing of Till may have happened in Sunflower County. I have looked into this. I can produce at least five witnesses at the proper time who will testify that Till was not killed in Tallahatchie County but killed in Sunflower County about three and a half miles west of Drew in the headquarters shed of the Clint Sheridan Plantation[,] which is managed by Leslie Milan, brother of J. W. Milan, one of the defendants and half-brother of Roy Bryant[,] the other defendant." Hicks, "White Reporters Double-crossed Probers." See also Till-Mobley & Benson, *Death of Innocence,* p. 161.

39. See Clark Porteous, "Next: 2 Face Kidnap Charges," *Memphis Press-Scimitar*, September 24, 1955, p. 1.

40. Quoted in Anderson, *Emmett Till,* p. 209.

to something out of what would be seen a few years later on Rod Serling's *Twilight Zone* TV series. (As it turned out, the then-young script-
writer was so struck by the injustice of it all that he prepared a screenplay for an episode based on the Till tragedy, but the idea was killed at
least twice by TV executives and advertisers.[41])

* * * *

There are trials and there are truths. When the wheels of the law
turn toward justice, the two coincide. But that did not occur in *State of
Mississippi v. J. W. Milam and Roy Bryant*. Worse still, evil took a new
turn when a freelance reporter named William Bradford Huie arranged
to secretly meet with defense lawyers John Whitten and J. J. Breland.
Sometime after the trial, a deal was struck to interview J. W. Milam and
Roy Bryant: $1,269 to their law firm plus 10 percent of magazine roy-
alties. Each of the cash-strapped defendants would get $1,575 plus a
purported portion of profits from magazine sales. Their "tell-all" story
of how they murdered Emmett Till would be revealed to the world, albeit with an assurance that the legal doctrine of "double jeopardy"
would prevent them from being retried. On January 24, 1956, *Look*
magazine ran the story titled "The Shocking Story of Approved Killing
in Mississippi." Six million copies were sold before the piece was reprinted for six million *Reader's Digest* subscribers. Then came yet another Huie-authored *Look* magazine piece on January 22, 1957, titled
"What's Happened to Emmett Till's Killers." And then there was the
1959 book *Wolf Whistle*, with its sordid, screaming red cover.[42]

In all of this Huie had his work cut out for him: his account had to
be cautiously and cleverly attentive to what was set out in the trial transcript. Additionally, his account had to be told in such a way as not to
incriminate the defendants and others—the pair could, after all, still be
indicted for kidnapping by a new grand jury since double jeopardy did
not protect them given that they had never been tried for kidnapping.

---

41. Whitfield, *A Death in the Delta,* pp. 83–84; Gorn, *Let the People See*, pp. 253, 356
nn. 12–13, 14 (the screenplay was named "Noon at Doomsday" and was first written for
ABC's *United States Steel Hour*; later Serling submitted something to CBS's *Playhouse 90*);
Anderson, *Emmett Till,* p. 461 n. 7. See also Jackie Mansky, "An Early Run-In with Cen-
sors Led Rod Serling to 'The Twilight Zone,'" *Smithsonian Magazine*, April 1, 2019.

42. See Anderson, *Emmett Till*, pp. 220-51.

In the revisionary process, some places and persons had to be rearranged or omitted to protect the guilty. On the one hand, Huie had to write a revealing story while, on the other, he had to retell the story so as not to reveal any incriminating truths. As explained in Part V of this book, it made for good copy, though as with the trial transcript, there was much in it that was simply false.

While the Black press had long been highly suspicious of Huie's "checkbook journalism," the most damning evidence came from FBI reports on the Till murder. Though Huie was favorably portrayed in the 1987 documentary *Eyes on the Prize*, rigorous studies by the FBI and biographers have offered a largely damning interpretation. For example, though the FBI was apparently unwilling to open an investigation in 1956,[43] in its 2006 "Prospective Report,"[44] the FBI authoritatively disproved important parts of Huie's account. That is, much in its depiction of events was deemed wrong or misleading. The FBI reported various falsehoods perpetuated by Huie, some having to do with the locale of the crimes and others relating to the actual size of the murder party, which Huie falsely reported to be two (J. W. Milam and Roy Bryant). In all instances, such falsehoods were likely intended to protect the guilty, be they the two defendants or other parties.[45] In his 2010 book, Simeon Wright (Moses Wright's son and an eyewitness to the criminal acts) entered this into the historical record: "In the end,

---

43. See *ibid.*, pp. 248–49. In a September 2, 1955, attorney general's internal memo (from Mr. F.L. Price to Mr. Rosen), it was stated that "considerable 'pressure' is being generated by Negro newspapers and colored organizations in an effort to have the Federal Government take some action in Mississippi." In an August 29, 1955, memo (from Mr. F.L. Price to Mr. Rosen), it was recommended that the "Memphis [FBI office] contact local authorities to obtain complete facts to determine if a Bureau violation [e.g., Federal Kidnapping Statute] has occurred." An addendum dated August 30, 1955, declared, "No indication of interstate transportation. Memphis following matter closely." https://fsu .digital.flvc.org/islandora/object/fsu%3A685427.

44. "The Emmett Till Case: The FBI Report," Famous Trials, February 9, 2006, https:// famous-trials.com/emmetttill/1765-fbireport. See also Margaret M. Russell, "Reopening the Emmett Till Case: Lessons and Challenges for Critical Race Practice," *Fordham Law Review*, vol. 73 (2005), p. 2101.

45. See, for example, Tell, *Remembering Emmett Till*, pp. 49–59, 64–65, 75–76, and Simeon Wright, *Simeon's Story*, pp. 133–36.

Huie got his story,"[46] through the perpetration of untruths, half-truths, and misleading claims.

* * * *

Those lawyers, J. J. Breland and John Whitten and the rest, hadn't really defended Roy Bryant and J. W. Milam so much as they defended a way of life.

—MAMIE TILL-MOBLEY[47]

They weren't just killing a boy, they were expressing something rooted in decades of animosity, fear, and anger.

—BRYAN STEVENSON[48]

"[W]e've got to have our Milams to fight our wars and keep the nig-gahs in line."[49] Those were the brazen post-trial words mouthed by J. J. Breland, lead counsel for the defendants. Offensive as they were intended to be, Breland's remark was rooted both in the state's past and in its present. For example, the Equal Justice Initiative has documented "4,084 racial terror lynchings in twelve Southern states between the end of Reconstruction in 1877 and 1950. . . ."[50] And in the "75 years before Emmett Till set foot in Mississippi, more than 500 Black people had been lynched in the state—most were men who had been accused with associating with white women."[51] Whatever system of justice there was in the South in general, and Mississippi in particular,[52] that system was largely bereft of justice for people of color.

---

46. Wright, *Simeon's Story*, p. 136.

47. Till-Mobley & Benson, *Death of Innocence*, p. 198.

48. "The Body of Emmett Till: 100 Photos," *Time*, November 17, 2016 (narrated by Bryan Stevenson), https://www.youtube.com/watch?v=4V6ffUUEvaM.

49. Quoted in Tyson, *The Blood of Emmett Till*, p. 49.

50. Equal Justice Initiative, *Lynching in America: Confronting the Legacy of Racial Terror* (3d ed., 2017), p. 4.

51. *The Murder of Emmett Till*, documentary, directed by Stanley Nelson (PBS, *American Experience* (2003)).

52. Even in 1955 it was reported that "[s]ince 1882, Mississippi has led the country in lynchings, holding the record of more than 11 percent of all in the country." William Gordon, "Reviewing the News: The Sins of Mississippi," *Atlanta Daily World*, September 4, 1955, p. 4.

Then there was *Brown v. Board of Education*, the landmark 1954 desegregation ruling, a case that threatened the legacy of racial submission and bigotry as a central tenet of the southern way of life. In Breland's mind, that was the link to the Till murder. "[T]hey wouldn't have killed him except for Black Monday [the day *Brown v. Board* was handed down]. The Supreme Court . . . is responsible for the murder of Emmett Till. . . ." Again, Breland's words.[53] By that logic, the Till murder and the jury's acquittal symbolized a fiercely defiant response to *Brown*[54] and to *Brown II,* which was decided three months before the Till murder. Breland, as many then knew, was echoing the words and ideas of Thomas Pickens Brady, then a Mississippi circuit judge and later a state supreme court justice and author of a widely circulated pamphlet titled *Black Monday: Segregation or Amalgamation—America Has a Choice.*[55] The tract was an overtly racist bluster urging whites to rise up and rebel against the *Brown* ruling. The white culture, its white women (the "loveliest and the purest of God's creatures"), and its white way of life had to be preserved at all costs.[56] And it is well to note that the trial of the two defendants occurred, thanks to the devious assumption of jurisdiction by Sheriff Strider, in Tallahatchie County— "ground zero in the fight over a 'southern way of life'. . . ."[57]

Writ large, the past again became present. That present—the tragedy of the Emmett Till murder—tilted forward in ways both promising and treacherous. There was the birth of a new and invigorated civil rights movement and the enactment of the Civil Rights Acts of 1957, 1964, and 1968, and the Voting Rights Act of 1965, along with a string of

---

53. Quoted in Gorn, *Let the People See*, p. 236; Tyson, *The Blood of Emmett Till*, p. 49.

54. See, e.g., Editorial, *Daily News* (Jackson, MS), May 18, 1954, p. 6 ("Human blood may stain southern soil in many places because of this decision, but the dark red stains of that blood will be on the marble steps of the United States Supreme Court building.").

55. Thomas P. Brady, *Black Monday*, Winona, MS: Association of Citizens' Councils (1954), discussed at length in Tyson, *The Blood of Emmett Till*, pp. 91–106.

56. Brady, *Black Monday*, p. 45; "Thomas P. Brady: Mississippi Judge," *New York Times*, February 1, 1973, p. 38 (obituary). The pamphlet "served as the guide for starting the Citizens Council movement to resist" the *Brown* ruling. *The Blood of Emmett Till*, p. 49. See also Neil R. McMillen, *The Citizens' Council Organized Resistance to the Second Reconstruction, 1954–64*, Champaign, IL: University of Illinois Press (1994), pp. 17–40.

57. Dave Tell, *Confessional Crises and Cultural Politics in Twentieth-Century America*, University Park, PA: Penn State University Press (2015), p. 84.

post-*Brown* civil rights Supreme Court rulings. Then again, there were the events of 1963: for example, Medgar Evers's murder and the Birmingham church bombing. There were also the tumultuous Watts and Harlem race riots of 1965 along with the assassination of Martin Luther King Jr. in 1968. By the time of the Kerner Commission Report (1968), ordered by President Johnson, the nation had moved toward "two societies, one black, one white—separate and unequal."[58] Much later came the "Black Lives Matter" movement of 2013, in response to countless incidents of police brutality and racially driven violence against African Americans. In the words of professor and author Christopher Lebron, it sparked haunting memories of "Emmett Till's face beaten and bloated as much by hatred as by the river waters that overtook his biology. . . ."[59] By the time of the 2020 George Floyd police murder and the homicidal manhunt for Ahmaud Arbery, the historical sweep of racial injustice pointed, yet again, to what has been described as "systemic and institutional failures."[60] As with so many others, the link directly back to Emmett Till was too great for Congressman Lewis to ignore.[61]

Like Roy Bryant, though in softer but nonetheless dismissive tones, too many modern-day Americans have grown weary of hearing about the evil of the Emmett Till murder and all that the legacy of racism came to represent in the events leading up to the murders of George Floyd and Ahmaud Arbery, among others. Such talk (as evidenced by Florida's Stop W.O.K.E Act of 2022) is viewed as an attack on them and their heritage. By their dim lights, racism is not troublingly widespread but distinctively individualistic, and it is not something that should impugn the reputations of once revered past or present public figures. But such attitudes are themselves monuments to bigotry. Hence, they do not topple easily.

A quarter-century ago, John Edgar Wideman wrote bluntly and prophetically about the lasting terror of the Emmett Till lynching and

---

58. Quoted in *The Essential Kerner Commission Report*, ed. Jelani Cobb, New York: Liveright (2021), p. xiv.

59. Christopher J. Lebron, *The Making of Black Lives Matter*, New York: Oxford University Press (2017), p. 161.

60. *The Essential Kerner Commission Report*, p. xviii (Cobb introduction).

61. See note 5, *supra*.

what it symbolized: "Emmett Till's murder was an attempt to slay an entire generation. Push us backward to the bad old days when the lives of Black people seemed to belong to Whites. When White power and racist ideology seemed unchallengeable forces of nature." Those forces were dominant then, and even today there is a current of the same force, if only because "Emmett Till's mangled face could belong to anybody's Black son who transgressed racial laws. . . ."[62] So much of the story of the killings of people of color is a history of race and law operating in a culture in which systemic racism is first indifferent to the inviolability of Black lives and then indifferent to laws designed to protect all lives. And in today's charged political environment, teachers who dare to speak up about racial injustice stand to be harassed or sacked.

When an entire race has been uprooted for centuries and then enslaved, there are collateral consequences that affect their cultural, legal, economic, and psychological history. They represent, in Simone Weil's perceptive words, "the supreme human tragedy."[63] Just how we deal with that complex and perpetual tragedy is the "truest barometer of American democracy and the test of the national creed."[64] By that measure, Emmett Till "can't stay dead"—the full and unvarnished truth is just too important to let die.

* * * *

A FEW ADDITIONAL FACTS

- A support fund, replete with contribution jars in local stores, had been organized to raise money for Bryant and Milam's legal defense.

- Nine days before the trial began, the African American *Chicago Defender* editorialized, "No country that *tolerates* the barbarous hate-killing of a child within its midst deserves, nor can it expect, the respect of the civilized world. There can be no compromise this time."

---

62. John Edgar Wideman, "The Killing of Black Boys," *Essence*, November 1997, p. 124.

63. Simone Weil, *The Need for Roots*, trans. Arthur Wills, New York: Routledge (1952), p. 119.

64. *The Essential Kerner Commission Report*, p. xviii (Cobb introduction).

- The courtroom, located in a then two-story courthouse, seated two hundred fifty. On the first day, and "[s]urveying the more than 400 Mississippi Delta residents jammed into every available space in the courtroom including the isles [*sic*], Circuit Judge Curtis Swango told the crowd: 'If a fire develops any place in the courthouse, a great tragedy will take place.' Smoking is permitted in Mississippi courtrooms."[65]

- The trial occurred in the courtroom that was situated on the second floor and accessible only by narrow stairs; its rules and arrangements were largely set by Sheriff H. C. Strider.

- The two defendants, clad in short-sleeved white shirts and khaki pants, were never handcuffed, including at the time outside when they approached the court.

- A room on the first floor of the courthouse was "converted into a makeshift press room with typewriters and teletype machines, and UP installed a telephone" for its reporter to give updates.[66]

---

65. "District Attorney Seeks More Time to Examine New State Witnesses," *Greenwood Commonwealth* (AP), September 20, 1955, p. 1.

Four women labor activists "were unable to get into the courthouse, so they spent the morning outside on the lawn, passing out copies of the UPWA District 8 Women's Conference resolution on the Till murder. During the midday recess, the women shared a picnic lunch under a nearby tree. Their interracial group met with 'disapproving and shocked glances' from locals. 'The three white ladies and I were sitting down and along came a white photographer and took our picture,' recalled Lillian Pittman. 'He asked us were [if] we from Chicago, and we all answered, "No, we are from Louisiana." He couldn't believe it.'" Matthew F. Nichter, "'Did Emmett Till Die in Vain? Organized Labor Says No!': The United Packinghouse Workers and Civil Rights Unionism in the Mid-1950s," *Labor: Studies in Working-Class History*, vol. 18, no. 2 (2021), p. 28.

Regarding the modern status of the courthouse, see Erica L. Green, "Biden Creates Monument to Emmett Till Amid Fights Over Black History," *New York Times* (July 25, 2023). Remarks by President Biden and Vice President Harris at Signing of the Emmett Till and Mamie Till-Mobley National Monument Proclamation, " and Establishment of the Emmett Till and Mamie Till-Mobley National Monument (July 25, 2023) (remarks by President Biden). See also Dave Tell, "A 700-Mile Road Trip with the Last Living Witness to Emmett Till's Murder," *Esquire* (July 28, 2023).

66. Herbers & Rosen, *Deep South Dispatch*, p. 61. "One room on the first floor of the courthouse had been converted into an editorial office that contained typewriters, tables, and a teletype machine. Representatives from the National Broadcasting Company and Columbia Broadcasting System also sent reporters, but in the era before instantaneous transmission, the networks had to put the film on a bus to Memphis, and then have it flown to New York." John R. Tisdale, "Different Assignments, Different Perspectives:

- *First day*: Defendant J. W. Milam's children were rowdy during the trial (e.g., they ran and jumped around, pointing toy pistols at each other).

- The courtroom was racially segregated both for reporters and the audience.

- Twenty-one reporters covered the trial for the "white press" and sat up front near the judge's bench.

- A total of twelve Black journalists covered the trial and the events leading up to it, though not all were in the courtroom at the same time. Some of the reporters included Moses Newson (*Tri-State Defender*), Simeon Booker (*Jet* and *Ebony* magazines), Jimmy Hickes (*Baltimore African-American*), Alex Wilson (*Tri-State Defender*), and Ruby Hurley (*The Crisis*, the official NAACP magazine). The courtroom photographers for the Black press were David Jackson and Mike Shea (*Jet-Ebony* team) and Ernest Withers (*Chicago Defender*). On the first day, they had to sit at a small card table off to the side near a window, though it was replaced the next day with a larger table. Sheriff Strider openly addressed them as "niggers"[67] and "greeted" other people of color by saying, "Mornin', niggahs." During

---

How Reporters Reconstruct the Emmett Civil Rights Murder Trial," *Oral History Review*, vol. 29, no. 1 (Winter/Spring 2002), p. 39, at p. 46.

67. See Simeon Booker, "A Negro Reporter at the Till Trial," *Nieman Reports*, January 1956. "The day before the trial opened, our *Jet-Ebony* crew ran into a truckload of gun-bearing whites on a truck near Money, Mississippi, which brought it home to us that our assignment was no good neighbor get-together." *Ibid.*

As to the importance of the Black press coverage, there is this: "In the pages of the *Chicago Defender*, alongside those of other leading Black newspapers, the drama of Emmett Till's murder dominated the headlines throughout the fall of 1955. For 19 consecutive weeks, the paper presented the accounts of the final hours of the teenager's life, the outcry of Mississippians (of all races) for swift justice against Till's murders, the NAACP's efforts to publicize Till's tragedy to the nation-at-large, [and] the gradual backlash of White Mississippians who felt slandered by the NAACP leadership and changed their allegiance from Till to the boy's assailants. . . ." Harvey Young, "A New Fear Known to Me: Emmett Till's Influence and the Black Panther Party," *Southern Quarterly*, vol. 45, no. 4 (Summer 2008), p. 22. See also Michael Randolph Oby, "Black Press Coverage of the Emmett Till Lynching as a Catalyst to the Civil Rights Movement" (MA thesis, Georgia State University (2007)) (available online).

noon recesses, Black reporters' chairs were stolen, requiring some to stand up.[68]

- Black witnesses were addressed solely by their first name or nickname, whereas all white witnesses were addressed by their surname.
- The jury was all white and all male.[69]

Ronald K.L. Collins
Lewes, Delaware

---

68. Till-Mobley & Benson, *Death of Innocence,* p. 165; James L. Hicks, "The Real Till Story," *Los Angeles Sentinel,* October 27, 1955, pp. 1, 4.

69. "In 1955, 30,486 persons lived in Tallahatchie County. No Negroes were registered; thus none could serve as jurors. So jury service was limited to the 3,163 white males over 21 years of age. . . . On September 8, 1955, on the motion of the state, Circuit Judge Swango ordered a special *venire* of 120 men to be drawn from the jury boxes, in open court, on September 12. The special *venire* gave the state a chance to get half of the jurors from the east side of the county, far from the homes of the accused. The regular *venire* had come entirely from west of the Tallahatchie River." Hugh Stephen Whitaker, "A Case Study of Southern Justice: The Murder and Trial of Emmett Till," *Rhetoric and Public Affairs,* vol. 8, no. 2 (Summer 2005), p. 189, at p. 205. Note: Whitaker was the son of a local sheriff's deputy and did his master's thesis on the trial. Among many others, Whitaker, who was related to Gerald Chatham, interviewed all of the living jurors. The additional notes and comments that accompany the trial transcript were added by the editor.

PART I

___

State of Mississippi v. J.W. Milam and Roy Bryant

The Annotated Trial Transcript[1]

Sumner, Mississippi

September 19–23, 1955

STATE OF MISSISSIPPI

VS.

J. W. MILAM[2] and ROY BRYANT[3]

---

1. The following transcript (save for numerous note entries, corrections, bracketed additions, formatting, and commentary) derives from what is posted online: https://diginole.lib.fsu.edu/islandora/object/fsu:390158. The online transcript was posted by Florida State University and based on the FBI's transcript: https://vault.fbi.gov/civil-rights?b_start:int=40 (partial version). The author retains copyright rights over all such changes and additions.

2. John William "J. W." Milam (1919–1980) "was born in Charleston, Tallahatchie County, Mississippi. . . . He married Juanita Thompson [in] 1949 . . . and they had two sons. He possessed only a ninth-grade education and fought in Europe during World War II. While in the military he won a purple heart, a silver star, and other medals. Soon after the trial and acquittal, he and Roy Bryant [half-brothers] sold their story confessing to the murder of Emmett Till to reporter William Bradford Huie for $3,150, and it was published in *Look* magazine. By 1956, Milam found he was unable to rent land and was refused a loan due to his notoriety in the case. The Milams moved to Texas for several years, and later returned to Mississippi. They moved to Greenville, Washington County, Mississippi in 1965. [Juanita] and J. W. were said to have later divorced, but he is listed as married to Juanita in his obituary, and there is no divorce record for them. . . . He had worked as a heavy equipment operator in Greenville, and was retired at the time of his death from cancer." Devery Anderson, "Who's Who in the Emmett Till Case," Devery Anderson.com, https://www.deveryanderson.com/whos-who-in-the-emmett-till-case. For a more complete discussion, see Anderson, *Emmett Till*.

3. Roy Bryant (1931–1994) "was born a twin in Charleston, Tallahatchie County, Mississippi. . . . He later spent three years in the military as a paratrooper (1950–1953). He married Carolyn Holloway [in] 1951, and the couple had three sons and a daughter. After

No. 2131

INDICTMENT—MURDER

Proceedings of Trial at September Term, 1955
in Sumner, Mississippi

In the Circuit Court

Second District of Tallahatchie County

Seventeenth Judicial District

State of Mississippi

September Term, 1955

———

J. W. MILAM & ROY BRYANT

INDICTMENT — MURDER[4]

---

the murder trial, due to [Blacks] boycotting of his store, he was forced to close. . . . Around this time he and Milam [half-brothers] sold their story confessing to the murder to reporter William Bradford Huie, [which] was published in *Look* magazine. . . . In 1956 he . . . learned welding with the help of the G.I. Bill. He worked as a welder and boilermaker for 16 years in East Texas and Louisiana. He and his family then moved to Ruleville, Sunflower County, Mississippi, in 1973. . . . Legally blind as a result of his years as a welder, he came to own another general store in Ruleville, which he ran until it burned down in 1989. As [with] his store in Money three decades earlier, the Ruleville establishment catered mainly to [Blacks]. He and Carolyn divorced in 1975; [he remarried in] 1980. In 1983, while running his grocery store, he was indicted for buying food stamps for less than their value and then selling them at full price. . . . He pled guilty to two counts of food stamp fraud, but due to the pleas of his attorney, he was sentenced to only three years' probation and a $750.00 fine. Four years later . . . he was again charged with food stamp fraud and was sentenced to two years in prison. However, he was released after only eight months. . . . Toward the end of his life, he spent most of his time at home, but sold watermelon and other fruit at a stand along the road in Ruleville in the summertime. Plagued with health problems, he nearly lost his feet due to diabetes and eventually died of cancer . . . in Jackson, Mississippi." Anderson, "Who's Who in the Emmett Till Case."

    4. "The foreman of the *grand jury* was Jerry Falls, one of the wealthiest men in the county, a Delta aristocrat steeped in the tradition of noblesse oblige. . . . After hearing testimony . . . , the 18-man grand jury returned ten true bills on Tuesday morning. Jury

Presiding: Hon. Curtis M. Swango, Jr.,[5] Circuit Judge, Seventeenth Judicial District of the State. Appearances:

For the State:

- Hon. Gerald Chatham, District Attorney;
- Hon. Robert B. Smith, III, Special Assistant to the District Attorney;
- Hon. Hamilton Caldwell, County Attorney.

For the Defendants:

- Hon. J. J. Breland, of Sumner, Mississippi;
- Hon. C. Sidney Carlton, of Sumner, Mississippi;
- Hon. J. W. Kellum, of Sumner, Mississippi;
- Hon. John W. Whitten, Jr., of Sumner, Mississippi;
- Hon. Harvey Henderson,[6] of Sumner, Mississippi.

Chairman Falls read, 'Roy Bryant and J. W. Milam did willfully, unlawfully, feloniously, and of their malice aforethought did kill and murder Emmett Till, a human being, against the peace and dignity of the State of Mississippi.' A similar indictment was handed down on the kidnapping charge. Under Mississippi law, conviction on *either* count could carry the death penalty." Whitaker, "A Case Study of Southern Justice," at p. 200 (notes deleted) (emphasis added).

5. Curtis M. Swango Jr. (1908–1968), then 47, "presided as judge at the Milam–Bryant murder trial. He graduated from Millsaps College in Jackson, Mississippi, and from the University of Mississippi law school. He was appointed to the Circuit Court bench in 1950 by then Governor Fielding Wright and was a judge of the Seventeenth Judicial District. He was praised by black and white journalists for the even-handed way he conducted the trial." Anderson, "Who's Who in the Emmett Till Case." See also Bill Minor, "Shame of the Till Murder Lives On," *Greenwood Commonwealth*, January 22, 2003 ("Circuit Judge Curtis Swango, whom I had known previously as a highly respected state legislative leader, maintained remarkable decorum throughout the trial, despite the emotional tension which hovered in the courtroom like the cloying summertime humidity of the Mississippi Delta."); Dan Wakefield, "Justice in Sumner," *The Nation*, October 1, 1955 ("Judge Curtis Swango, a tall, quietly commanding man, combined order with a maximum of freedom in the court. . . .").

6. Robert Harvey Henderson Sr. (1921–2007). "At 34, he was the youngest of the legal team. He had been a life-long resident of Tallahatchie County and had been in practice since 1947. As the last surviving member of the defense team, his death came just five days after Tallahatchie County apologized to the Till family for the injustices of the trial on October 2, 2007." Anderson, "Who's Who in the Emmett Till Case." Apart from once reading the jury instructions, he played no visible role in the trial. In later years, Henderson "approached local architect Richard Dickson about saving the courthouse. While

Witness for the State:[7]

1. Moses Wright

2. Chester A. Miller

3. C. A. Strickland

4. George Smith

5. Robert Hodges

6. B. L. Mims

7. John Ed Cothran

8. C. F. (Chick) Nelson

9. Mamie Bradley[8]

10. Willie Reed

11. Add Reed

12. Amandy Bradley

Witness for the Defendants:

1. Mrs. Roy Bryant

2. Mrs. J. W. Milam

3. H. C. Strider

4. Dr. L. B. Otken

5. H. D. Malone

6. Lee Russell Allison

7. Lee McGarrh

8. L. W. Boyce

---

there was not tax money to repair the courthouse, there was grant money to restore the courthouse to its 1955 condition. When his job was on the line, Harvey Henderson jump-started the push to restore the courthouse and remember Emmett Till." Dave Tell, "Emmett Till Interpretive Center," Emmett Till Memory Project, https://tillapp.emmett-till .org/items/show/19?tour=2&index=0. See also Tell, *Remembering Emmett Till*, pp. 100– 106.

7. The prosecution did not ask for the death penalty. See "Prosecution Doesn't Say if Death Penalty Sought in Trial of White Men," *Jackson Daily News*, September 12, 1955; "State Will Not Ask Death Penalty in Trial of White Men at Sumner," *Greenwood Commonwealth*, September 19, 1955.

8. Mamie Till-Bradley (later Till-Mobley).

9. James Sanders

10. Harold Terry

ORGANIZATION OF COURT

BE IT REMEMBERED that a regular term of the Honorable Circuit Court of the Second District of the County of Tallahatchie, State of Mississippi, convened in the town of Sumner, in said County and State, on this, the 19th day of September, 1955, at the time and place designated by statute for the convening of said Court:

Present and presiding:

- Hon. Curtis M. Swango, Jr., Circuit Judge, Seventeenth Judicial District of the State; present,

- Hon. Gerald Chatham, District Attorney;

- Hon. Robert B. Smith, III, Special Assistant to the District Attorney;

- Hon. Hamilton Caldwell, County Attorney;[9]

- H. C. Strider, Sheriff;

- Charlie Cox, Circuit Clerk; and

- James T. O'Day, Court Reporter:

Indictment: Murder[10]

---

9. "County prosecuting attorney [James] Hamilton Caldwell [1898–1962] was recovering from a recent heart attack and was unable to bear much of the burden of the prosecution. He opposed asking the grand jury for an indictment because the case was lost from the start. 'A jury would turn loose any man who killed a Negro over insulting a white woman.'" Whitaker, "A Case Study," at p. 200, citing "personal interview" with Caldwell, August 15, 1962. That same year Caldwell drowned.

10. As noted in the prologue, the defendants were originally charged with kidnapping and murder, but for jurisdictional reasons they were tried only for murder in one county and then arrested but not indicted for kidnapping in another county. Had the two crimes been tried together (and they should have since the kidnapping and murder probably occurred in the same jurisdiction), the prosecution could have tried them for second degree murder under Mississippi law: "When done in the commission of an act eminently dangerous to others [e.g., kidnapping] and evincing a depraved heart, regardless of human life, although without any premeditated design to effect the death of any particular individual, shall be second-degree murder." Mississippi Code Title 97. Crimes

This day this cause came on to be heard, on this the 19th day of September, A. D. 1955. Comes the District Attorney, came also the defendants, each of them in his own proper person and represented by counsel and announced ready to proceed herein.

PROCEEDINGS:[11]

Indictment: Murder[12]

This day this cause came on to be heard, on this the 19th day of September, A. D. 1955. Comes the District Attorney, came also the defendants, each of them in his own proper person and represented by counsel and announced ready to proceed herein. Whereupon, came a jury[13] selected[14] from the regular panels of the week and a special venire from this County, composed of

---

§ 97-3-19(1)(b). Thus, murder could have been established by proving that a death occurred in the course of a kidnapping, regardless of the absence of any intent to murder.

11. Trial Witness Index omitted.

12. The defendants elected to be tried jointly and not to testify, presumably to decrease the likelihood of incriminating themselves. Although the defendants had been indicted on *both* kidnapping and murder charges on September 6, 1955, District Attorney Chatham opted to try them on murder charges first. Depending on the outcome of the murder trial, the idea was that defendants could later be indicted and tried on kidnapping charges.

13. "As a graduate student in 1962, [Hugh Stephen Whitaker] was assigned to revisit the trial for his master's thesis in political science. *He says the jurors, who received him openly because he had grown up in the county, told him they did not doubt that Mr. Bryant and Mr. Milam had been responsible for the killing.*" Shaila Dewan & Ariel Hart, "FBI Discovers Trial Transcript" (emphasis added). The transcript was not publicly released until 2007, albeit with one page missing and without the exhibits that had been part of the record. See also Whitaker, "A Case Study of Southern Justice."

14. "In order to obtain a jury . . . the state asked the following questions on the voir dire: (1) Will you start out not only to give the defendants but the State of Mississippi a fair trial? (2) Would you be prejudiced because of race? Do you know the accused personally? (3) Did you contribute to the fund for the defense, or would you have contributed if asked to? (Chiefly, funds came from the Delta [west] side of the county.) (4) Did any of the defense attorneys ever represent you in a lawsuit?" Whitaker, "A Case Study," p. 206, citing *Commercial-Appeal*, September 20, 1955, p. 1, 15. See also John Herbers, "The Trial Bogs Down in Jury-Picking Job," *Delta Democrat Times*, September 19, 1955, p. 1. The jurors selected were drawn from a pool of some 120 white men. (In order to be selected for jury service, one had to be male and registered to vote. Since no men of color were registered, none could be selected.)

1. J. A. Shaw, Jr.,

2. Ed Duvaney,

3. Bishop Matthews,

4. L. L. Price,

5. Howard Armstrong,

6. Ray Tribble,

7. Davis Newton,

8. James Toole,

9. George Holland,

10. Travis Thomas,

11. Gus Ramsey and

12. Jim Pennington,[15]

all good and lawful men,[16] being specially sworn to try the issue. Thereupon the cause proceeded to trial before the Judge afore-

---

Decades later it was reported that Whitaker had discovered that "the man in charge of picking the jurors was the county attorney; the county attorney at the time was John Whitten Jr." Marion Brooks, D.S. Shin, & Tom Jones, "Emmett Till Murder Case: Author of 1963 Thesis Investigation Shares New Trial Revelations to NBC Chicago," NBC 5 Chicago, January 10, 2023, https://www.nbcchicago.com/news/local/emmett-till-murder -case-author-of-1963-thesis-investigation-shares-new-trial-revelations-to-nbc-chicago /3041716/ (documentary video footage in *The Lost Story of Emmett Till: Then and Now*, https://www.nbcchicago.com/news/local/watch-nbc-chicagos-docuseries-on-emmett -till/3021225/). According to Whitaker, Whitten had "hand-picked the jury to be sure that the list from which the jury was taken had only people that he was pretty certain that they were racist and who would think nothing of killing an African American." Brooks, Shin, & Jones, "Emmett Till Murder Case."

15. "The prosecution and the defense each had twelve preemptory [*sic*] challenges, allowing each of them to reject a juror without giving a reason. . . . The state ended up using eleven of its twelve challenges. [The defense, per lawyer J. J. Breland], asked each potential juror if he believed the state must prove beyond a reasonable doubt that the body in the river was Till's. . . ." Some of the *voir dire* questions asked by the prosecution included queries about race and whether it would prejudice their decision, whether any of them had ever been represented by any of the five defense lawyers, and whether any of them had contributed to the fund for the defendants. Gorn, *Let the People See*, pp. 89–90, 322 n. 22.

16. At the time of the trial, only men could serve on juries in Mississippi. It was not until 1968 that Mississippi lawmakers passed a law allowing women on juries. Mississippi was the last state in the nation to take that step. "Women on Mississippi Juries." *New*

said, and the Jury aforesaid,[17] when proceedings were had, as follows:

THE COURT Do you gentlemen desire to make any preliminary statement?

MR. CHATHAM:[18] No, Sir.

The District Attorney, for and on behalf of the State of Mississippi, then and there introduced the following testimony and evidence, that-is-to-say:

FOR THE PROSECUTION
DIRECT EXAMINATION BY
DISTRICT ATTORNEY CHATHAM

York Times (AP) June 15, 1968. And not until 1986, in the case of *Batson v. Kentucky*, 476 U.S. 79, did the Supreme Court rule that the exclusion of Blacks from juries in criminal cases was unconstitutional.

17. "Ten of them were farmers, one a carpenter, one an insurance salesman, and one a retired carpenter." Whitaker, MA thesis, p. 145. "The locals were uniformly confident that any juror who dared vote in favor of a conviction would be killed in short order." Nichter, "'Did Emmett Till Die in Vain?,'" p. 30 (footnote omitted).

18. Gerald Chatham (1906–1956) "was the district attorney who prosecuted J. W. Milam and Roy Bryant in their murder trial. He had practiced law in the district since 1931. He had also served as a state representative, county superintendent of education, and county prosecuting attorney before he was elected district attorney in 1942. He held that office until 1956. Unfortunately, he died of a heart attack at home one year after the trial in Sumner. His family blames his health issues on stress related to the Till case." Anderson, "Who's Who in the Emmett Till Case."

Chapter 1

THE STATE'S CASE
MEN IN THE NIGHT—THE KIDNAPPING

There was no doubt in our minds that the State faced insurmountable odds.

—SIMEON BOOKER[1]

The jurors having been selected, the proceedings continued with the prosecution's putting on its case, though apparently without the benefit of an opening argument and with little time to investigate the matter and locate witnesses. Gerald Chatham[2] took the lead by calling the State's main witness, Moses Wright, Emmett's great uncle on his mother's side. The testimony of the sixty-four-year-old sharecropper and minister is key since he was an eyewitness to the kidnapping, which began at his home. That is, he saw the defendants, Roy Bryant and J. W. Milam, the night they came armed to his house in search of the boy who whistled. At this point in the prosecution it is important to note that the defendants were only being tried for murder; after the murder trial ended, a grand jury in another county would decide whether to indict the two on the kidnapping charges for which they were also arrested.

---

1. Booker & Booker, *Shocking the Conscience*, p. 68.
2. "The state had had two weeks since the indictment to gather evidence. Sheriff Strider refused to aid the prosecution by obtaining evidence. District Attorney Chatham and special prosecutor Smith had to try to do police work, riding country roads to look for witnesses and searching" for evidence. Whitaker, "A Case Study of Southern Justice," p. 207.

As to the facts, on August 27th the defendants and others arrived at Mr. Wright's home at around two o'clock in the morning. As of that date, Moses Wright was unaware of what had happened at the Bryant grocery store; had he known, he probably would have whisked Emmett back to Chicago immediately. Hence, he was both surprised and terrified when white men with guns came to his home in the middle of the night. He was in the house with his wife and three grandsons, Curtis Jones, Simeon Wright, and Wheeler Parker; and his great nephew, Emmett. Wright's testimony is important because it puts the State's case in motion by way of a chain of events designed to link the defendants to the murder. His testimony is also critical in that he was able to identify the body pulled from the Tallahatchie River as Emmett's.

"J. J." Breland took the lead for the defense on cross-examination. The tactic the defense employed with this witness and others was to create confusion to make all of the prosecution's claims doubtful. To that end, the defense grilled Wright as to whether he was certain of the identities of both Bryant and Milam, and whether he was sure who was outside his home other than the defendants, and also whether he could say with absolute assurance that the badly disfigured body pulled from the river was Emmett's.

Sidney Carlton, another one of the defense's five attorneys, came in for the second half of the cross-examination of Wright. He pursued the same strategy of attempting to discredit the witness by creating doubt as to who and what Moses Wright saw. Carlton's cross-examination also revealed that the defense team had deposed Wright shortly before the trial; Carlton used those statements in an attempt to confuse Wright and likewise to contradict his trial testimony.

Throughout it all, Moses Wright held his own in endless rounds of dizzying and particularized questions strategically prepared by five defense lawyers. And he did so even though he had little formal schooling and was testifying before a courtroom packed with hundreds of white men hostile to everything he had to say. Wright was also aware of the lingering threat made to him the night Bryant and Milam came to his home: "Well, if you know any of us here tonight, then you will never live to get to be sixty-five."

MOSES WRIGHT,[3] a witness introduced for and on behalf of the State, being first duly sworn, upon his oath testified as follows:

[DISTRICT ATTORNEY CHATHAM]

Q   Will you please state your name to the Jury?

A   Moses Wright.

Q   Uncle Moses, where do you live?[4]

A   Money.

Q   Is that Money, Mississippi?

A   Yes, Sir.

Q   And where is Money with reference to Philipp in Tallahatchie County?

A   It is—I think it is about north, maybe northeast.

Q   Do you mean Philipp is north of Money?

A   Yes, Sir, that is what I think.

Q   How long have you lived in that community, Uncle Moses?

A   Ever since '46.

Q   And on August 28th, of this year, where were you living near Money?

---

3. Moses Wright (1892–1977) "was the great-uncle of Emmett Till, who visited Chicago in August 1955 and brought Emmett and Wheeler Parker to Mississippi. He was born in Mississippi and married Lucinda Larry on December 16, 1911. After her death, he married Elizabeth Smith around 1925. Until 1949 he preached at a black church in Money, Mississippi, and also worked as a sharecropper, and since 1946, worked on a plantation in Money owned by Frederick Grover. . . . After the trial, he moved to Argo, Illinois [a subdivision of Summit annexed by the village in 1911], with his family and did some speaking engagements on the Emmett Till case that were sponsored by the NAACP. Due to his notoriety in the case, he was offered a lifetime job in a nursery in Albany, New York. However, he chose to move to Argo, where he lived quietly after the case died down and his speaking engagements ended, working as a janitor in a night club in Chicago and at a restaurant in Argo. He died in the White Oak Nursing Home in Indian Head Park, Illinois." Anderson, "Who's Who in the Emmett Till Case."

4. "Moses was sworn in at nine-fifteen Wednesday morning. He had been waiting there in the court over the last two days just for this moment. On Tuesday, he had stood around because there were no vacant seats. He just stood, waiting to be called. Then the court was recessed so that the surprise witness could be found, and that he'd had to wait overnight." Till-Mobley & Benson, *Death of Innocence*, p. 173.

A   Where was I living?

Q   On whose place were you living?

A   Mr. G. C. Frederick.

Q   And in which direction from Money is Mr. Frederick's place?

A   East.

Q   And about how far from Money is that?

A   Three miles.

Q   Uncle Moses, are you a married man?

A   Yes, Sir.

Q   How much family do you have?

A   Oh, I have twelve.

Q   You have twelve in your family?

A   But they are not all with me, you know.

Q   In August of this year, how many of your family were living with you there at your home, living with you and your wife there?

A   There was only me, and my wife and three children.

Q   There was you, and your wife and three children living there at that time.

A   Yes, Sir.

Q   What kind of house do you live in, Uncle Moses?

A   We live in a six-room house.

Q   Will you tell the jury how those rooms are arranged?

A   I think so.

Q   Well, tell them, please.

A   Well, the house in the east is a living room, and on the west there is a living room, in the front, you know, and there is a screened-in front porch facing north; and there is a kitchen between those rooms, and there is a door that enters into the east room, but it goes right on through to the south room, you know. Of course, there is a partition there, and we have got to go through this door there, and it is the same way over on the other side. There is a west door that enters into the west room. And then we just go on around there and that is the way we enter the side of the other rooms there. That is where the bedrooms is.

Q From your explanation of the floor plan of your house, I take it that there are two rooms on the front, is that right?

A Two on the front, that's right.

Q And your house faces north, is that right?

A Yes, Sir.

Q How close is your house to the road?

A It is fifty some feet, I think, about fifty feet.

Q Are there any trees in your yard between your front porch and the road?

A Yes, sir.

Q Now, specifically on the night of August 27th, Saturday night, August 27th, who was there at your home at bedtime?

A Well, at bedtime, there was Curtis Jones, my grandson; and Wheeler Parker, my grandson; and Emmett Louis Till, my nephew—I am his [great] uncle; and Lillybeth Wright, my wife; and Maurice and Robert and Simon [sic], my sons.

Q Uncle Moses, tell the jury about what time that Saturday night your family went to bed.

A My wife was already in bed. Of course, myself and the boys, we went to bed about one o'clock. We had went to Greenwood that night, and we came in about one o'clock.

Q Had you, and your wife and all the members of your family been to Greenwood that night?

A My wife didn't go. It was just the boys that went.

Q And she remained at home, is that right?

A Yes, Sir.

Q And you got back with them about one o'clock?

A Yes, Sir.

Q And you immediately went to bed, is that right?

A Yes, Sir.

Q Now, I want you to tell the jury in which room of your house did Emmett Till go to bed?

A Well, the east room, my wife and I sleep there.

Q Then we will call it the east front room, is that right?

A That's right. And there is a door that leads out to the side room there. That is where Emmett Till was.

Q And who went to be[sic]d with Emmett Till that night?

A Simon [sic], my baby.

Q And Simon and Emmett Till were the only two people in that room that night?

A That's right.

Q Now, Uncle Moses, after you and your family had gone to bed that night, I want you to tell the jury if any person or if one or more persons called at your home that night, and if they did, what time was it?

A About two o'clock.

Q What was the first thing that attracted your attention to the fact that there was someone about your premises?

A Well, someone was at the front door, and he was saying, "Preacher— Preacher." And then I said, "Who is it?" And then [h]e said, "This is Mr. Bryant. I want to talk to you and that boy."

Q Do you know Mr. Bryant?

A I just know him since he came up here. I couldn't see him that night so well, only with that flashlight there, and I could see that it was this other man. Mr. Milam. But I know Mr. Milam.

Q You know Mr. Milam, do you?

A I sure do.

Q And then what did you do?

A Well, I got up and opened the door.

Q And what did you see when you opened the door?

A Well, Mr. Milam was standing there at the door with a pistol in his right hand and he had a flashlight in his left hand.

Q Now stop there a minute, Uncle Moses. I want you to point out Mr. Milam if you see him here.

A There he is (pointing).[5]

Q And do you see Mr. Bryant in here?

A (The witness pointed with his hand.)

Q All right—about how big a porch is this there on the front of your house, Uncle Moses? How wide is it?

A It ought to be something like about nine feet.

Q You would say it is about nine feet wide, is that right?

A Yes, Sir.

Q And does that porch run the full length of your house?

A That's right.

Q That is, it runs the length of those two front rooms, is that right?

A That's right.

Q And I believe you have already testified that it is a screened-in porch, is that right?

A That's right.

Q Now tell the jury, Uncle Moses, when you opened the door and looked out at that time, and you saw Mr. Bryant and Mr. Milam there, where were they standing?

MR. BRELAND:[6] We object to that, Your Honor. He said that he didn't recognize them out there. He said he just saw the flashlight.

---

5. "At this point, disregarding the judge's prohibition against taking photographs during testimony, Ernest Withers [a photographer for the *Tri-State Defender* (Memphis)] raised his camera and took a photograph of Moses Wright, a slight figure in yellow and brown suspenders over a white, long-sleeved shirt and a thin black tie. . . ." Booker & Booker, *Shocking the Conscience*, p. 74.

6. Jesse Josiah "J. J." Breland (1888–1969) "was one of five defense attorneys representing Bryant and Milam in their murder trial. He was a graduate of Princeton University and began to practice law in Sumner, Tallahatchie County, Mississippi, in 1915. . . . He later went on to become Tallahatchie County chairman of the Republican Party." Anderson, "Who's Who in the Emmett Till Case."

THE COURT: The objection will be sustained. The witness stated that he didn't recognize Mr. Bryant at that time.

> Q   When did you see those two men that night?
>
> A   That was about two o'clock in the morning.
>
> Q   But did you see them before you opened the door or after?
>
> A   It was after I opened the door.
>
> Q   And where were they standing?
>
> A   Mr. Milam was standing there at the door, and there was one man standing at the screen door, and Mr. Bryant was standing kind of out away from the door.

MR. BRELAND: We object to that, if the Court please. He said that he didn't recognize him.

THE COURT: I believe the witness has stated that he did not see Mr. Bryant, that he didn't see him out there that night because it was dark.

THE WITNESS: I saw him but I couldn't see his face.

THE COURT: The objection will be sustained. He has stated that he didn't recognize Mr. Bryant.

MR. BRELAND: And we would like to ask the jury to disregard that statement.

THE COURT: You gentlemen of the jury will disregard the statement made by the witness about Mr. Bryant at this time.

> Q   When this man first called out to you that night, Uncle Moses, did he tell you who it was?
>
> A   Yes, Sir.
>
> Q   And who did he tell you it was?
>
> A   He said he was Mr. Bryant.
>
> Q   And do you see the man here in this courtroom now who was standing on your porch that night that said he was Mr. Bryant?
>
> A   Yes, Sir.

MR. BRELAND: We object to that, Your Honor. He said that he didn't recognize him.

THE COURT: The objection at this time will be sustained unless the witness can say that he was able to identify him and recognized him that night.

Q   Now, Uncle Moses, what did you say J. W. Milam had in his hand that night when you saw him there on your porch?

A   He had a pistol in his right hand.

Q   And what else did he have?

A   And he had a flashlight in his left hand.

Q   And what did he say to you?

A   Well, he asked me if I had two boys there from Chicago?

Q   And what did you say?

A   I said, "Yes, Sir."

Q   And will you tell the jury who those boys were?

A   Wheeler Parker,[7] my grandson, and Emmett Till.

Q   How long had they been visiting in your home with you?

A   They was there a week that same day.

Q   Now, Uncle Moses, after you told Mr. Milam that you did have two boys there from Chicago, and that they were there in your house, what did he say and do then?

A   Then Mr. Milam said, "I want that boy that done the talking down at Money."

---

7. Wheeler Parker (1939–) "was a cousin of Emmett Till who accompanied him to Mississippi from Chicago to visit relatives. He was with Emmett at the Bryant Grocery and Meat Market the night that Emmett whistled at Carolyn Bryant. He was in the home of Moses and Elizabeth Wright the night that Emmett was abducted. He was born in Mississippi and moved with his parents and two siblings to Argo, Illinois, in 1947. He operated a barber shop in Argo until 2007. He also became a minister in 1977. In 1993, he became pastor of the Argo Temple Church of God in Christ, the church Alma Spearman, Emmett's grandmother, helped to found." Anderson, "Who's Who in the Emmett Till Case." See also "Full Interview: Rev. Wheeler Parker, Emmett Till's Cousin, on the Derek Chauvin Conviction and Racial Justice," CBS News Chicago, April 21, 2021, https://www.cbsnews.com/chicago/news/full-interview-rev-wheeler-parker-emmett -tills-cousin-on-the-derek-chauvin-conviction-and-racial-justice/; Wheeler Parker Jr. & Christopher Benson, *A Few Days Full of Trouble: Revelations on the Journey to Justice for My Cousin and Best Friend, Emmett Till*, New York: One World (2023).

Q   And what did he do?

A   Well, we went right over to the east room, the front room there, and I called, and he wasn't in there.

Q   When you say "We," who do you mean by that? Who was there then?

A   Mr. Milam and Mr. Bryant.

MR. BRELAND: We object to that, Your Honor. And we ask that his statement be excluded.

Q   At any time after you first saw the man with Mr. Milam that you first could not recognize, did you later on recognize him in or about your house as being a man that you knew? Did you ever recognize him that night?

A   That is the first time I remember seeing him.

Q   Where was the first time you remember seeing him?

A   In my house.

Q   The first time you ever saw him was in your house?

A   That's right.

Q   And who was that man?

A   Mr. Milam.

Q   And who else did you see in your house?

A   Mr. Bryant.

MR. BRELAND: Now just a moment, please . . .

THE COURT: Let Mr. Chatham ask a further question about that, if you will, please.

Q   Did you at any time that night recognize Mr. Bryant as one of the men in your house?

A   Yes, Sir.

MR. BRELAND: We object to that, Your Honor. That is just a repetition of the question.

THE COURT: The objection will be overruled there. I believe he stated he didn't recognize him at first. Now let's find out if he ever did recognize anyone there that he could identify as Mr. Bryant.

> Q Uncle Moses, do you see any man in this courtroom now who was with Mr. Milam that night at your house?
>
> A Yes, Sir.

MR. BRELAND: We object to that, if the court please. That is purely a leading question, and having the party here present at this time and sitting in the courtroom, that would not be a proper identification anyway. And his statement to begin with, he said that he never recognized him.

THE COURT: I believe he said he didn't recognize him at the door. The objection will be overruled at this time.

> Q And will you point that man out, Uncle Moses?
>
> A Yes, Sir.
>
> Q Well, point him out for the benefit of the jury.
>
> A Yes, Sir.
>
> Q And who was that man?
>
> A It was Mr. Bryant, he told me he was.
>
> Q Now, after Mr. Milam and Mr. Bryant got in your house that night, tell the jury what you did.
>
> A Well, we went to this first room, we went to the first bed there, and Emmett Till wasn't in there. And so I walked out the door into the side room there. Of course, there wasn't anyone sleeping in the first room. And then I passed another door, and in this second room there, we found him and Simon in bed.
>
> Q Now, what, if anything, was said by Mr. Milam or Mr. Bryant to Emmett Till?
>
> A Well, before we entered into the room, Mr. Milam said, "If this is not the right boy, then we are going to bring him back. If it is not the right boy, we are going to bring him back and put him in the bed."

Q   Did you ask them what they wanted with the boy?

A   No, Sir, I sure didn't.

Q   And what did they do then?

A   Then we come on to where this boy was in the room there, and he was there in the bed, and they told him to get up.

Q   Who did?

A   Mr. Milam said for him to get up.

Q   And what did he have in his hand then?

A   He had the pistol and the flashlight.

Q   And what did Emmett Till do?

A   He got up and dressed. He sat on the side of the bed and dressed.

Q   And what happened after that, Uncle Moses?

A   Well, when he got up, and they started out, then he asked me if I know anybody there and I told him, "No, Sir. I don't know you." And then he said to me, "How old are you?" And then I said, "Sixty four." And then he said, "Well, if you know any of us here tonight, then you will never live to get to be sixty five."

Q   And was that in the room where Emmett was in bed?

A   That's right.

Q   And then did they leave out of your house with Emmett Till?

A   That's right.

Q   Did they go out the same way they came in? When they left your house, did you go back to the door the same way you came in?

A   No, Sir. We went through some room there, you know, the door was open, and we went through this other bedroom there. That is where we went through on the way back.

Q   Was that the room where you and your wife sleep?

A   Yes, Sir.

Q   And when you went through that room, did either Mr. Bryant or Mr. Milam have anything to say to your wife?

A   Yes, Sir, they did.

Q   And what did they say?

A   Well, she had gotten up out of bed, and then he said to her, "You get back in that bed, and I mean, I want to hear the springs."

Q   He said that he wanted to hear the springs?

A   That's right.

Q   And what did she do then?

A   Well, she got back in bed.

Q   And did Mr. Milam still have the pistol in his hand then?

A   He kept it in his hand all the time.

Q   Before you got out of the house, Uncle Moses, or before Mr. Milam or Mr. Bryant got out of the house with Emmett Till, I want you to tell the jury if either you or your wife tried to induce them not to carry the boy out.

A   Yes, Sir.

Q   What did you or your wife say to them?

MR. CARLTON:[8] We object to that, Your Honor. That would be hearsay testimony.

THE COURT: If anything was said it would have been in the presence of the defendants. The objection is overruled.

Q   Go ahead, Uncle Moses, and tell us what was said.

A   Well, my wife, she said that we will pay you whatever you want to charge if you will just release him. She said that we would pay them for whatever he might have done if they would just let him go.

Q   And what did they say?

A   They didn't say a word.

Q   And did they remain there after that?

A   Well, just for a few minutes, and then they walked on.

---

8. Caleb Sidney Carlton (1915–1966) "was one of five defense attorneys representing the defendants. He was admitted to the bar in 1939 and began practicing law in Sumner, Mississippi, in 1945. He later became president of the Mississippi Bar Association." Anderson, "Who's Who in the Emmett Till Case."

Q   Where did they go?

A   They entered a car and drove off towards Money.

Q   And what did you do, Uncle Moses? Did you go to the front door when they went out of
the house?

MR. BRELAND: We object to that. That is a leading question.

THE COURT: I want to ask all counsel to please refrain from leading questions so far as possible.

MR. CHATHAM: I am sure that rule will work both ways, Your Honor.

THE COURT: That applies to all counsel.

Q   Uncle Moses, after Mr. Milam and Mr. Bryant left out of your house that night with Emmett Till, what did you do?

A   Well, I came out towards the screen door, and I stood there on the porch.

Q   Is that the screen door on the porch which you described at the beginning of your testimony?

A   That's right.

Q   And from that point, could you see out near the road in front of your house?

A   I couldn't see very clear because there wasn't no light.

Q   What, if anything, did you see out there when Mr. Milam and Mr. Bryant took Emmett Till out in front of your house?

A   I saw a car moving off towards Money.

Q   And which way was that car parked?

A   It was parked towards Money.

Q   Before Mr. Milam and Mr. Bryant got to the car with Emmett Till, did you hear them make any statement or ask anybody out there any question in that car?

A   I sure did.

Q   Will you tell the jury what that was?

A   They asked if this was the boy, and someone said, "Yes."

Q Was that a man's voice or a lady's voice you heard?

A It seemed like it was a lighter voice than a man's.

Q Did you say it seemed like a louder voice?

A Lighter.

Q And what did they do with Emmett Till after they received that response from the person who was in the car?

MR. BRELAND: If he knows, Your Honor.

THE WITNESS: Then they drove off towards Money.

Q Do you know what kind of an automobile it was?

A No, Sir. They didn't turn on no lights. I just heard it and I kind of saw it there in the dark. It was kind of dark, you know, and there was no lights on it.

Q The lights weren't burning on the car?

A No, Sir.

Q Did you watch the car as it drove off towards Money?

A Well, I stood on the porch there for maybe twenty minutes or more.

Q As far as you know, did they ever turn on any lights on the car?

A I never did see it.

Q Where is the next house situated and what is the closest house from your place in going towards Money?

A I reckon it is about two hundred yards from there.

Q Mr. Frederick lives up that way, is that right?

A That's right.

Q And the closest house from you is about two hundred yards going towards Money?

A Yes, Sir.

Q And what about any house in the other direction?

A I guess about half the distance.

Q In other words, there is no other house close by you, is that right?

A That's right.

Q Now, Uncle Moses, have you since that night ever seen Emmett Till alive?

A No, Sir.

Q Did Mr. Bryant or Mr. Milam ever bring him back to your house that night?

A No, Sir, they haven't.

Q Or have they ever brought him back?

A No, Sir.

Q Now tell the Court and Jury when was the next time after they took Emmett Till away from your house that you saw him or his body.

A I saw him when he was taken out of the river. He was in a boat then. I don't know just which day it was.

Q Was that on the Wednesday following the Saturday night that they took him away from your house?

A That's right.

Q And when you saw Emmett Till there, was he living or dead?

A He was dead.

Q Where was Emmett's body there at the point in the river where you went when you first saw him after that?

A They had him in a boat. He was in a boat there.

Q And who was there handling the boat, if you remember?

A They already had him out. There wasn't anyone handling it when I got there. It was already on shore.

Q It was already on the shore when you got there?

A That's right.

Q And who went with you over there, Uncle Moses?

A It was the Deputy Sheriff, I think. I don't know the names. There was two of them.

MR. BRELAND: We object to his stating what he doesn't know.

MR. CHATHAM: The old man is endeavoring to tell the truth. Do you object to that?

THE COURT: Counsel will please direct all remarks to the Court. These side remarks to each other are not necessary.

Q Then you don't know the Sheriff of this County?

A I just know him since I have been here is all.

Q Well, was Mr. Strider[9] there?

A He sure was.

Q Do you know Mr. Garland Melton, one of his deputies?

A I sure know him, too.

Q Was he there?

A Yes, Sir.

Q And was there a lot of more white people there?

A Yes, Sir.

Q And were there two or three young boys there?

A Yes, Sir.

Q Who came and notified you to come up there, that there might have been some person there for you to see?

A It was the Deputy Sheriff from Greenwood. I don't know his name.

Q You don't know whether it would have been Mr. John Ed Cothran or not?

A Well, I know Mr. Smith, the Sheriff. It wasn't Mr. Smith.

---

9. Henry Clarence "H. C." Strider (1904–1970) "was sheriff of Tallahatchie County from 1951–1955. . . . [H]is actions behind the scenes bore out his support for [the defense]. He was prominent in the press during the Till affair and made no friends among the black press during the trial. He owned a large plantation, and after the trial, five black families moved off of his land because of his actions at the trial. In 1957, he was seated in his car at a general store in Cowart, Mississippi, when a bullet was fired into the vehicle. He narrowly missed being hit in the head. In 1959, he decided to run for the sheriff's office again, but withdrew at the urging of his wife, who feared for his safety. He declined to run again in 1963 for the same reasons. From 1964 until his death, he served as a state senator for Grenada and Tallahatchie counties. In this role, he served as vice chairman and chairman of the Game and Fish Committee, member of the Public Property, Transportation, and Water and Irrigation committees, and chairman of the Penitentiaries Committee. He died of a heart attack while at a deer camp in Issaquena County, Mississippi. Two years after his death, a portion of Mississippi Highway 32 was designated 'Henry Clarence Strider Memorial Highway.'" Anderson, "Who's Who in the Emmett Till Case."

Q Who did you carry with you when you went up there? Did any members of your family go up there with you?

A No, Sir.

Q When you got there, was the body of Emmett Till laying on the bank?

A It was in a boat.

Q I want you to tell the jury whether or not you could tell whose body it was?

A Yes, Sir.

Q And who was it?

A Emmett Till.

Q During the time you were there where you first saw the body, did you notice whether or not the undertaker or any Deputy Sheriff took a ring off of Emmett's finger?

A Yes, Sir.

Q And was that ring taken off his finger in your presence?

A That's right.

Q What did you do after that, Uncle Moses, with reference to the body?

A What is that?

Q What did you do after that with reference to Emmett's body? What did you do with his body?

A Well, we taken it back. The undertaker man took it back to Greenwood.

Q And what undertaker man was that, Uncle Moses?

A Mr. Miller.

Q Is that Chester Miller?[10]

---

10. Chester A. Miller (1903–1986) "managed the Century Burial Association in Greenwood, Mississippi, which received Emmett Till's body after its discovery in the Tallahatchie River. He made initial preparations of the body by placing it in a casket, while law officials planned a burial in Money, Mississippi. He testified [as] to the condition of the body as it was pulled from the river and placed in a boat. He had been called

A   Yes, Sir.

Q   And he is the undertaker man over at Greenwood?

A   That's right.

Q   And he is the man who took the body from the point on the river where you first saw it there?

A   That's right.

Q   And where was it that you next saw Emmett's body after Chester Miller took it away from the river?

A   After he took it away from the river, I didn't see it any more.

Q   Did you supervise the arrangements for the burial of Emmett's body?

A   That's right.

Q   And where did you have it sent?

A   At Money. Where I live, we have a church and graveyard there.

Q   And did they bury the body there?

A   They sure didn't.

Q   What did they do with the body?

A   They carried it back to Greenwood.

MR. BRELAND: We object, Your Honor. He has already said that he didn't see it any more.

THE COURT: The witness can only state what he knows, Mr. Chatham.

Q   Did you give any instructions to the Sheriff, or to the undertaker man, or to anybody as to where the body should be sent for burial?

A   That's right.

Q   And where was that?

A   At Money.

------

to the scene of discovery by Sheriff H. C. Strider." Anderson, "Who's Who in the Emmett Till Case."

Q   But you say they didn't bury the body at Money?

A   They sure didn't.

Q   Well, did you give anyone instructions as to where the body was to be sent for burial?

A   Yes, Sir. I called the boy's Grandmother in Chicago, and she told me. . . .

MR. BRELAND: We object to that, Your Honor.

THE COURT: The witness cannot repeat any conversation that was not made in the presence of the defendants.

Q   After you had this conversation, what instructions did you give as to where the body was to be sent for burial?

A   I said not to carry it to Greenwood and bury the body there, and I made other arrangements.

Q   Did you give the undertaker man there at Greenwood any instructions as to where he was to send the body?

MR. BRELAND: We object, Your Honor. He said that he didn't see the undertaker.

THE COURT: I don't think he testified as to that. I think he said that he had not seen the body after it had been taken away.

MR. BRELAND: Well, find out if he saw the undertaker.

MR. CHATHAM: Mr. Breland, we will conduct this examination, if you don't mind.

THE COURT: You gentlemen will have to direct your remarks to me.

Q   Uncle Moses, what I am trying to get at is this: Where does Emmett's Mother live?

A   In Chicago.

Q   Now will you tell the jury whether or not, whether you gave any instructions to anyone to send the body up to Chicago?

MR. BRELAND: We object to that. We object to the leading form of the question.

THE COURT: Will you rephrase your question, Mr. Chatham?

Q   After the body had been brought to Money, where did you tell the undertaker to send the body from Money?

MR. BRELAND: We object to that, Your Honor. He hasn't said he told him anything about that.

THE COURT: If he told him, he can testify to that.

Q   Did you tell the undertaker where to send the body?

A   I didn't.

Q   Now, Uncle Moses, getting back to the point where you saw Emmett's body there on the river, what river was that?

A   Tallahatchie.

Q   Will you give the jury some idea as to about where on Tallahatchie River the body was when you saw it that Wednesday morning?

A   It was in a boat and the boat was out of the water.

Q   And was it between some towns? What communities or towns was it between or near?

A   It was between Philipp and Tippo.

Q   And you stated you were present there when Miller took the ring off of Emmett's finger?

A   I was looking right at him, that's right.

Q   And what did Miller do with that ring?

A   He put it on the seat there when he taken it off.

Q   Do you mean the seat in the funeral coach?

A   That's right.

Q   Was that ring ever given to you?

A   That's right. I asked for it.

Q   When did you ask for it?

A   Shortly after they got the body in the coach.

Q   And did he give it to you?

A   That's right.

Q   Now I hand you a ring, Uncle Moses, and I ask you to tell the Court and Jury if that is the ring that Chester Miller took off of Emmett's finger and gave to you that morning?

A   Yes, Sir, it is.

Q   How long did you keep the ring after that?

A   Until we got home.

Q   And then what did you do with it?

A   I gave it to the Sheriff.

Q   Sheriff who?

A   To the Deputy. I don't know his name.

Q   Was that a Deputy in this County?

A   Leflore County.

Q   And until today that is the last time you saw this ring, is that right?

A   That's right.

Q   And you say you gave it to the Deputy in Leflore County?

A   That's right.

MR. CHATHAM: TAKE THE WITNESS.

CROSS EXAMINATION BY
MR. CARLTON:[11]

Q   Moses, I believe you testified on direct examination that Emmett was sleeping in the east room right behind your bedroom, is that correct?

A   That's right.

Q   And also that he was in the bed with your son, Simon?

A   That's right.

Q   Who was next to the wall in that bed?

---

11. Caleb Sidney Carlton had also previously represented defendant Roy Bryant's mother in a divorce case.

A   Simon.

Q   And how close was the side of the bed where Emmett was to the doorway into your room?

A   The head of the bed was jammed up against the wall and the door was right there.

Q   And who else was asleep in that room?

A   Robert and Maurice.

Q   I believe on direct examination, he testified there was nobody in there but Simon [sic] and Emmett.

A   Well, that is the way it was. They was in there with Emmett.

Q   Do you mean you are changing your story now from what you said a while ago?

A   I didn't say it.

Q   You didn't say that those were the only two in that room?

Q   They was the only two in the bed, and I didn't say in the room.

Q   Well, who else was in the room?

A   Robert and Maurice. They was both in the bed.

Q   Those are both your boys?

A   That's right.

Q   How old are they?

A   Robert is fourteen and Maurice is sixteen.

Q   When they came to your house that night, as you say, and called out, "Preacher—Preacher," where was Mr. Milam?

A   He was standing right at the door.

Q   And as soon as you opened the door, you saw him?

A   That's right.

Q   Now, will you get up and show the jury just how he had the pistol and the flashlight in his hands, as you say?

A   He had the pistol right in this hand (indicating).

Q   He had the pistol in his right hand?

A   Yes, Sir.

Q   And how did he have the flashlight?

A   In this hand (indicating).

Q   And he had the flashlight in his left hand, is that right?

A   Yes, Sir.

Q   And where was the flashlight pointed?

A   It was out like this (indicating with his hand).

Q   Do you mean it was out in front of his body, in front of the other hand in which you say he had the pistol?

A   That's right.

Q   Was there any light in your house that night?

A   No light.

Q   Did anybody ask you to turn on a light?

A   No, Sir—Well, they asked me to.

Q   Did anybody ask you to turn on the lights?

A   Yes, Sir.

Q   But you didn't turn on the lights?

A   No, Sir.

Q   Were there ever any lights turned on in your house while those men were in there?

A   No, Sir.

Q   How many flashlights were in there, in your house that night?

A   I didn't see but one.

Q   And where did he keep that flashlight while he was in your house?

A   It was right in his hand.

Q   He held it right in front of him all the time?

A   That's right.

Q   Did he ever turn it up and shine it in his face?

MR. CHATHAM: In whose face?

Q   Did he ever turn it in his own face?

A   Well, he had it something like that when we was going through the house (indicating with his hand).

Q   Who was in front of you as you were going through the house?

A   Well, me and Mr. Milam was side by side.

Q   And this other man was behind you, is that right?

A   He was behind.

Q   And did he always keep the flashlight out in front of him?

A   That's right.

Q   Did he ever shine it in his face?

A   Well, I could see from the light, you know, how it will shine out from the side like that.

Q   But did he shine it in Emmett's face?

A   Yes, Sir, he did.

Q   Did he ever shine it in Simon's face?

A   I don't know about that. He was on the back there.

Q   When you went in the room where Emmett was, was Emmett asleep?

A   That's right.

Q   Who wakened him up?

A   He told him to get up and put his clothes on.

Q   Did he have anything on at the time when he was in bed? Was he sleeping with clothes on?

A   I think he had on his shorts and maybe a shirt. I don't think he had pajamas.

Q   And when he told him to get up and put his clothes on, what did he put on then?

A   He put on a shirt and trousers.

Q   Did he put on any shoes?

A   Yes, Sir.

Q   And he got dressed, did he?

A   That's right.

Q   What kind of clothes did he put on?

A   I can't remember what kind.

Q   Well, you stated that you were there looking at him, didn't you?

A   That's right.

Q   And you were standing right there, weren't you?

A   That's right.

Q   And there Mr. Milam was standing there in front of your door, when you opened your door that night, you saw him right there at that time, did you?

A   That's right.

Q   And where was this other man that you say was there who went through the house with you?

A   He was standing back behind Mr. Milam.

Q   Could you see him standing there then?

A   No, Sir, I didn't see him right then.

Q   Then how could you see him when you say that you saw him standing back there then?

A   Well, he was on the porch.

Q   But the light wasn't on, was it?

A   That's right.

Q   When you opened the door and saw Mr. Milam there and saw this other man standing behind him, could you see the car out there then?

A   No, Sir, I didn't see the car.

Q   Well, how could you see the man standing back there if you couldn't see the car?

A   Well, like I said, he was up on the porch.

Q   And you say the light wasn't on?

A   That's right.

Q   But it was so dark out there that you couldn't see the car?

A   I couldn't see the car out in the road, no.

Q Was there anybody else there at that time?

A There was one man who stood there at the screen door.

Q How was he standing?

A Well, he was standing kind of with his head down like this here (demonstrating) peering. He was trying to hide, it looked like.

Q In other words, you think he was trying to hide to keep you from seeing him?

A That's right.

Q And I believe you told me before that you thought he was a colored man, isn't that right?

A He acted like a colored man.

Q Where was this second man when you walked into this other room, this other front room?

A Well, all three of them was almost together.

Q Who was in that other bedroom near the company room?

A There was Wheeler Parker,[12] my grandson, and Curtis Jones.[13]

Q And when you started through the house, you looked at them, did you?

A That's right.

Q Well, how did you know what boy they were looking for?

A I heard someone say that this boy had done something, or had done some talking down at Money. I think that was on Thursday or maybe Friday.

Q You already knew about it, did you?

A That's right.

---

12. See note 7, *supra*.

13. Curtis Jones (1938–2000) was "a cousin of Emmett Till. He traveled from Illinois to Mississippi to spend time with Moses Wright's family shortly after Emmett and Wheeler Parker had left, and was in the Wright home the night Emmett was abducted. He is quoted in the film *Eyes on the Prize* as having been at the store at the time of the incident between Emmett Till and Carolyn Bryant, although he had not yet arrived in Mississippi. He served with the Chicago Police Department for years." Anderson, "Who's Who in the Emmett Till Case."

Q   Had you talked to Emmett about it?

A   I sure did.

MR. SMITH:[14] We object to that, if the Court please.

THE COURT: The objection is sustained.

Q   Did you punish Emmett for that?

MR. SMITH: We object, Your Honor.

THE COURT: The objection is sustained.

Q   When you went into the company room, you went into the second room on the east side, is that right?

A   The South side.

Q   And that would have been the side towards Money, is that right?

A   Yes, Sir.

Q   And there is a door going from the company room into that room, is that right?

A   That's right.

Q   And there is no door between your room and the company room?

A   That's right.

Q   There is a chimney there, isn't that right?

A   That's right.

Q   And there are some pictures there on the mantel, is that right?

A   That's right.

---

14. Acting as a special prosecutor, former FBI agent Robert B. Smith III (1914–1967) of Ripley, Mississippi, was appointed by then attorney general J.P. Coleman to assist in the prosecution of the defendants. After the trial, he returned to Ripley to practice law with his uncle. On December 4, 1967, Smith, who suffered from alcoholism, committed suicide (shot himself). *Clarion Ledger*, September 13, 2018. "Smith played a key role in finding, and providing protection, for several of the state's vital witnesses, including Moses Wright and 17-year-old black youth Willie Reed, who placed the two accused white men at the suspected murder scene." *Daily Journal* (Jackson, Mississippi), January 23, 2003; Anderson, "Who's Who in the Emmett Till Case."

Q   Whose pictures are on the mantel there?

MR. SMITH: We object to that, Your Honor. That has nothing to do with this case at all. It has no bearing on this matter whatsoever.

THE COURT: Unless it is shown to be pertinent to this trial, the objection is sustained.

Q   Was there anybody sleeping in the second room there at all?

A   There sure wasn't.

Q   That is a bedroom there too, isn't it?

A   That's right.

Q   And then you go from that room into the room where Emmett was sleeping?

A   That's right.

Q   And back of that room in your house, back from where Emmett was, you go into a place which is something like a hallway, between there and the dining room, isn't that right?

Q   That's right.

Q   And there is a little place in there on the east side between the dining room and the kitchen, isn't that right?

Q   That's right.

Q   And the kitchen is over on the left side as you are going through there?

A   Yes, Sir.

Q   By the way, do you have electricity there?

A   Yes, Sir.

Q   And you have an electric refrigerator, do you?

A   Yes, Sir.

Q   And you also have electric lights, do you?

A   Yes, Sir.

Q   And you say that one of the men asked you to turn the lights on that night?

A   Yes, Sir.

Q But you still didn't turn the lights on?

A I sure didn't.

Q Did you ever see this man that you pointed out as Mr. Bryant, did you ever see the light shining on his face that night?

A Did not.

Q Had you ever seen him before that night?

A Not to know him.

Q Had you ever been in his store?

A I never have.

Q And the first time you ever saw him was in the courtroom this week, wasn't it?

A The first time I saw his face, that's right.

Q Now, let's go back to Mr. Milam—you testified that he was standing in the doorway of your house with a pistol in his right hand and a flashlight out in front of him in his left hand, is that correct?

A That's right.

Q And the flashlight was sticking out in front about six or eight inches, about six or eight inches in front of the pistol, is that right?

A I don't know about that. I didn't measure it.

Q Had you ever seen Mr. Milam before that night?

A I never had.

Q Did you ever see the lights flashing on his face that night?

A Sure. He had it up to his face. That is the way I know him.

Q Moses, you talked to me over at this law office over here (pointing with his hand) last week, is that right?

A That's right.

Q And do you remember this gentleman here, Mr. Breland, being present at that time?

A Yes, Sir.

Q   And do you remember Mr. Henderson[15] being present there that day (indicating another gentleman)?

A   That's right.

Q   And this gentleman over there in the blue coat, Mr. Kellum, was he present that day also?

A   That's right.

Q   You remember him being there, do you?

A   Yes, Sir.

Q   And isn't it a fact, Moses, that you on that day told each one of those gentlemen and me that the only reason you thought this was Mr. Milam in your house that night was due to the fact that he was a big man and had a bald head? Isn't that true?

A   That's right.

Q   And the first time that you ever saw him was in this courthouse later on when they came into the courtroom, isn't that right?

A   I don't believe I understand.

Q   The first time you ever saw him was in this courtroom, isn't that right?

A   No Sir. I knowed him that night.

Q   And the reason you say you know him is because the man had a bald head, isn't that right?

A   Well, I noticed his face and his stature. And I knowed his face just like I see him there now.

Q   Then you have changed your story from what you told us the other day, haven't you?

A   They was at my house.

Q   And the only thing you saw at your house, the only man you saw, was a bald headed man, is that right?

A   That's right.

---

15. He was one of the defense attorneys.

Q Moses, isn't it a fact that before you saw Mr. Milam up here, you saw Mr. Milam's picture in the newspapers, that is, before he came in here and you saw him up here? Isn't that true?

A I don't know whether I have or not. I can't remember.

Q Now isn't it a fact that you told me and these other gentlemen here last week that you saw him in the newspaper before you saw him here in the courtroom?

A I don't remember saying that.

Q Do you deny that?

A I don't remember.

Q What were Emmett's initials, Moses?

A I don't know.

Q Are his initials "L. T."?

A That is his Daddy's name, Louis Till.[16]

Q But are they Emmett's initials?

A That is Louis Till, his Father's initials.

Q But they are not Emmett's initials, is that right?

A That's right.

Q Now, you say you saw a car out there when you first came out on the porch, and you say you saw it first when they went out there with Emmett, is that right?

A I saw it when they went out there with the boy. I could see something black up on the road.

Q But you say you couldn't see a car out there on the road when you first opened the door?

A That's right.

---

16. Louis Till (1922–1945) married Mamie in 1940, but the two separated in 1942—he was physically abusive towards Mamie. He served in the military during World War II. He was found guilty of murder and rape and then executed by the U.S. Army in 1945. After the trial Emmett Till's murder gained international media attention when Mississippi senators James Eastland and John C. Stennis uncovered confidential details about Louis Till's reported crimes and execution.

Q But you could see a man standing out there?

A When I first came on the porch there, sure, I saw him.

Q Now, this car you say you saw out there afterwards, was the car pulled up to your porch or was it out on the road?

A It was in the space between the road and my house.

Q It wasn't up in the gravel road, was it?

A No, Sir.

Q And it is just about fifty feet out to the gravel road, isn't that right?

A It is something like that.

Q And what kind of trees are in the yard there?

A Cedar trees and Persimmon trees.

Q And those trees are about thirty or forty feet from the road, isn't that right?

A No, Sir.

Q Then how far are they?

A I guess about maybe ten or twelve feet, something like that.

Q Is there plenty of room for a car to pull off there?

A There is plenty of room for a car. I park there.

Q And you saw the car parked there, did you?

A When it pulled off.

Q Then you didn't see a car before it pulled off?

A I didn't see it before he pulled off.

Q Then you didn't see Emmett get into the car, did you?

A I didn't see that.

MR. CHATHAM: If the Court please, I would like to ask Mr. Carlton to please give the Witness time to answer his questions.

THE COURT: The Witness will have plenty of opportunity to answer the questions. And I must ask Counsel to direct all remarks to the Court.

Q   You didn't see Emmett get into the car, did you?

A   I did not.

Q   And you didn't see anybody put him in the car, did you?

A   I did not.

Q   And you did not see either one of these men who were at your house get into the car, did you?

A   I did not.

Q   And you didn't see anybody in that car when it drove off, did you?

A   I did not.

Q   Did you see any headlights on the car?

A   There wasn't no lights on.

Q   Did you see any tail light on the car?

A   I did not.

Q   When they opened the door to get in the car, did any lights turn on?

A   I didn't see it.

Q   How many folks were in that car?

A   I don't know.

Q   Was this voice you say you heard out there the voice of one of these three men you had already seen there?

A   It was just a voice. They took him out there, and somebody said, "Is this him?" and then a voice said, "Yes." But it wasn't one of them.

Q   And the only reason you thought Mr. Bryant was there that night was because somebody came up there and told you or said that he was Mr. Bryant, is that right?

A   That's right.

Q   How old is Emmett Till?

A   Fourteen.

Q   What grade was he in?

A   The 9th.

Q   And how did he walk? Did he walk natural?

A   He walked right.

Q   Did he walk good?

A   That's right.

Q   And how did he talk?

A   Well, he had a stammering speech. Sometimes he couldn't get a word out.

Q   Did you understand him all right?

A   Yes, when he got it out.

Q   And he could make you understand him, is that right?

A   That's right.

Q   And how tall was he?

A   Well, it looked like Emmett was about five feet and three or four inches.

Q   And how much did he weigh?

A   One hundred and fifty.

Q   Did he look like he was pretty well grown? Was he a pretty good sized man?

A   He looked like a man.

Q   When this car drove off from there that night, how many people were in there when it drove off?

A   I don't know.

Q   Well, you say you stood there and watched it drive off, is that right?

A   Yes, Sir.

Q   Was the moon shining?

A   It was not.

Q   There was no light there at all?

A   No light.

Q   And you didn't turn on the lights in your house?

A   That's right.

Q   And you say you stood there for about twenty minutes before you did anything?

A   That's right.

Q   Now, let's go up there to the morning on the river, Moses. When you went up there, how many folks were in the car that you went up there in?

A   There was three.

Q   Do you know who they were?

A   I don't know their names. They said it was the Deputy Sheriff of Greenwood; Mr. Cothran, I think.

Q   Did you stop anywhere on your way up there?

A   We stopped at Philipp.

Q   Why did you stop there?

A   They stopped to inquire where the body was?

Q   You stopped there at Philipp and then you went on up the road to where the body was?

A   Yes, Sir.

Q   And you went with them up there?

A   I sure did.

Q   When they parked the car there, what did you do?

A   We all got out and walked down to the river.

Q   You got out of the car and then walked down a ways to go down to the river where the body was?

A   Yes.

Q   Could you see the body in the river?

A   I couldn't see good. It was in the boat.

Q   There wasn't any trees or anything like that from where the car was parked to where the body was, is that right?

A   Yes, Sir.

Q   And you could look to where the body was from where the car was parked?

A   Yes, Sir.

Q   And did you walk down to where the body was with Mr. Cothran?

A   I sure did.

Q   And did he ask you on the way down there if that looked like the boy's body?

A   I can't remember now whether he did or not.

Q   Then you were close to him, were you, when you first decided it was Emmett's body?

A   I was standing right up over him.

Q   And you didn't say anything to him when you were about fifteen or twenty yards back from the boat, you didn't say that it looked like him when you were that distance away?

A   I don't remember.

Q   You didn't tell Mr. Cothran that before you got down to the boat.

A   I don't remember.

Q   Do you mean to say that you did not tell him that it looked like Emmett when you were some distance away before you reached the boat?

A   I can't remember.

Q   On the river down there, what was done with the boat?

A   What was that?

Q   Was the boat still in the water?

A   It was out of the water.

Q   It was out of the water just like it had been pulled out on the bank out of the water?

A   It was just kind of pulled out, yes, Sir.

Q   And how was the body in the boat there?

A   It was in the boat.

Q   Well, was it laying face down or on its back?

A   On its face.

Q   And what part of his body was up towards you as you were coming up there to the boat?

A   His head.

Q   And all you could see lying there in the boat was just his head and back, is that right?

A   They turned him over, and then I saw all of it.

Q   Now wait just a minute, Moses—when you first came up there, all you saw was just the head and back, is that right?

A   That's right.

Q   When you got down there, did you have any conversation with the officers there after that as to whether that was Emmett or not?

A   I can't remember.

Q   Who turned the body over?

A   I can't remember that either. But someone turned it.

Q   Someone turned the body over, is that right?

A   That's right.

Q   And then you looked at him, did you?

A   That's right. That is when I began viewing him.

Q   And you were sure that was Emmett Till?

A   That's right.

Q   When did you first see this ring?

A   The same day that he was taken out there, I saw him on the boat there, and that is the first time I seen the ring.

Q   As I understand, you brought him down from Chicago with you didn't you?

A   Yes, Sir.

Q   And you brought him down on the train with you, is that right?

A   That's right.

Q   And I believe, as I understand it, you left there on Saturday morning and arrived Saturday afternoon, is that correct?

A   That's right.

Q   Then you saw him with that ring, didn't you?

A   Well, he didn't wear it all the time. He didn't wear it every day. I think they had to put some tape around it, or something. It was too big.

Q   Do you mean to say that he was there in your home all week and you didn't see that ring?

A   I sure didn't.

Q   Then you had never seen that ring before?

A   No, Sir.

Q   Did it have tape on it then?

A   It didn't then.

Q   But you say it was too big?

A   That's right.

Q   Just how do you know that is was too big?

A   Well, I know when they got it of his finger, well, it was all swollen, and it was slipping off then.

Q   But you didn't really know it was too big, did you?

A   It was too large.

Q   But you had never seen it before, is that right?

A   I never seen it.

Q   And you don't know of your own knowledge that it was Emmett's ring, do you?

A   Yes, Sir, I do.

Q   Just how do you know that, Moses?

A   Simon and Robert told me.

Q   Somebody told you it was his ring, is that right?

A   Simon and Robert told me.

MR. CARLTON: I would like to ask the Court to disregard that.

MR. BRELAND: If Your Honor please, we ask the Court to instruct the jury to disregard the statement that he knew it was Emmett's ring.

THE COURT: You gentlemen will disregard the statement that he made where he said that he knew it was Emmett's ring.

MR. SMITH: If the Court please, Mr. Carlton asked the witness the question, himself, and the witness was just replying to his question.

THE COURT: Will you ask the question over again, Mr. Carlton. I didn't get the response to that particular question.

MR. CARLTON: Inasmuch as the Court has told or instructed the jury to disregard his last statement, I will pursue another line of questioning.

Q   Now, Moses, you say that the only reason you identified that man there that night as being Mr. Bryant is that he said he was Mr. Bryant, is that right?

A   That's right.

Q   And you also say that, the only reason you identified Mr. Milam as being there that night is the fact that he is a big man and bald headed, is that right?

A   That's right.

Q   Now, Moses, isn't it a fact that you told these same four gentlemen that I have pointed out previously—those three gentlemen over there and myself—that you told them that the only reason that you could identify that body in the boat as being Emmett Till was because he was smooth faced? Isn't it a fact that you said because the body didn't have any whiskers and was smooth faced, and because Emmett was missing, then you identified that body there in the boat as being Emmett Till? Isn't that correct?

A   I didn't mention no missing.

Q   Moses, do you deny that you made this statement to Mr. Breland, Mr. Henderson, Mr. Kellum and me[17] that the only reason you could identify that body in the boat as being Emmett Till was because he was clean faced or smooth faced, and because Emmett Till was missing?

A   I did not say it.

Q   You did not make that statement?

A   No, Sir, I did not make it.

Q   Moses, when you were talking to those four defense lawyers over there in Mr. Breland's office, did we treat you nice?

A   I think so.

---

17. These were the attorneys for the defendants.

MR. CHATHAM: We object to that, Your Honor. He is leading the witness and telling him what to say.

THE COURT: The objection will be sustained. I will let you ask him how he was treated, but let him state it, himself.

Q   Well, how were you treated over there, Moses?

A   I was treated all right.

Q   Were you treated just about like the State's attorney treated you when he talked to you?

A   That's right.

Q   Did anybody threaten you over there?

A   They did not.

Q   And were you told there in that office that all we wanted to know there was just what you knew about it?

A   That's right.

MR. SMITH: If the Court please, we will admit—we know these five gentlemen here, and we will admit of our knowledge that Moses was not mistreated and that he wasn't brow-beaten, and we will admit that all that is true. We admit that. We know they wouldn't do a thing like that.

THE COURT: All right, I think that is enough.

Q   Moses, on this Wednesday night that the incident[18] happened in Money, where were you?

A   At church.

MR. SMITH: We object to anything that happened on Wednesday night, if the Court please. That has nothing to do with whatever is involved in this lawsuit.

THE COURT: I think it calls for a conclusion and would be hearsay evidence. And I think it is objectionable there unless it is further qualified.

---

18. Notice that the defense refers to the kidnapping as "the incident."

Q Now, on the Wednesday night before this incident, on the Wednesday night down there at Money. . . .

MR. SMITH: If the Court please, we object to anything that happened on Wednesday night.

THE COURT: I will let Mr. Carlton ask the question before I rule on any question or on any objection to a question.

Q On the Wednesday night preceding the night that Emmett Till disappeared from your home, where were you?

MR. SMITH: We object to that, Your Honor.

THE COURT: The objection is overruled.

Q Where were you, Moses, on the Wednesday night before Emmett Till disappeared from your home?

A At the church.

Q And who was at church with you?

A Oh, there was a good many people there. I can't recall.

Q I mean, who was with you from your family group in your house?

A My wife.

Q Were the boys with you?

A No, Sir.

MR. SMITH: If the Court please, we object to all questions that have to do with anything that happened prior to the night that Emmett Till disappeared. That has nothing to do with the case at all.

THE COURT: The objection will be overruled. He can state that. But the witness is not going to be permitted to state something that he doesn't know of his own knowledge.

Q Were your boys at church with you that night?

A They was not.

Q Was Emmett Till at church with you that night?

A No, Sir.

Q Do you know where they were?

THE COURT: Just of his own knowledge now, not by hearsay.

THE WITNESS: I sure don't.

Q Did they have your car that night?

A That's right.

Q Now, Moses, when they came to your door that night—these four men—did you know what boy they wanted to see?

A That's right.

Q Then I take it you know who they wanted?

A They told me who they wanted.

Q What did they tell you?

A They said they wanted the boy that done the talking at Money.

Q And you knew who that boy was, did you?

A That's right.

Q After the men who had come in your home that night, after they left and after Emmett went out the door, what did you do?

A I stood on the porch, I think, for about twenty minutes after they left.

Q And what did you do after that? What did you do after you left your porch? Where did you go?

A I went to the store and got some gasoline.

Q Did you go in your car?

A That's right.

Q And who was with you when you went after the gasoline?

A My wife.

Q Where were the boys? Where were your boys?

A They stayed at home.

Q The five of them stayed there at home? That is, your three boys and Wheeler Parker and Curtis Jones?

A That's right.

Q   Did you go back to your house that night after you bought the gasoline?

A   I don't think so.

Q   When did you next come back to your house after you left there that night to get some gasoline?

A   I reckon it was about eight o'clock Sunday, something like that.

Q   Did you leave any adult, any grown person, there with your boys during that time you were gone?

A   I sure didn't.

Q   About what time did you leave to go to the store after the gasoline?

A   I reckon it was about forty minutes after it happened, I guess, as near as I can remember.

Q   And you say it happened about two o'clock, is that right?

A   Something like that.

Q   Then that would make it about a quarter to three when you left your home to get some gasoline?

A   Maybe something like that.

Q   And you say you left there at that time and didn't come back there to your house until about eight o'clock Sunday morning?

A   I guess it was about that.

Q   And you left the boys there—you left them there for about five hours by themselves, is that right?

A   I guess something like that. I don't know exactly. I didn't keep time.

Q   Tell me, Moses, if Emmett Till had not disappeared, would you have identified the body in the boat as Emmett Till?

A   What do you mean? Do you mean the same identification I had before?

Q   If Emmett Till had not been missing, would you have thought that was Emmett Till's body in that boat?

A   With the evidence I had on him?

Q   Yes.

A   Yes, Sir.

Q   And because he had this ring on his finger, I take it, and because your boys told you that was Emmett's ring, is that right?

A   That's right.

Q   But you had never seen the ring before?

A   That's right.

Q   And all you know about the ring is what your boys told you, is that right?

A   That's right.

Q   Was this a dark night. Moses, that these men came to your house?

A   That's right.

Q   And there was never any light in that house that night except from just one flashlight, is that right?

A   That's right.

Q   And it was so dark that you couldn't even see the car out in your front yard, is that right?

MR. CHATHAM: Your Honor, I think that is about the third time he has gone over that. We will be here all week if he keeps up that type of questioning.

THE COURT: I will ask you to please limit your questioning and not repeat questions, if possible to do so. But we will let him ask that question.

Q   My question was, Moses—it was so dark that night that you couldn't even see a car in your front yard, is that right?

A   I couldn't make out what it was, what kind of a car it was.

Q   And you don't know whether it was a Ford or a Chevrolet, is that right?

A   That's right.

Q   And you don't know whether it was a truck or whether it was just a car, is that right?

A   That's right.

Q All you know is that some vehicle was out in front of your house and that it drove off towards Money after these men went out of your house, is that right?

A I saw something dark out there, but I couldn't make out what it was.

Q And you don't know whether it was a car or a truck, do you?

A Well, when it passed the trees, I saw something dark. But I couldn't make out just what it was, what kind it was.

Q Was there more than one car there?

A I don't know if there was more than one. I just seen one car.

Q Which way was the car facing?

A Towards Money.

Q Could you see that it was facing towards Money?

A Yes, Sir. They didn't ever have to turn around at all. They just drove right off with it.

Q Could you see that it was facing towards Money?

A That's right.

Q Do you mean to say that you could see it was facing towards Money, but you couldn't tell whether it was a car or a truck out there?

A That's right. I saw it when it passed the trees, when it was going towards Money. I could see it then easy.

Q Then what kind of a car was it if you could see it so easy?

MR. SMITH: If the Court please, he has already testified to that.

THE COURT: I think that question has been covered.

MR. CARLTON: That is all.

MR. CHATHAM: I think that be all we have with this witness.

(WITNESS EXCUSED.)

* * * *

(At the request of the Prosecution, the Court took a recess from 10:25 a.m. until 10:50 a.m., this date, at which time the proceedings were resumed.)

MR. BRELAND: If the Court please, the Clerk of this Court has just handed Defense Counsel a list of additional witnesses which the Clerk states he has subpoenaed both for the State and defense. We now move the Court that the defendants' counsel have the opportunity of examining these witnesses in the witness room before they are offered as witnesses by the State.

The names of these witnesses are as follows:

- Amandy Bradley,
- Walter Billingsley,[19]
- Ed Reed,
- Willie Reed,
- Frank Young,[20] and
- C.A. Strickland.

THE COURT: Have subpoenas been issued for them for the defendants?

MR. BRELAND: They have, Your Honor.

---

19. Walter Billingsley (1923–?) "was slated as a witness for the prosecution in the Milam–Bryant murder trial, but was not called to testify. He was a milkman on the Sturdivant plantation near Drew, Sunflower County, Mississippi, and heard the sounds of the beating in the barn on the morning after Emmett Till was kidnapped in Money. This plantation was managed by Leslie Milam, brother of J. W. Milam and half-brother to Roy Bryant. He was supposed to testify at the trial but, at the last minute, told prosecutors that he did not see or hear anything. His life after the trial remains unknown at present." Anderson, "Who's Who in the Emmett Till Case."

20. Frank Young (1920–?) "was a field worker who volunteered names of accomplices of J. W. Milam and Roy Bryant in the kidnapping and murder of Emmett Till to Dr. T.R.M. Howard, as well as leads to possible witnesses. It was intended that he testify on behalf of the prosecution at the Milam–Bryant murder trial, but for whatever reason, he left the courthouse and did not testify." *Ibid.* See also Beito & Beito, *T.R.M. Howard,* pp. 135–37, 140.

THE COURT: Then you will have an opportunity to examine them before they are put on the witness stand.

MR. SMITH: If they have been subpoenaed for the defense also, then we have no objection to them talking to the witnesses. But I will make this further statement, that none of these witnesses will be offered until after the noon recess, unless some change in our plans comes up which we cannot foresee.

THE COURT: If they have been subpoenaed by the defense, then they will have an opportunity to talk to them before they are put on the stand.

* * * *

Chapter 2

———

THE STATE'S CASE
IDENTIFYING THE BODY AND
THE CAUSE OF DEATH

Robert B. Smith and Gerald Chatham, arguing on behalf of the State, called seven witnesses: Chester Miller (undertaker), C.A. Strickland (identification officer), George Smith (arresting sheriff), Robert Hodges (fisherman who discovered the body), B.L. Mims (at the scene when the body was found), C.F. "Chick" Nelson (owner of the funeral home that embalmed Till's body), and John Ed Cothran (deputy sheriff at the scene of the discovery of body).

The main purpose of their testimony was to identify, by various means, the bloated and disfigured body found in the Tallahatchie River as that of Emmett Till. The prosecution could not establish murder unless it first proved with reasonable certainty the identity of the corpse. For all one knew, and as the defense argued, Emmett Till could still have been alive. Though the identity question came up during the testimony of Moses Wright, the prosecution felt it needed to introduce more evidence to establish this principle element of the crime of murder. Likewise, it sought to introduce evidence as to the cause of death.

We also learn that the undertaker had been instructed by Officer Strickland to bury the body promptly,[1] which would have made it yet more difficult to identify. (Recall that Emmett was not buried in Mis-

———

1. The author Angie Thomas put it well: "Why is the sheriff even making that [burial] decision? When have you heard of a sheriff deciding where a body would be buried?" Quoted in *Let the World See*, ABC docuseries, episode 1 (January 6, 2022).

sissippi as his mother intervened to claim his body and have it shipped to Chicago. Soon thereafter, he was buried at Burr Oak Cemetery in Alsip, Illinois.) In the rush and agony of it all, no autopsy was then conducted. Additionally, during this portion of the trial transcript, we learn of the cotton gin fan that had been affixed to Emmett's neck with barbed wire; we also learn of a ring that had been found on the body with the date "May 25, 1943," and the big initials "L. T." inscribed on it—the ring of Emmett's father, Louis. This was submitted as evidence to identify the body as that of Till.

J. J. Breland again took the lead for the defense in cross-examining the State's witnesses. Time and again Breland, assisted by Sidney Carlton, sought to prove that given the disfigured state of the body, it was impossible to identify it. Importantly, the defense team also sought to keep out of evidence Roy Bryant's and J. W. Milam's conversations with and confessions to Sheriff Smith and his deputy sheriff John Ed Cothran.

Also, in an exchange with Sheriff Smith, Breland went to great lengths to discredit the officer who first took a confession from Roy Bryant as to *kidnapping*. Eleven years before the Supreme Court's landmark custodial interrogation ruling in *Miranda v. Arizona*, Breland sought to exclude from evidence anything Bryant said to Smith that might be incriminating, even in the absence of any force used by the sheriff: "[T]he witness should not be permitted to testify," Breland argued, "on the grounds that any statement made to the witness was made as a matter of confidence, and any statement that was made, whatever it was, would not be competent in this case." He also objected to the sheriff's testimony being allowed since the "corpus delicti" (actual evidence of the death of the victim) had yet to be established. With such procedural moves, he hoped to prevent Sheriff Smith's testimony of Roy Bryant's *kidnapping* confession from being admitted into evidence in this *murder* trial. An identical tact was taken by Sidney Carlton when Deputy Sheriff Cothran was cross-examined. In the end, Judge Swango overruled the objections.

CHESTER A. MILLER,[2]

A witness introduced for and on behalf of the State, being first duly sworn, upon his oath testified as follows:

DIRECT EXAMINATION BY
MR. SMITH:

Q Your name is Chester A. Miller?

A Yes, Sir.

Q Where do you live, Chester?

A I live in Greenwood.

Q Greenwood, Mississippi?

A Yes, Sir.

Q What is your occupation?

A I am an undertaker.

Q How long have you been in the business of an undertaker?

A Sixteen years.

Q Do you own your own establishment or not?

A No, Sir.

Q You do not?

A No, Sir.

Q You just work there as an undertaker, is that it?

A I am there as manager.

Q You are manager of it?

A Yes, Sir.

Q Chester, have you been continuously employed in that occupation for sixteen years, for the sixteen years that you have been there?

A Yes, Sir.

---

2. See Chapter 1 note 10, *supra*.

Q Now, on or about the 31st day of August, 1955, were you called upon to come to Tallahatchie County to pick up a body?

A Yes, Sir.

Q Who came with you on that occasion? Who came from your funeral home up here with you?

A One of my helpers.

Q One of your nephews?

A No—one of my helpers.

Q Where did you go when you came up here?

A I went beyond Philipp, back in there on the river.

Q You went down to the river?

A Yes, Sir.

Q Who called you and requested you to come up there?

A Mr. Cothran.

Q Who is Mr. Cothran?

A He is a deputy sheriff of Leflore County.

Q When you got up there, what did you do?

A When we got there, they ordered us to turn the body over.

Q Well, when you got there, did you see a body?

A Yes, Sir.

Q Was it living or dead?

A It was a dead body.

Q Where was it when you got there?

A It was lying in a boat.

Q And where was the boat relative to being up on the bank or in the stream?

A The boat was up on the bank.

Q Was the body laying face down or face up when you first got there?

A Face down.

Q Then what did you do relative to the body at that time, you and your helper?

A   Well, we got ready to move the body.

Q   How did you move it? What did you do?

A   We just turned it over. We first turned it over.

Q   Was that while it was still in the boat?

A   Yes, Sir.

Q   All right—then what did you do? What did you do with the body then?

A   Well, we—someone—some of the law officers asked us to go and move that ring off his hand. After we turned it over, then we discovered this ring on one of his fingers.

Q   What kind of a ring was that?

A   It was kind of silver. It was a big ring up in here (indicating with his hand), but it was kind of small underneath.

Q   Would you recognize that ring if you saw it again?

A   Yes, Sir.

Q   I hand you here a ring that has marked on it, engraved on the front of it, "May 25, 1943," and with the Large initials, "L. T." I will ask you if that is the ring you removed off the finger of that dead body?

A   Yes, Sir.

Q   You can positively identify that as the same ring?

A   Yes, Sir.

Q   Now then, Chester, who took the ring off?

A   My helper, because he had the gloves on, and when we got the call, we rushed off and only had one pair of gloves with us. And when one of the law officers said, "Take the ring off that finger," well, he had the gloves on, and then I said to him, "Take it off." And then he took it off and handed it to me.

Q   Did you or did you not see the ring taken off of the finger of that hand?

A   Yes, Sir.

Q   And when the ring was taken off, what did you do with it?

A   Well, he gave it to me. I was standing right there by his side when he took it off.

Q And what did you do with it?

A I laid it over on the floorboard of the ambulance, on the left-hand side there.

Q That was your ambulance that you took up there for the body?

A Yes, Sir.

Q And afterwards what did you do with the ring?

A Well, after we got the body turned over, then we decided to load it, and then he took the ring off, and I put it away there where I told you, on the floorboard of the ambulance. And then we decided to get ready to load the body and move it away. And then we went and got the casket—or rather it was kind of like a regular shipping case, you might call it. You see, the body was swollen so, and we had this casket and box there, and we took the shipping case, which is really a metal article, you know. It was there on top of the regular casket case. And then we taken it out and put it aside, and then we taken the lid off the casket box, the outer box, you know, and then we taken this casket, and we set it there by the side of the body. And then I and my helper, we lifted the body and taken the body out and laid it there in the casket. And then we closed the casket as best we could, and then we put the casket in this outer box, and we took the box, the entire box, and we pushed it up in the ambulance.

Q Now, go back to the time the body was still in the boat—was there any other thing in the boat there with the body?

A Yes, Sir.

Q What was it?

A Well, there was a big wheel there.

Q A big wheel?

A A [cotton gin] wheel and a strand of barbed wire.[3]

Q Was that barbed wire attached to the big wheel? Was it wrapped around it or attached to it in any way?

---

3. The cotton gin wheel fan was in the courthouse basement, then tossed out, thereafter retrieved by someone, and ultimately discarded, never to be seen again. *See* Anderson, *Emmett Till*, pp. 337–38, 475 n. 86.

A I just don't remember whether it was attached to the wheel or not.

Q Was it attached to the body?

A Yes, Sir.

Q The barbed wire was.

A Yes, Sir.

Q And the barbed wire—how was it attached to the body?

A It was right around the neck.

Q In what manner was it right around the neck? Was it wrapped around?

A Yes, Sir, it was wrapped around; well wrapped.

Q It was around the neck of the body?

A Around the neck, yes, Sir.

Q Now then, you said you put the ring in the funeral coach, or the ambulance, this vehicle you took up there with you, then what happened to that ring after that?

A Well, we pretty much got everything taken care of, and then I went up there—well, I went up to some colored men who was standing there, and I asked if this boy had any relatives that they knowed about, and then someone pointed to this old man standing there, and someone said, "This old man is his Uncle or some relation." And then I went up and I asked him, "Will you identify the body as the boy who was taken from the house. . . ."

MR. BRELAND: We object to that, Your Honor.

THE COURT: The objection will be sustained. You can't state anything that would be hearsay. And I will ask you, gentlemen on the jury, to disregard that statement.

Q Did anyone present there at the scene identify the body as any particular person?

A Yes, Sir.

Q And who did they identify it as being?

THE COURT: That is, if you know.

MR. BRELAND: We object, Your Honor. That calls for a conclusion.

THE COURT: The objection is overruled.

Q   Who did they identify that body as being, if you know?

A   The body of Emmett Till.

MR. BRELAND: We object, Your Honor, because that was a statement made there.

THE COURT: The objection is overruled.

Q   Did you later find out who the person was who identified the body that you testified to?

A   Yes, Sir.

Q   And who was that?

A   Moses Wright.

Q   Have you seen Uncle Moses since then?

A   Yes, Sir, I have seen him since then.

Q   And you know that was Moses Wright?

A   Yes, Sir, I know him well.

Q   Now then, I will ask you, in your business as an undertaker for sixteen years, have youseen a number of dead bodies in that time?

MR. BRELAND: I object to that leading form of the question.

THE COURT: Objection overruled.

Q   Have you or not seen lots of dead bodies during the time you have been in your profession?

A   Yes, Sir.

Q   In your opinion, was the body that was there in the boat that you took out of the boat and put in your ambulance, was it possible for someone who had known the person well in their lifetime to have identified that body?

A   Yes, Sir.

MR. BRELAND: I object to that, Your Honor. That definitely calls for a conclusion.

THE COURT: The objection is sustained. And the jury will disregard that answer.

Q Now, Chester, when you got the body up, you testified you got the body up and then put it in a casket, and put it in a box, and then you put it in your ambulance—then what did you do with that body thereafter?

A I taken it to my place, to the funeral home.

Q And where was that?

A Greenwood.

Q What instructions were you given relative to what to do with the body? Now don't tell what anybody said, but just what instructions you may have received as to what to do with it after you got it.

A Well, we were instructed to unload it because there had to be some more investigation made of it.

Q Did anyone take any pictures of that body while it was down there?

A Yes, Sir.

Q And who took them?

A Mr. Strickland.[4]

Q And who is Mr. Strickland?

A He is one of the police officers there in Greenwood.

Q And that was while the body was down there in your place?

A Yes, Sir.

Q What instructions were you later given as to what to do with the body?

A To take it to burial.

---

4. Charles Alvin "C. A." Strickland (1904–1994) "was an identification officer who worked for the Greenwood, Mississippi, police department, and served as a witness for the prosecution. . . . He photographed Emmett Till's body as part of the inquest while it [lay] in Greenwood at the Century Burial Association." Anderson, "Who's Who in the Emmett Till Case."

Q   Where?

A   We had planned to take it to Money.

Q   Now, to go back, how long was it after the body was taken from the river that Mr. Strickland made those pictures. Chester?

A   About two hours.

Q   And I believe I understood the answer to your question was that you were instructed to prepare the body for burial at Money, Mississippi, is that right?

A   Yes, Sir.

Q   Did you carry out those instructions?

A   Yes, Sir. I delivered the body to the cemetery at Money.

Q   And when you got there with the body, what happened?

A   When I got there, Moses wasn't there, but he left word. . . .

MR. BRELAND: We object to what he was told or what word had been left, Your Honor.

THE COURT: Don't tell what you heard. Just state what you know.

THE WITNESS: Yes, Sir.

Q   Did you bury the body there or not?

A   No, Sir.

Q   What did you do with it?

A   I taken it back to my funeral home at Greenwood.

Q   And who did you later deliver it to?

A   To the undertaker there at Tutwiler.

MR. BRELAND: WE object to that, if Your Honor please, unless he did it himself.

Q   What is the man's name at Tutwiler to whom the body was delivered?

A   I don't remember.

Q   Now then, Chester, I asked you about the ring a while ago, and we got up to the place where you laid it in the ambulance, or the funeral coach—what did you do with that ring thereafter?

A   I gave it to Moses Wright.

Q   You gave the ring to Moses Wright?

A   Yes, Sir.

Q   And you have never had that ring since?

A   No Sir.

MR. SMITH: Take the witness.

CROSS EXAMINATION BY
MR. CARLTON:

Q   Chester, this body that you had there, did you carry it to Tutwiler, yourself?

A   No, Sir.

MR. BRELAND: Now, we move the Court to exclude the statement made by the witness that he took it to Tutwiler.

THE COURT: The witness says it was delivered to Tutwiler, and he is the manager of the funeral home. He should know where he sent the body.

MR. BRELAND: Well, he can still state just what he did.

MR. CHATHAM: One other question, Your Honor, if you will permit it, I think it might save some time.

THE COURT: All right, Sir, I will permit it.

REDIRECT EXAMINATION BY
MR. SMITH:

Q   When that body was laying there in the boat at the time you got there, Chester, how was the body clothed, if it was clothed?

A   It wasn't clothed.

Q   Did it have anything on it whatsoever except that piece of barbed wire?

A   No, Sir.

Q   I believe you stated that you are the manager of the funeral home down there, is that right?

A   Yes, Sir.

Q   Will you state whether or not the body was delivered to Tutwiler at your directions?

MR. BRELAND: If the Court please, we object unless he knows.

THE COURT: The objection will be overruled.

Q   Was it delivered to Tutwiler at your directions?

A   Yes, Sir.

MR. BRELAND: If the Court please, we move to exclude that witness' statement as being a mere conclusion on his part, as he did not go with the body to Tutwiler.

THE COURT: The objection is overruled.

Q   Did you direct anyone in your establishment there to deliver the body that you got out of the river to Tutwiler?

A   No, Sir.

Q   What?

A   No, Sir.

Q   Did you understand my question, Chester? I said, did you give directions from someone or to someone in your establishment to deliver the body which you found in the river, or which you got from the river, to Tutwiler?

MR. BRELAND: If the Court please, we object to that as being a leading question.

THE COURT: I think it would be better if the witness were to state the directions that were given, if any, and if so, what they were.

Q The body that was down there at your funeral home, what directions did you give and to whom did you give them to deliver the body to Tutwiler?

MR. BRELAND: We object, Your Honor. That is leading.

THE COURT: The objection is overruled. Let's proceed.

THE WITNESS: Well, I don't remember instructing anyone the way to go from Greenwood to Tutwiler.

Q Who did you instruct to take the body up there to Tutwiler?

MR. BRELAND: We object, Your Honor. That is still leading the witness.

THE COURT: The objection is overruled.

THE WITNESS: Crosby Smith.

Q Will you state whether or not the body which left your funeral home with Smith was the body that you took from the river down there?

A Will you say that again, please, Sir?

Q Will you state whether or not the body which Smith left there to take to Tutwiler was the same body that you picked up down there at the river?

A Yes, Sir.

MR. BRELAND: We object to that, Your Honor.

THE COURT: The objection is overruled.

MR. BRELAND: But he has not said that Smith left there with anybody.

THE WITNESS: Well, I went to Tutwiler the next morning to see if the body was going to be shipped, and it had a bill or a tag with the name "Emmett Till" on the casket. And I helped load it on the coach in the train.

MR. BRELAND. We object to that, if your Honor please. The witness was not asked about that at all.

THE COURT: The objection is sustained. You gentlemen will please disregard that statement made by the witness.

Q   Will you describe the body generally that you picked up down there on the river out of the boat? Would you tell the court and jury generally just what kind of body it was?

A   Yes, Sir.

MR. CARLTON: If the Court please, we object to this. This is not proper cross examination.

THE COURT: The objection is overruled. I believe they asked permission to ask additional questions.

MR. WHITTEN:[5] But, if the Court please, it was just one question that they wanted to ask.

THE COURT: The objection is overruled.

Q   Will you give the jury a description of that body as to size, age, weight and so forth?

A   Well, it looked to be about five foot four or five inches in height; weight between one hundred and fifty or sixty pounds. And it looked to be that of a colored person.

Q   Could you tell whether or not it was the body of a young person, or middle age or an old person?

A   Yes, Sir. Well, the flesh in the palm of the hand, well, it looked like it was the body of a young person. And from certain parts of the body—well, in my experience in handling those kind of bodies, by certain parts of the body it looked like a youth more so than a grown person or an older person.

---

5. John Wallace Whitten, Jr. (1919–2003) "was born in Tallahatchie County and began practicing law in Sumner in 1940. He served as Tallahatchie County chairman of the Democratic Party, and attorney for the board of supervisors. . . ." Anderson, "Who's Who in the Emmett Till Case." Whitten was the defense lawyer who, after the trial, brokered a deal with *Look* magazine for William Bradford Huie to interview the defendants. See Chapter 15, *infra*. See also Ellen Whitten, "Injustice Unearthed: Revisiting the Murder of Emmett Till," (granddaughter of John W. Whitten, Jr.), http://dlynx.rhodes.edu/jspui /bitstream/10267/23921/1/2005-Ellen_Whitten-Injustice_Unearthed-Shirley.pdf.

MR. SMITH: That is all.

MR. BRELAND: We will excuse the witness at this time, Your Honor.

(WITNESS EXCUSED.)

* * * *

C. A. STRICKLAND,

A witness introduced for and on behalf of the state, being first duly sworn, upon his oath testified as follows:

DIRECT EXAMINATION BY
MR. SMITH:

Q Will you state your name, please, Sir?

A C. A. Strickland.

Q Where do you live, Mr. Strickland?

A Greenwood.

Q What is your occupation?

A Identification Officer for the Collision Department.

Q Of Greenwood?

A Yes, Sir.

Q How long have you been serving in that capacity?

A Most of twelve years.

Q Now, as an identification officer for the Police Department of Greenwood, did it fall within your province to take photographs and so forth?

A Yes.

Q On or about the 31st day of August, 1955, were you called upon to take photographs of a dead body and other articles there in Greenwood?

A Yes, Sir.

Q And where were they?

A The body was at the Century Burial Funeral Home there in Greenwood.

Q Is that the funeral home operated by Chester A. Miller?

A Yes, Sir.

Q And did you take photographs of a dead body there, and a fan or wheel, or something of that sort there?

A A fan was there at the same place where the body was. I taken both pictures but at different times. And I did photograph the body there.

Q And the body was there at the funeral home?

A Yes, Sir.

Q Did anybody point out to you the body that you were to take pictures of?

A Yes, Sir.

Q And who pointed it out?

A Deputy Sheriff Cothran.

Q And he is a deputy sheriff of Leflore County, is that right?

A Yes, Sir.

Q I now hand you a photograph and ask you to identify that and tell the court and jury what that is.

A That is a picture of the body that I photographed on the 31st of August, at about three p.m. in the afternoon. It was on a table at the back of the Century Burial Funeral Home there in Greenwood.

Q Now I will ask you whether or not this photograph represents the true situation that was there when you photographed that body?

A It does.

Q And you took it with what kind of photographic equipment?

A I used a 4 by 5 Crown graphic camera.

Q And is that the kind of camera you use normally in your work?

A Yes, Sir. I take the pictures, and develop them too. I took the pictures there, and I printed the film and developed it myself.

Q And that has been in your possession all the time, is that right?

A Yes, Sir.

Q Now I hand you another photograph and ask you to identify that, please.

A This is a photograph of the [cotton] gin fan that I photographed on the 1st day of September in the Leflore County Sheriff's office. It was in the office of the sheriff.

Q And who directed you to take this photograph?

A Sheriff Cothran—I mean Deputy Sheriff Cothran. He was also with me when I made that picture.

Q And you were also the same person who printed and developed the film of that?

A Yes, Sir.

MR. SMITH: Your Honor, we would like to make these photographs exhibits to the testimony here.

MR. CARLTON: We object to the writing on the back of the photograph.

MR. SMITH: We admit that is not competent. We will obliterate it in some manner.

THE COURT: All right. But see that it is done before the exhibit is shown to the jury.

THE WITNESS: You see, I take that information for my own use so I can positively identify the pictures.

MR. BRELAND: If the Court please we are going to object to the picture of the gin fan at this time.

THE COURT: All right. The objection will be sustained as to the gin fan picture. The photograph of the body will be admitted providing what is written on the back of the photograph is marked out or obliterated so that it cannot be read or identified.

(A photograph is marked as Exhibit 1 to the testimony of C. A. Strickland by the reporter.)[6]

---

6. The exhibits accompanying the trial record have been lost.

MR. BRELAND: As I understand it, Your Honor, the photograph of the gin fan is not admissible, is that correct?

THE COURT: I held that the photograph of the gin fan had not been properly identified.

MR. SMITH: Yes, Sir. That is not important anyway at this time. Take the witness.

MR. CARLTON: No questions.

(WITNESS EXCUSED.)

* * * *

GEORGE SMITH,[7]

A witness introduced for and on behalf of the State, being first duly sworn, upon his oath testified as follows:

DIRECT EXAMINATION BY
DISTRICT ATTORNEY CHATHAM:

Q Is this Mr. George Smith?

A Yes, Sir.

MR. BRELAND: Just a preliminary question, if Your Honor please— has this witness been in the courtroom during the trial of the cause?

THE WITNESS: No, Sir.

Q Mr. Smith, what official position do you now have in Leflore County, Mississippi?

A Sheriff.

---

7. George Wilson Smith (1902–1975) "was sheriff of Leflore County at the time of the . . . trial. He arrested and booked . . . Bryant and . . . Milam . . . on kidnapping charges and was the one who received the initial confession of Bryant that he had kidnapped . . . Till. He testified at the trial and later at the grand jury hearing seeking an indictment of Milam and Bryant on kidnapping charges. He had served as a police officer from 1935– 1948 and from 1948–1952 as deputy sheriff of Leflore County. His term as sheriff lasted from 1952–1956. He ran for state representative in 1955 but lost. He served a second term as Leflore County sheriff from 1964–1968. . . ." Anderson, "Who's Who in the Emmett Till Case."

Q   How long have you held that position?

A   Well, it will be four years this January.

Q   Were you sheriff of Leflore County on August 31st, 1955?

A   Yes, Sir.

Q   I want you to tell the court and jury whether or not along about August 28th or August 31st, 1955, you had occasion to investigate the death of Emmett Till.

A   Yes, Sir.[8]

Q   And in your investigations, please tell the jury whether or not you had a conversation with Mr. Roy Bryant, one of the defendants in this case?

MR. BRELAND: If the Court please, if he is going to bring out any admission or any conversation had with the defendant, then we ask that it be properly qualified, that the testimony be properly qualified in the absence of the jury.

THE COURT: Is that what you are leading up to, Mr. Chatham?

MR. CHATHAM: We are leading up to a statement made to the witness.

THE COURT: Then the jury will be excused from the room at this time.

(The jury retired to the jury room, and the proceedings continued in the absence of the jury.)

Q   Mr. Smith, where was Mr. Bryant when you had this conversation with him?

A   In front of his store, sitting in my car, Sunday afternoon, August the 28th, at about two o'clock.

Q   And where is that store located?

A   In Money, Mississippi.

---

8. "The Governor also assigned two Highway Patrol inspectors to aid in the investigation." Whitaker, MA thesis, p. 131. "Sheriff Strider, however, refused to aid the prosecution by obtaining evidence." *Ibid.*, p. 146.

Q   Did you offer Mr. Bryant any hope of reward or immunity if he made a statement to you concerning the death of Emmett Till?

A   No, Sir.

Q   Did you threaten him in any way in order to intimidate him to make a statement?

A   No, Sir.

Q   And was the statement that he made to you then and there voluntarily made?

A   Yes, Sir.

MR. CHATHAM: We think that qualified the statement, Your Honor.

CROSS EXAMINATION BY
MR. BRELAND:

Q   How long have you known Mr. Bryant, Mr. Smith?

A   Mr. Breland, I guess he has been in that county for about two years.

Q   And you have known him since that time?

A   Yes, Sir—not too well, but I know who Roy was.

Q   Now, your deputy, Mr. Cothran, ran for Sheriff of Leflore County in this past election, did he not?

A   Yes, Sir.

Q   And you supported him in that, did you not?

A   No, Sir.

MR. CHATHAM: We object to that, if Your Honor please. That has no bearing on this whatsoever.

THE COURT: I will reserve my opinion on that.

Q   Did you support your deputy for sheriff down there in Leflore County?

A   Mr. Breland, I had two deputies running out of my office, and I prefer not to answer that question if I can.

Q   And that is for personal reasons?

A   Yes, Sir.

THE COURT: I don't see that this would have any bearing on the case unless it can be shown that such an inquiry is material.

Q   Mr. Smith, you, yourself, did run for representative down there in your county this time, is that right?

A   Yes, Sir.

Q   And Mr. Bryant supported you in that race, did he not?

A   I don't know, Sir. I didn't ask him to vote for me or anybody else.

Q   But he told you that he supported you, isn't that true?

A   I don't know.

Q   Well, you considered him your friend and he considered you as his friend, isn't that true?

A   Well, I have been friends with several of them in the family; yes, Sir.

Q   And when you went there that day he was asleep in his bedroom, wasn't he?

A   He was asleep, yes, Sir, as I understand.

Q   And you asked him to come out away from his family, didn't you?

A   Mr. Cothran did.

Q   And that was so you could talk to him confidentially?

A   Yes, Sir.

Q   And you wanted him away from the members of his family?

A   Yes, Sir.

Q   And the impression was left by you and Mr. Cothran that you were going to talk confidentially with him at that time?

A   Well, I don't know about the impression.

Q   Well, that could have been the impression, could it not?

A   It could have been.

Q   And he trusted you, did he not, and also Mr. Cothran?

A   I guess so.

Q   And it was on that basis that he made any statement to you, was it not?

A   Well, there was very little statement made, Mr. Breland.

Q   I understand—but what statement was made, that was true?

A   Yes, Sir.

Q   And you didn't tell him that you actually came up there for the purpose of arresting him or anything like that, did you?

A   Well, I didn't right at that moment.

Q   I mean before any statement was made to you?

A   No, Sir.

Q   In other words, when he was talking to you, he thought that he was talking to a confidential friend and in a confidential manner, didn't he?

A   Well, I couldn't answer that question.

MR. BRELAND: We submit, Your Honor, that the witness should not be permitted to testify on the grounds that any statement made to the witness was made as a matter of confidence, and any statement that was made, whatever it was, would not be competent in this case. And we object further, Your Honor, because the corpus delicti has not been established. There has been no testimony here that this body that was taken from the river was the body of Emmett Till. And any admission, if the corpus delicti has not been established, then such admission or admissions that might have been made, as far as any admission of guilt is concerned, that is certainly not competent in this case.

THE COURT: Any conversation as to guilt or any admission of guilt in the crime of murder cannot be shown at this time because the corpus delicti has not been shown.

MR. BRELAND: And further, Your Honor, that cannot be considered as *res gestae* at this time, and therefore, such an admission is not competent.

THE COURT: Suppose we see what the witness is going to testify to before I rule on this.

MR. BRELAND: And we would like for that to be traced before the jury comes in and hears it.

THE COURT: Yes. The corpus delicti has not been proven as yet.

REDIRECT EXAMINATION BY
DISTRICT ATTORNEY CHATHAM:

Q Mr. Smith, on that particular day that you say you talked to Mr. Bryant, what statement did he make to you concerning the disappearance of Emmett Till?

A He said he went down there and went to his house and got him out and then brought him up to the store. And he said he wasn't the right one so then he turned him loose.

Q And to whose house did he say he went to get him?

A He said he went down to Moses Wright's.

Q Did he make any further statement to you as to where he went after he released Emmett Till?

A He said he went somewhere to play cards. I don't remember where just now.

Q Did he say how long he had been up that night?

A Well, he said he played cards the rest of the night, over at some of the family's house.[9]

Q And who did he say went down to Moses's house with him?

A He didn't say.

Q And did you later have an opportunity to talk to Mr. Milam?

A I didn't, no, Sir.

THE COURT: Mr. Chatham, the court is of the opinion that before the witness can testify to these things, the corpus delicti should be proven. There has been no proof of any criminal agency shown here as far as a corpus delicti is concerned. These gentlemen are charged with the crime of murder. And before this evidence can be received, I think a corpus

---

9. Gerald Chatham would challenge this claim in his closing arguments. See Chapter 9.

delicti should be proven. But as yet, there has been no corpus delicti in this case.

MR. CHATHAM: Will the court permit me to continue along that line?

THE COURT: Yes, Sir; go right ahead.

Q   Mr. Smith, did you have an opportunity to see the body that was taken from the Tallahatchie River on August 31st by Chester Miller at the point between Philipp and Masel any time after it got into Miller's possession?

A   I did not.

Q   When did you see that body?

A   I did not see the body.

Q   You did not see the body?

A   No, Sir.

MR. [ROBERT] SMITH: In view of the Court's ruling, we will excuse Mr. [George] Smith at the present time and call Chester Miller back.

(WITNESS EXCUSED.)

* * * *

(The jury returned to the courtroom, and the proceedings continued with the jury present.)

CHESTER A. MILLER

Recalled as a witness for and on behalf of the State, having been duly sworn, upon his oath testified as follows:

REDIRECT EXAMINATION BY
MR. SMITH:

Q   Now you are Chester A. Miller, is that right?

A   Yes, Sir.

Q   And you are the same Chester A. Miller who testified here a while ago?

A   Yes, Sir.

Q   And you are an undertaker at Greenwood?

A   Yes, Sir.

Q   Now, we asked you about the body of a person taken out of the Tallahatchie River on August 31st, 1955, and you testified to that. Did you examine that body while it was in your possession or while you observed it?

A   Yes, Sir.

Q   Did you make a close or casual examination of it?

A   I would say casual.

Q   Did you notice anything unusual about the body relative to wounds or anything of that nature?

A   Yes, Sir.

Q   Where were those wounds?

A   It seemed like a bullet wound . . .

MR. BRELAND: We object, Your Honor.

THE COURT: The objection is sustained.

Q   Chester, just describe the situation. Describe what you saw.

A   Well, the whole crown of his head, from here above (indicating with his hand) was just crushed in.

Q   Where there any other wounds about the body?

A   No, Sir.

Q   Were there any other wounds on the head? Any other indications of a wound on the head?

A   There was no other wound except it looked like a pistol wound . . .

MR. BRELAND: We object, Your Honor.

THE COURT: The objection is sustained. The witness should not state his own conclusion. Just state what you know.

Q   Just describe what any wound about the head looked like. Was it a round hole, or a square hole or what?

MR. CARLTON: We object to counsel testifying, Your Honor.

THE COURT: The objection is overruled.

THE WITNESS: The crown of his head was just crushed out and in, you know, and a piece of his skull just fell out there in the boat, maybe three inches long or maybe two and a half inches wide, something like that.

Q   Now don't tell what your conclusion is, but just state what the wound was there about his head.

A   Well, that is about all the wound I know of.

Q   I believe it was objected to your testifying about something over his ear. What did that look like?

A   It looked like a bullet hole.

MR. BRELAND: We object, Your Honor.

THE COURT: The objection is sustained.

Q   Chester, just describe it. Don't tell your conclusion as to what caused it. Just state what it looked like. What did you see there?

A   I saw a hole in the skull.

Q   And how big a hole was it?

A   Oh, about—maybe half an inch square, something like that.

Q   And where was that hole? Will you point on your head to where it was?

A   It was somewhere around there, above the ear (indicating with his hand).

Q   And that is about three-quarters of an inch above your right ear, is that right?

A   Yes, Sir.

Q   Was there any hole or similar thing over on the other side of his head?

A   Well, it was crushed on the other side. You couldn't tell too much it was crushed so. And it was all cut up and gashed across the top there.

Q   Will you state whether or not the wounds which you have described here were sufficient to cause his death?

MR. BRELAND: We object to that, Your Honor. He is no expert to that. And the jury knows as much as he does about that. I think that is within the province of the jury.

THE COURT: I am going to let the witness answer the question.

Q   Will you state whether or not the wounds which you have described here were sufficient to cause his death?

A   Yes, Sir.

Q   I believe I asked you this, but I am not sure. You testified that there was some barbed wire in the boat, but did I ask you whether or not the barbed wire was on the person of the deceased?

A   Yes, Sir, you asked me.

Q   Was it?

A   Yes, Sir.

Q   Where was it?

A   Around the neck.

RE-CROSS EXAMINATION BY
MR. BRELAND:

Q   Chester Miller?

A   Yes, Sir.

Q   What you saw about that body was a decomposed condition. You couldn't tell what caused that condition, could you?

A   Well, yes, Sir, it was blown from some kind of instrument.

Q   It was caused from some outside agency? Would you say that? That is all, you can say, is it?

A   What do you mean, by outside agency?

Q   Well, you said a blow or something, isn't that right?

A   It was a bruise caused by some instrument, I would say.

Q   Then you would say that there was a bruise or something there?

A   Well, some of the wounds I noticed were caused from some instrument of some kind and some I saw might be something like from a gun.

MR. BRELAND: The Court has already ruled on that, and we move that it be excluded.

THE COURT: The conclusion of the witness will be disregarded by the jury.

Q   Now, what you saw about the condition of that man as to his head, you couldn't tell whether it was caused before or after his death, could you?

A   No, Sir.

Q   And you couldn't tell whether it was caused in a car accident or otherwise, could you? You couldn't tell that to be truthful about it, could you? You couldn't tell could you?

A   No, Sir.

MR. BRELAND: That is all. Take the witness.

MR. SMITH: That is all.

(WITNESS EXCUSED.)

(At this point in the proceedings, 11:45 a.m., the Court took a recess until 2:45 p.m., this date, at which time the proceedings were resumed.)

*   *   *   *

ROBERT HODGES,[10]

A witness introduced for and on behalf of the State, being first duly sworn, upon his oath testified as follows:

DIRECT EXAMINATION BY
MR. SMITH:

Q   What is your name, please?

A   Robert Hodges.

Q   Where do you live, Robert?

A   Down in Philipp, Mississippi.

Q   And what county is that you live in?

A   Tallahatchie.

Q   Now old are you, Robert?

A   Seventeen.

Q   Are you a fisherman?

A   Yes, Sir.

Q   And you live right out on the river, I believe.

A   Yes, Sir.

Q   Now, Robert, on the last day of August of this year, of 1955, on the 31st day of August, did you go fishing that morning?

A   Yes, Sir.

Q   And I believe you said that you had set out some lines and went out to see them, is that right?

A   Yes, Sir.

Q   Robert, did anything unusual happen while you were out there setting out the lines?

A   Yes, Sir. I seen two knees and feet.

Q   Just describe to the jury and court what you saw there.

---

10. Robert Hodges (c. 1938–2019) "was the young fisherman who discovered . . . Till's body in the Tallahatchie River at a spot called Pecan Point, near Philipp, on August 31, 1955." Anderson, "Who's Who in the Emmett Till Case."

A   Well, I saw right along here, up and down, both of them (indicating with his hands).

Q   And that would be from the top part of the legs and knees down, is that right?

A   Yes, Sir.

Q   And the front part of the feet, is that right?

A   Yes, Sir.

Q   Robert, where did you find that?

A   Well, it was about one mile from my house.

Q   Which side of the river was it on?

A   On the left side going down the river.

Q   Would that be in Leflore County or Tallahatchie County? Was that on the Leflore County side or Tallahatchie side?

A   Tallahatchie.

Q   What was the reason for it being there? Was it hung up or floating?

A   Yes, it was hung up there on a snag in the bottom of the river.

Q   When you saw those two feet and legs sticking up there, what did you do then, Robert?

A   Well, I had a few more set out down below there, and then I went on and run them, and then I came down and told my Father about it. And then my Father. . . .

MR. SMITH: You can't tell what you told your Father.

THE COURT: Don't tell any conversation you might have had with anyone.

Q   Then after you had run your lines, what did you do?

A   I reported it to my Father.

Q   Do you know of your own knowledge what he did about it?

A   Well, he told the landlord that we live with, and then he reported it . . .

Q   Who is your landlord?

A   B. L. Mims.[11]

Q   And what time of the morning was that?

A   It was between six thirty and seven o'clock.

Q   In the morning?

A   Yes, Sir.

Q   Did anybody do anything about that body down there during the rest of the day?

A   No, Sir—didn't nobody go down there.

Q   Did somebody go down there later in the day?

A   Three men was the only ones that went down there and there was the Deputy Sheriff.

Q   Did they go down there with Mr. Mims or by themselves or how?

A   No, Sir; in B. L. Mims' boat.

Q   Is that B. L. Mims?

A   Yes, Sir.

Q   Who were those men?

A   Well, the Deputy Sheriff.

Q   Mr. Melton?

A   Yes, he was one of them; and there was Charlie Fred Mims and my Father.

Q   Do you know whether that was in the Sumner Court District of Tallahatchie County?

A   Yes, Sir, in the Sumner Court District.

Q   That is where the body was found?

A   Yes, Sir.

Q   Robert, when you all went back down there, I believe you took two boats, did you not?

11. Benjamin "B. L." Mims (1925–2001) "was in the boat with Garland Melton when . . . Till's body was pulled from the Tallahatchie River on August 31, 1955. . . . He served as a witness for the prosecution and testified to the condition of Emmett's body." Anderson, "Who's Who in the Emmett Till Case."

A   Yes, Sir.

Q   When you got back down there, was the body there in the same place?

A   Yes, Sir, in the same place. It hadn't been moved.

Q   And was it still in the same position?

A   Yes.

Q   When you got down there, tell the court and jury what you all did.

A   Well, the first thing we done, one boy went down there—the first thing we done—the first boy—let me see now—when the first boy went down—Bo Mims and Mr. Melton,[12] I think that was the deputy's name, and Fred Mims—well, they came back to the house and got me and my Daddy, and we went down there at first.

Q   And then what happened?

A   Well, they brought the rope back there, and then me and this other boy was in a boat, and Mr. Melton was there, and they had the rope around the boy's legs and then they hung it on there, and they had it on this other boat, and then they carried it down the river and took it out on the other side there.

Q   How did you hang it there?

A   Well, they pulled up the river a little ways and got it unhung, so that they could move it, and then they got this rope around the legs, and then we carried it on up the river, and then we just come on across and pulled it over on the bank in the boat.

Q   When you pulled it back up the river, did the body float?

A   Yes, Sir, I think so.

Q   When you pulled it out on the bank, what if anything, was attached to the body?

A   An iron weight.

----

12. Garland Melton (1907–1962) "was deputy sheriff of Tallahatchie County who arrived at the scene at the Tallahatchie River when Emmett Till's body was found. He and Robert Hodges (who discovered the body) took separate boats into the river in order to retrieve the body. He married Myrtha Campbell in 1939 in Charleston, Tallahatchie County." Anderson, "Who's Who in the Emmett Till Case."

Q   What?

A   A weight.

Q   What kind of a weight was it?

A   A gin fan.

Q   Robert, how was that weight or fan, as you say, attached to the body?

Q   With a piece of barbed wire.

Q   How was the barbed wire attached to the body?

A   It was wrapped around his neck, as best I can remember.

Q   Would you remember that fan or weight if you saw it again?

A   Yes, Sir, I believe I would.

Q   Will you come around and take a look at this (indicating an object on the floor)?

A   It looks like it.

Q   Does that look like it?

A   Yes, Sir.

Q   And does that look like the barbed wire that was attached to it?

A   Yes, Sir. It looks like it except the mud has been cleaned off it.

Q   And you say when you pulled it out on the bank that the barbed wire was wrapped around the neck of this body and that it was attached to the fan, is that right?

A   Yes, Sir.

Q   And that was serving as a weight for the body, is that correct?

A   Yes, Sir.

Q   Did you have a chance to observe the body there relative to any blows or any wounds of any kind?

A   It was beaten pretty bad in the back.

Q   On the back?

A   Yes, Sir, and hips.

Q   What about the head?

A   It was also gashed in on the side.

Q   What was done with the body then after you drug it out on the bank with that weight?

A   Well, this . . .

MR. BRELAND: Your Honor, we want to object to the statement of the witness that the body was beaten on the back.

THE COURT: You can tell what the condition of the body was, but not your conclusions as to what caused that. You can state to the jury what the condition of that body was with reference to any marks, wounds, or anything else that you could actually see. But you can't draw your own conclusion as to what might have caused that.

THE WITNESS: No, Sir, I can't.

THE COURT: And you gentlemen (to the jury) will, of course, disregard that statement made by the witness.

Q   What did the marks on his back look like?

A   Well, it looked to me like it was blood-shot.

Q   Robert, what was done with the body after you all pulled it out on the bank with that weight attached to it?

A   Well, they unconnected the barbed wire from the weight. I believe that was the first thing. And then they put the body in the boat, and they got the weight and set it in the back end of the boat.

Q   And where was the boat taken, if anywhere?

A   We carried it up to the landing there.

Q   Is that the landing you normally used there?

A   Yes, Sir.

Q   And when you got back up there, what did you do with the body and with that weight?

A   Well, the undertaker came down—will you repeat that? I didn't get that.

Q   After you got the body up there in the boat, and it was in the boat, what did you do with the body and this weight up there at the landing?

A   Well, they just left it in there. And then after that the ambulance come, or the coach, or whatever you want to call it.

Q   Did you stay there until the ambulance came?

A   Yes, Sir.

Q   Do you know who the undertaker was that was driving or operating with that ambulance?

A   Chester Miller, I believe his name was.

Q   You saw him come there, did you?

A   Yes, Sir.

Q   And you were there when he got the body?

A   Yes, Sir.

Q   And when the undertaker got there, what did he do with the body?

A   He put it in a box.

Q   And what did he do with the box?

A   He set it back in the coach.

Q   Now, Robert, did you see anything on this boy's hands or fingers?

A   There was a ring.

Q   What kind of a ring was it?

A   A silver ring.

Q   Did you examine that ring? Did you look at it?

A   No, Sir. I didn't get close to it.

Q   Would you recognize it if you saw it again?

A   I might.

Q   There is a ring, Robert, that has engraved on it "May 25, 1943" and the big initials "L. T." Do you recognize that as being the ring that was on the finger of that body?

A   It looked like it. I didn't get close enough to see the initials.

Q   But that looks like the ring though?

A   Yes, Sir.

Q   Who took charge of this weight out there, Robert?

A   Who was in charge of it?

Q   Yes. Who took charge there and took it away from there?

A   There was some sheriff—I forgot who it was—from Greenwood. I can't remember his name.

Q   Was it Mr. Cothran, if you know?

A   It could have been. I don't remember.

MR. SMITH: Take the witness.

MR. BRELAND: No questions.

(WITNESS EXCUSED.)

* * * *

B. L. MIMS,

A witness introduced for and on behalf of the State, being first duly sworn, upon his oath testified as follows:

DIRECT EXAMINATION BY
MR. SMITH:

Q   You are Mr. B. L. Mims?[13]

A   That's right.

Q   And I believe you spell that M-I-M-S, is that right?

A   Yes.

Q   Where do you live, Mr. Mims?

A   About five miles north of Philipp.

Q   Is that in Tallahatchie County?

A   Yes, Sir.

Q   And I believe you live right down there, right at the river, is that correct?

A   That's right.

Q   And that is the Tallahatchie River?

A   Yes, Sir.

---

13. See note 11, *supra*.

Q   Mr. Mims, do you recall the occasion back on August 31st, 1955, when a body was found down there at the river near your home?

A   Yes, Sir.

Q   Who notified you about that fact?

A   It was one of these boys on the place there. I am not sure exactly who did notify me about it. But somebody told me about it.

Q   And you then called the officers about it, is that right?

A   Beg pardon.

Q   Did you call the officers?

A   No, Sir.

Q   You didn't call them?

A   No, Sir.

Q   Mr. Mims, I believe someone down there did notify them, is that correct?

A   Yes, Sir; that's right.

Q   Did you go down there to the river after you heard about this?

A   Yes, Sir.

Q   When was the first time you saw this body?

A   I went down the river. I used my outboard motor and boat, and I went down the river to look for him, and we found him.

Q   Who was with you at that time?

A   Deputy Sheriff Garland Melton.

Q   Was there anyone else along?

A   Yes, Sir. There was two men behind us in another boat.

Q   Who were they?

A   Well, my brother Fred Mims, and Robert Hodges.

Q   Will you just describe what you saw when you got there?

A   Well, we saw a person—from his knee on down and including his feet—we saw that sticking up above the water. And we could tell by looking at it that it was a colored person. That is all we could see, just from the knee on down, both knees.

Q   Why was that body there? Was it hung up, or floating or what?

A   Yes, Sir, it was hung. It was hung.

Q   Then what did you and the others do relative to that body?

A   Well, we went up there and looked at it, and we decided that we was going to have to have a rope in order to unhang him. And so we sent one of the boats back after a line and to bring it down so that we could unhang the body.

Q   And after you got the line, what did you do?

A   Well, we tied it on the feet and then pulled the feet together. We tied it around the ankles and then pulled it loose from the bottom.

Q   When you pulled it loose, did the body float there in the water?

A   Well, I am not sure about that. I wouldn't say it did float, and I say that because the deputy was there in the front end of the boat holding on to the line. And I didn't notice whether there was any slack that was loose enough for the body to be floating there or not. I didn't notice that.

Q   What did you all do then with the body?

A   We towed it downstream to a shallow bank there and then we landed there and pulled the body out.

Q   Then was there anything attached to that body?

A   Yes, Sir, there was.

Q   What was it?

A   It was a weight, part of a gin fan.

Q   Would you recognize that fan if you saw it again?

A   Yes, Sir, I believe I could.

Q   Would you come around here and look at this fan here on the floor?

A   Yes, Sir. (The witness observed the think [*sic*] that is it.)

Q   Is that it?

A   I believe it is, Yes, Sir.

Q   It looks like it, does it?

A   Yes, Sir.

Q   Now, how was that fan attached to the body?

A   It was tied around his neck and then it was around the fan.

Q   It was tied with what?

A   A piece of barbed wire.

Q   When you all got it out there on the bank, what did you do then?

A   The Deputy Sheriff disconnected the weight from the body there when we pulled it out.

Q   And what did you do with the body and the weight?

A   We pulled the body over there in an extra boat that we had there to tow him back in, and we put the weight there in the boat also, in the same boat.

Q   And then what did you do?

A   Then we connected it on behind my boat and towed it upstream to the landing.

Q   And then what was done with the body?

A   We pulled the boat, out on the bank about fifteen steps, I would say, from the water. And that is the way was when I left. I didn't stay there but a little while after that.

Q   You are familiar with the river and the land and so forth down there in that section, are you not?

A   Yes, Sir.

Q   And I believe you are a landowner down there, is that right?

A   A renter.

Q   At the place you found that body, will you state to the jury and to the court whether it was on the Tallahatchie County side or on the Leflore County side of the river?

A   Well, I am not sure about how the line goes there. I understand the river is not exactly the way the line is. But I would guess it was in Tallahatchie County.

Q   And would that be in the Second Court District of Tallahatchie County or the Sumner Court District?

A   Yes, Sir.

MR. SMITH: Take the witness.

MR. CARLTON: No questions, Your Honor.

(WITNESS EXCUSED.)

* * * *

GEORGE SMITH,

Recalled as a witness for and on behalf of the State, having been duly sworn, upon his oath testified as follows:

REDIRECT EXAMINATION BY
DISTRICT ATTORNEY CHATHAM:

Q   Is that Mr. George Smith?

A   Yes, Sir.

Q   Mr. Smith, what official position do you hold in Leflore County, Mississippi?

A   Sheriff.

Q   How long have you held that position?

A   Four years.

Q   As Sheriff of Leflore County, Mr. Smith, I want you to tell the court and jury whether or not during the period between August 28th and August 31st, 1955, you had occasion to investigate the death and disappearance of Emmett Till?

A   Yes, Sir.

Q   And during that investigation did you have an opportunity to talk to the defendant, Roy Bryant?

A   Yes, Sir.

MR. BRELAND: Now, if the Court please, we are going to interpose here the same objection that we did before the preliminary examination of this witness, for two reasons. And the first reason is that it is not shown here in the preliminary examination that any statement incriminating this defendant was freely and voluntarily made. And that has already been decided by the Supreme Court of Mississippi. And if they are going to ask any additional questions to qualify the witness or any statement that he might have made, then that should be made or done in the absence of the jury.

THE COURT: Suppose you go ahead and ask your questions, Mr. Chatham. The objection at this time will be overruled.

Q Mr. Smith, where was Mr. Bryant when he made the statement to you?

A In my car, sitting there in front of his store, in Money, Mississippi.

Q And on what day of the month of August was that?

A It was Sunday afternoon, August 28th.

Q Sunday afternoon, August 28th?

A Yes, Sir.

Q Were there any other persons present at the time Mr. Bryant made the statement to you?

A No, Sir.

Q Now, before making any statement to you at that time, Mr. Smith, did you threaten or intimidate Mr. Bryant in order to get him to make a statement?

A No, Sir.

Q Did you offer him any hope of reward or immunity from prosecution? Did you promise him any reward for making any statement to you?

A I did not.

Q And was the statement freely and voluntarily made by him to you?

A Yes, Sir.

Q I wish now, Mr. Smith, that you would please tell the jury what your conversation was with Mr. Bryant at that time in regard to the disappearance or murder of Emmett Till.

MR. CARLTON: We object, Your Honor.

THE COURT: The objection is overruled.

MR. CARLTON: We want to renew our objections at this time which we made earlier during the preliminary examination of this witness and for the same reasons that we stated then.

THE COURT: Let the record show that the objections of the defendants are renewed at this time as they were stated in the preliminary hearing made this morning relating to the same matters, and that the objections are now renewed at this time as they were given this morning.

MR. CARLTON: And if the Court please, the defendants would like to object further on the grounds that the corpus delicti has not been definitely established.

THE COURT: The objection is overruled.

Q   Mr. Smith, go ahead and tell about the statement that Mr. Bryant made to you that Sunday afternoon.

A   Well, I just asked him about it.

Q   What did you ask him?

A   I asked him about going down there and getting that little nigger.

Q   Will you please go over that again?

A   I asked him why did he go down there and get that little nigger boy, and he said that he went down and got him to let his wife see him to identify him, and then he said that she said it wasn't the right one, and then he said that he turned him loose.

Q   And where did he say that he turned him loose?

A   He said right in front of his store.

Q   Did he say that he went down to Moses Wright's house to get him?

MR. BRELAND: We object, Your Honor. That is a leading question.

THE COURT: I don't believe there has been any testimony in that respect.

Q   Did he tell you where he went to get Emmett Till?

A   To Moses Wright's.

Q   And when you drove up to Roy Bryant's store in Money that Sunday afternoon, was the store open?

A   No, Sir.

Q   Where was Mr. Bryant at that time?

A   He was asleep in back of the store.

Q   And what time of the day was that?

A   It was around two o'clock approximately.

Q   Did he offer any explanation to you at that time as to why he was asleep?

MR. BRELAND: We object to that, Your Honor. That has nothing to do with the case at all.

THE COURT: The objection is sustained.

Q   Did he say where else he had been the night before other than going down to Moses Wright's house?

A   He said he went to some of his people—I don't remember just who he said now—and he said he played cards there the rest of the night.

Q   He said he played cards the rest of night?

A   Yes, Sir.

MR. CHATHAM: Take the witness.

RE-CROSS EXAMINATION BY
MR. BRELAND:

Q   Mr. Smith, how long have you lived in the Greenwood neighborhood?

A   Since 1921.

Q   And did you live in the city during that time or out in the country around Greenwood?

A   I lived in the city since '28.

Q   And prior to 1928, where did you live?

A Well, I lived around Crahen or Moorhead (?), and I was there for about five years, and then I was at Minter City for two years.

Q And you have been Sheriff of that County for the past four years, is that right?

A Yes, Sir.

Q And by virtue of being an officer of that County, you got over the County very much during your administration, is that right?

A Yes, Sir.

Q And during that period of time you got acquainted with Mr. Roy Bryant, did you?

A Yes, Sir.

Q And of course, Mr. Roy Bryant was acquainted with you?

A Yes, Sir.

Q And you were all friends, is that right?

A Yes.

Q And you trusted him about matters, and he trusted you about matters, isn't that right?

A I hope so; yes, Sir.

Q Now, in this last summer, in the last primary, you ran for representative in Leflore County, didn't you?

MR. SMITH: We object to that, Your Honor. That has nothing to do with this at all.

THE COURT: The objection is overruled.

Q That is correct, isn't it?

A That is right.

Q And Mr. Roy Bryant supported you for office didn't he?

A Well, I hope so. That office, . . .

Q But you understood that he supported you, isn't that true?

A Well, I didn't make any campaign for it, but if he did, I appreciated it.

Q   But if you thought that you were his friend, then you expected it, didn't you?

A   I hope he did.

Q   And you believe he did, isn't that true?

A   I am not going to doubt it, no, Sir.

Q   And when you went up to Money that afternoon, when you went up there and went to his store, he was asleep back there in his living quarters, and you awakened him up or had him waked up is that right?

A   Yes, Sir.

Q   Were the other members of his family, the other members who were there, were they awake?

A   I don't think anyone else was there but he.

Q   No one was there but he?

A   That's right.

Q   Wasn't his wife there?

A   I didn't see her.

Q   Did you see the little children?

A   No, Sir.

Q   Did you see anybody else there at all?

A   Yes, Sir, I saw some others. They came there when we were there.

Q   Did you see his Mother?

A   No Sir.

Q   Who did you say you saw?

A   Some others.

Q   Where they friends of his?

A   No, Sir; relatives.

Q   And they were there in the store at the time you were there, were they?

A   When I was talking to Roy, they were there in the store.

Q And they were there when you got there?

A No, Sir. They followed me up.

Q But they were there before you took him out to your car to talk to him, is that right?

A I guess they was.

Q And you requested him to go out to your car where you could talk to him in private, is that right?

A Mr. Cothran told him to go out there, that I wanted to talk to him.

Q Was Mr. Cothran in the car when you talked to him?

A No, Sir.

Q Then Mr. Cothran stood aside there and was not present when you talked to him?

A No, Sir.

Q It was just you and he there together, is that right?

A That is all, sir.

Q In other words, the purpose of that was so that you could talk to him confidentially and privately, isn't that right?

A Well, I went up there to see what I could do about this trouble.

Q But the purpose of that was so that you could talk to him in private away from anybody else, even away from members of his family or relatives, and even your deputy sheriff, isn't that right?

A Well, they didn't come out there.

Q But you asked him to come out there for that purpose, didn't you?

A Yes, Sir.

Q And of course, he left the impression that he was going to talk to you confidentially, and you left that impression with him, isn't that right?

A Well, I asked him about the trouble down there.

Q Now let's go further on that—when you asked him to come out there, when you said that you wanted to talk to him, he naturally got the impression that you wanted to talk to him confidentially, isn't that right? In other words, when he came out and got in the car with you alone, you closed the door of the car, and you were both alone in there, isn't that right?

A   Well, I imagine that is right.

Q   And that was so that you could talk to him there confidentially, isn't that right?

A   Well, he came out to talk, yes, Sir.

Q   And you talked to him alone and separate from his kinfolks and also separate from your deputy sheriff, isn't that right?

A   Well, they was standing off to the other side there.

Q   But they were not within hearing distance, were they?

A   No, Sir.

Q   And what was said there in the car was just between you and Roy Bryant, isn't that right? Just between you two?

A   That right, Sir.

Q   Now, Mr. Smith, when you came up there to see Mr. Bryant, and he came out to your car and got in the car, and you got in the car with him there, you didn't tell him that you had come up there to arrest him, did you?

A   Not at that particular time.

Q   And you didn't mention that fact at all, did you?

A   Not right then.

Q   I mean, until he made that statement to you, isn't that right?

A   Well, my general purpose was to go up there and arrest him.

Q   But you didn't tell him that, did you?

A   Well, not to come on, no, not right then.

Q   And you didn't have a warrant for him, did you?

A   Not at that time.

Q   Did you tell him that you were investigating the case for the Sheriff's Office?

A   Yes, Sir—well, he knew that.

Q   I am asking you if you told him that?

A I wouldn't say that I told him exactly that.

Q But you went up there that afternoon as far as appearances were concerned, and as far as a reasonable man would think, where he might have been concerned, you went up there just as a friend to talk privately with him, isn't that right?

A Well, I got him in the car, yes, Sir.

Q Of course. And you didn't tell him that any statement that he might make to you anywise incriminating him might be used against him did you?

A There wasn't no statement hardly made, Mr. Breland.

Q But you didn't tell him that, did you?

A No Sir, I did not.

Q And did you later arrest him?

A Yes, Sir.

Q Did you tell him that you were arresting him?

A Yes, Sir.

Q Just what were the words you said?

A I told him I was going to have to arrest him and take him in, and he asked me to let him go in and put on some clean clothes; which he did.

Q Did you tell him what you were arresting him for?

A I told him what I was arresting him for, yes.

Q And you took him right on to jail in Greenwood, did you?

A A few minutes later, yes, Sir.

Q In other words, you waited for him so that he could dress and change clothes?

A Well, he waited on some customers and so forth first.

Q And you didn't have him in handcuffs or anything like that?

A No, Sir.

Q You just took him along with you to Greenwood and put him in jail, is that right?

A   Yes, Sir.

Q   And he stayed there in your jail from that time on until he was brought to Tallahatchie County, is that right?

A   Yes, Sir.

MR. BRELAND: That is all.

REDIRECT EXAMINATION BY
THE DISTRICT ATTORNEY:

Q   Mr. Smith, the town of Money is in Leflore County, is that right?

A   Yes, Sir.

Q   How long has Mr. Bryant been in business at Money, to your knowledge?

A   Approximately—I don't know exactly, but I wouldn't say not over two years, I don't think.

Q   And during that time you became acquainted with him and he with you, is that right?

A   Yes, Sir.

Q   And when you talked to him on this particular Sunday afternoon, he knew you were Sheriff of Leflore County, is that right?

A   That's right, Sir.

Q   After he made the statement to you that he did go down there to Moses Wright's house that night and got Emmett Till, and then he found out he was the wrong man . . .

MR. WHITTEN: I don't believe any of that part was testified to, Your Honor.

THE COURT: I think it was. Go ahead, Mr. Chatham.

Q   (Continuing)—and found out that he was the wrong boy and then put him out of the car and released him where did he say that he released him?

A   There in front of his store.

Q   And his store is in the town of Money, is that right?

A Yes, Sir.

Q Do you know how far that point would be from Moses Wright's house where he had gotten him?

A Approximately three miles, something like that.

Q Did he offer any explanation to you at that time as to why he did not carry the boy back home when he found out he was the wrong boy?

A He said he figured he knew the way back.

MR. CHATHAM: That is all.

MR. BRELAND: Now, if the Court please, we move to exclude this witness' testimony with reference to that statement. And any confession or statement made by Mr. Bryant to the Sheriff at that time would not be admissible, because it has been shown that any statement he did make was not made free and voluntarily to the Sheriff, and he was not properly advised of his rights.

THE COURT: That motion will be overruled. The witness was the Sheriff of Tallahatchie County, and as such, it was his duty to investigate any and all crimes and alleged crimes.

MR. CHATHAM: I believe Your Honor used the word "Tallahatchie" County, but I believe you meant to say Leflore County.

THE COURT: Yes—excuse me—I meant to say he was the sheriff of Leflore County.

MR. CHATHAM: That is all we have for this witness.

(WITNESS EXCUSED.)

MR. BRELAND: Your Honor, we don't like to be repetitious but the District Attorney in propounding questions to the witness used the words or name "Emmett Till." And there has been no evidence here to show that either party knew the name of Emmett Till at that time.

THE COURT: It is the Court's recollection that Emmett Till's name was mentioned in direct examination.

MR. BRELAND: Then we would like to call Mr. Smith back to the stand, if you please.

GEORGE SMITH,

Recalled as a witness for further cross examination by the defense, having been duly sworn, upon his oath testified as follows:

RE-CROSS EXAMINATION BY
MR. BRELAND:

Q If we understand your testimony correctly Mr. Smith, you asked Mr. Bryant at that time why he went down there and got that little ole boy, and you just asked him about a boy, and you didn't mention the name "Emmett Till," is that right?

A I didn't know Emmett Till's name at that time.

Q And so far as you know, neither did Mr. Bryant?

A No, Sir, I don't know that he did.

MR. BRELAND: Now, if the Court please, we ask that his testimony be excluded.

REDIRECT EXAMINATION BY
THE DISTRICT ATTORNEY:

Q Mr. Smith, on that Sunday afternoon when you were talking to Mr. Bryant, and he told you that he had found out that the boy he had gotten from the house of Moses Wright was the wrong boy, and he said that he had released him after that, where did he say he released him?

A In front of his store.

MR. BRELAND: That is repetition, Your Honor.

THE COURT: That question was asked before.

MR. CHATHAM: But before when I questioned him about this, I used the words "Emmett Till" and that is what they objected to. And I am just going back to the testimony about the boy that was taken out of the house and later, so he said, he was released. I am just clearing that up as far as the testimony is concerned.

THE COURT: That is correct.

MR. CHATHAM: And I would like for the rest of his [pages missing from surviving transcript[14]]

[JOHN ED COTHRAN[15]]

[BY MR. CHATHAM]

. . . . [*Apparently, the first round of questions presented to Sheriff John Cothran was made outside the presence of the jury in order to determine if they might be excluded or included in the trial record.*]

Q   Greenwood, Leflore County, Mississippi?

A   Yes, Sir.

Q   How long have you been in that County?

A   Thirty years.

Q   Thirty years?

A   Yes, Sir.

Q   And during the past four years, have you occupied any official position in that County?

A   I have.

Q   And what was that position?

A   Deputy Sheriff.

---

14. Devery Anderson informed me that Mr. Allan Hammons of Greenwood, Mississippi, purportedly has a copy of the missing page. I sent e-mails to Mr. Hammons, including one as late as February 2023, but was unsuccessful in securing a copy of the missing page.

15. John Ed Cothran (1914–2008) "was deputy sheriff to Leflore County sheriff George Smith. He arrested J. W. Milam on charges of kidnapping Emmett Till and was a witness for the prosecution. . . . He later served as sheriff of Leflore County from 1960–1964. He later lived in Moorhead, Mississippi, where he was questioned by the FBI during the course of its 2004–2006 investigation. He could not provide them with details, having forgotten much about the case, but did remember the events leading to Milam's arrest." Anderson, "Who's Who in the Emmett Till Case."

Q You were a deputy under Sheriff George Smith, is that right?

A Yes, Sir.

Q Were you serving in that capacity during the month of August, 1955?

A I was.

Q As Deputy Sheriff working under Mr. Smith, did you have occasion to assist him in investigating the death or disappearance of a negro boy by the name of Emmett Till?

A Yes, Sir.

Q And in your investigation, did you have occasion to talk to Mr. J. W. Milam, one of the defendants in this case?

A Yes, Sir.

Q And when was it that you talked to him, Mr. Cothran?

A It was in the Leflore County jail.

Q You talked to him in Leflore County jail?

A Yes, Sir.

Q Do you remember how many days after the body was found it was that you talked to him, or was it before that?

A It was after the boy had disappeared, but it was after he was placed under arrest for the commission of an alleged crime.

Q Who was present when you had this conversation with Mr. Milam?

A No one but him and myself.

Q And you say that was in the Leflore County jail over in Greenwood?

A Yes, Sir.

Q Did you offer or promise Mr. Milam any reward for making a statement to you?

A He didn't make a statement. [Note: below it is stated that "he *did* make a statement." (itals. added)]

Q But you say you talked to him?

A Yes, Sir.

Q And in that conversation you had with him, he did make a statement, isn't that right? [Note: above it is stated that "He *didn't* make a statement." (itals. added)]

A That's right.

Q Before that statement was made, did you offer him or promise him any reward or hope of immunity afterwards if he would make any statement to you?

A No, Sir.

Q Did you threaten him or intimidate him in any way at any time in order to get him to make a statement to you?

A No, Sir.

Q Was any statement made to you on that day in the Leflore County jail by Mr. Milam?

A Yes, Sir.

Q And was the statement made to you on that day, at that particular time, freely and voluntarily made?

A Yes, Sir.

Q Mr. Cothran, will you tell the Court in the absence of the jury what your conversation was at that time with Mr. Milam?

A I asked him if they went out there and got that boy.

Q When you said "they," did you call them by name?

A I didn't call anyone by name. I just asked if they went out and got that boy. And then he said, yes, they had got the boy and then turned him loose at the store afterwards; at Mr. Bryant's store.

Q Did he say why they turned him loose there?

A He just said that they brought him up there and talked to him, and then they turned him loose.

Q Did he say why he went down to get the boy at Moses Wright's house in the first place?

A No.

Q Did he offer any explanation to you as to why they didn't carry the boy back down to Uncle Moses's house after that?

A   I didn't ask him.

Q   And he didn't offer any explanation to you about that?

A   No.

MR. CHATHAM: I believe that is all we have in qualifying the witness for the State.

CROSS EXAMINATION BY
MR. CARLTON:

Q   Mr. Cothran, give to the Court the exact language of the question which you asked "J. W." on this occasion?

A   I asked him if they went out and got that boy, out at Moses Wright's house.

Q   Then you said, "Did they go out and get that boy from Moses Wright's house?"

A   I just said "Did you all."

Q   And what was his exact answer to you?

A   He said, yes, but they put him out there at the store.

Q   And when he said, yes, but they put him out there at the store, did he say who put him out at the store?

A   No, he didn't say.

Q   And when he gave his answer to you, did he say "They" or "We"?

A   I don't remember whether he said "We" or "They."

Q   Now who was present when you had this conversation with Mr. Milam?

A   You mean when I talked to Mr. Milan?

Q   Yes, Sir. Who was present at that time?

A   Nobody but me and him.

Q   Was Roy Bryant present?

A   No.

Q   Mr. Cothran, you were a candidate this year for Sheriff of Leflore County, isn't that right?

A   That's right.

Q   And Mr. Campbell, a brother-in-law of Mr. Milam down there at Minter City, supported you in that campaign for Sheriff, isn't that true?

A   I think so.

Q   And Mr. Milan supported you in that campaign, isn't that true?

A   I think so.

Q   And there was a brother over at Itta Bena[16] who supported you, isn't that right?

A   I think so.

Q   In fact, the entire family supported you in your campaign for Sheriff, isn't that right?

A   I believe they did.

Q   And you are a good friend of that entire family?

A   Yes.

Q   And you no doubt believe that they are all good friends of yours?

A   Yes, Sir.

Q   And you knew J. W. Milam before that time, did you?

A   Yes, Sir.

Q   And you all were good friends in the past?

A   Yes, Sir.

Q   Did you know that any statement he might make to you would be used against him?

A   No, Sir.

Q   And on what day did this particular conversation occur?

A   It was on Monday.

Q   Then it was on Monday, August 29th, after the boy had disappeared and before the body was found, is that right?

16. A small city in Leflore County, Mississippi. On a march between Itta Bena and nearby Greenwood, coordinated by the Student Nonviolent Coordinating Committee (SNCC) but led by Martin Luther King Jr., Stokely Carmichael coined the rallying phrase "Black power!" See Peneil Joseph, *Stokely: A Life*, New York: Civitas Books (2014).

A   Yes, Sir.

Q   Mr. Cothran, do remember the occasion about a week ago when you conferred with Mr. Breland, Mr. Henderson, and Mr. Kellum, and myself,[17] and also Mr. George Smith,[18] when we were all together over there in the office?

A   I do.

Q   And on that occasion, Mr. Cothran, did you not make the statement to us that you had never talked to "J. W." at all about this and that he had never made any statement about it?

MR. CHATHAM: If the Court please, this doesn't go into the admissibility of the statement.

THE COURT: No, it doesn't; but it is all right to ask it now.

MR. CARLTON: Well, we will hold that for now. But we will object to the admission of this testimony and this alleged admission on the grounds that it was not freely and voluntarily made, and that if any statement was made, it was made under improper circumstances without the defendant being properly advised of his rights. And we say that it is inadmissible for that reason. And we also have a further objection to this witness's testimony at this time on the grounds that the corpus delicti has not been proven, and that there has been no showing whatsoever in the record that the body taken from the Tallahatchie River and alleged to be that of Emmett Till, that the death of that body was caused by any criminal agency whatsoever.

THE COURT: The objections will be overruled. Let the jury come in.

(The jury returned to the courtroom, and the proceedings continued with the jury present.)

Q   Is this John Ed Cothran?

A   Yes, Sir.

Q   Mr. Cothran, where do you live?

A   Greenwood.

---

17. These were the attorneys for the defendants.
18. George Wilson Smith was sheriff of Leflore County.

Q Greenwood, Leflore County, Mississippi?

A Yes, Sir.

Q How long have you lived in Leflore County?

A Thirty years.

Q What, if any, official position have you held in that county during the past four years?

A Deputy Sheriff.

Q Deputy Sheriff?

A Yes, Sir.

Q And you have been a deputy under Sheriff George Smith, is that right?

A Yes, Sir.

Q In your capacity as Deputy Sheriff, I want you to tell the Court and jury whether or not in the latter part of August, 1955, you had occasion to investigate the murder or disappearance of Emmett Till?

A I did.

Q And in that investigation, did you have occasion to talk to J. W. Milam, one of the defendants in this case?

A Yes, Sir.

Q Where was he when you talked with him?

A In the Leflore County jail.

Q Do you remember the day of the week it was that you talked with him?

A Monday.

Q You talked with him on Monday?

A Yes, Sir.

Q And had he been arrested that day or was it the day before?

A That day.

Q Who was present in the jail, Mr. Cothran, when you talked with him?

A No one but he and myself.

Q Now, before he made any statement to you, and before you asked him any questions, did you threaten him or intimidate him in any way in order to compel him or force him to make any statement against his will?

A No, Sir.

Q You did not?

A No, Sir.

Q And before he made any statement to you, did you promise him any reward or hold out any hope of immunity for him if he made any statement to you?

A No, Sir.

Q And was any statement that he made to you in the jail at that time on that Monday, was that statement freely and voluntarily made?

A Yes, Sir.

Q Now, will you tell the jury, Mr. Cothran—and speak out so the last man sitting over here on the back row can hear you, will you state what you had to say to "J. W." that day in the jail and what he had to say to you in regard to the murder of Emmett Till?

A I asked him if they went out there and got that little boy and if they had done something with him. And he said that they had brought him up there to that store and turned him loose, there at Roy Bryant's store.

Q Did you say they went and got the boy, or did he say we went and got the boy?

A I don't remember whether he said "we" or "I." I wouldn't say for sure.

Q Did he say where they got the boy?

A Over at Moses Wright's.

Q He told you they had gotten the boy at Moses Wright's house?

A Yes, Sir.

Q Did he say what time of the night or morning it was when they went out and got him?

A No, Sir.

Q   Do you remember whether you asked him specifically the hour that he got him from Uncle Moses's house?

A   No, Sir.

Q   What did he say, Mr. Cothran, with reference to what he or they did with the boy after they got him from old man Moses's house?

A   He said they brought him up there and talked to him, and then they let him go.

Q   Where did he say they brought him to talk to him?

A   Up to Mr. Bryant's store.

Q   Where is Mr. Bryant's store?

A   In Money, Mississippi.

Q   And Money is in Leflore County, Mississippi, is that right?

A   Yes, Sir.

Q   Do you know about how far it is from Uncle Moses's house to Mr. Bryant's store at Money?

A   I would say around three miles.

Q   How long did they say they kept him up there before they released him?

A   He didn't say.

Q   Did he offer any explanation to you as to why they didn't carry the boy back home, back down to Uncle Moses's house?

A   No, Sir.

Q   Did he tell you where he spent the rest of the night after that?

A   He told me he went home.

Q   He said he went home after that?

A   Yes, Sir.

Q   Do you know where he was living at that time?

A   No, Sir.

Q   How long had you known Mr. Milam prior to this conversation you had with him?

A   I imagine around a couple of years.

Q Would you say that you knew him well and that he knew you well?

A Yes, Sir, I knew him.

Q So that, at the time you were talking to him in the jail there in regard to this alleged crime, he knew you were a deputy sheriff of that county under Sheriff George Smith, is that right?

A Yes, Sir.

Q And I believe it is the fact that you arrested him and brought him to jail, is that correct?

A Yes, Sir.

Q Now, Mr. Cothran, in your further investigation of this alleged crime, did you go down to the point on the Tallahatchie River between Philipp and Masel where the body was found?

A Yes, Sir.

Q And that was a body said to have been the body of Emmett Till, is that right?

A That's right.[19]

Q When did you go down there?

A It was on Wednesday morning about—around ten o'clock.

Q Then that would have been Wednesday morning, August 31st, is that right?

A Yes, Sir.

Q And it was this year, 1955?

A Yes, Sir.

Q And you say that was about ten o'clock in the morning?

A Yes, Sir.

---

19. Before the trial, Deputy Sheriff Cothran was quoted in no fewer than three papers that the body found in the river was that of Emmett Till. Years later, in an interview with journalist Paul Hendrickson, Cothran said otherwise: "I never said I knew the body was Emmett Till's for sure. I never saw Emmett Till alive. How would I know? All I said was I that I didn't know myself but that the boy's uncle was positive it was him. That's all I said." Paul Hendrickson, *Sons of Mississippi: A Story of Race and Its Legacy*, New York: Vintage (2003), pp. 111, 112.

Q   And what was the occasion for your going to that particular place? In other words, did you receive some message to go there or some request?

A   Yes, Sir.

Q   Do you remember who made that request of you or the sheriff?

A   Mr. McCool, the office deputy, called me and told me . . .

MR. BRELAND: We object to any conversation, Your Honor.

THE COURT: Don't repeat any conversation.

Q   But you did receive a request from someone in the sheriff's office to go to that place thereon the Tallahatchie River between Phillip and Masel, is that right?

A   Yes, Sir, that's right.

Q   And did you go there immediately?

A   Yes, Sir.

Q   Who went there with you?

A   Mr. Weber.[20]

Q   And who is Mr. Weber?

A   A deputy sheriff.

Q   Did you stop on the way there anywhere between Greenwood and the point of your destination?

A   We did.

Q   Where did you stop?

A   At Moses Wright's.

Q   Was Moses at home?

A   Yes, Sir. He was picking cotton.

Q   And did you pick him up?

A   Yes, Sir.

---

20. At the time, Ed Weber was "a deputy sheriff in Tallahatchie County and assisted when Till's body was discovered in the river. He and Leflore County deputy sheriff John Ed Cothran went to Moses Wright's home and brought Wright to the river to identify the body." Anderson, "Who's Who in the Emmett Till Case."

Q And where did you and Moses and Mr. Weber go after that?

A We went up on the Tallahatchie River, up on the other side of Philipp.

Q What did you find there when you got to that particular point on the river?

A We found a body that they had taken out of the river.

Q And where was the body when you and Uncle Moses first got there?

A It was laying in a boat there at the edge of the river.

Q And where was the boat? Was it in the water or out on the bank?

A On the bank.

Q Do you remember who else was around there assisting in getting the body there in the boat, and the details connected with it?

A Well, Mr. Strider was there, the Sheriff. And there was several people around there. There was Mr. Smith. He was over there. And I don't know just who all was there. There was several more.

Q Was there a number of your people around there?

A Yes, Sir.

Q Do you recall the negro undertaker at Greenwood?

A Chester Miller?

Q Yes, Chester Miller?

A Yes, Sir.

Q Was Chester there?

A Yes, Sir.

Q Was he there when you first got there?

A No, he came right after I got there.

Q And did he have his funeral coach with him?

A Yes, Sir.

Q And I believe you said that boy was in the boat when you first got there, is that right?

A Yes, Sir.

Q And how long was it after you got there that the body was removed from the boat?

A   Oh, I imagine around twenty minutes, maybe more or maybe not.

Q   What did they do with the body after it was taken out of the boat? How did they handle it?

A   They took some big brown wrapping paper and put it around the body and then put it in a casket.

Q   When you first saw the body there, was it lying on its back or face down?

A   On its face.

Q   And was it turned over before it was taken out of the boat?

A   Yes, Sir.

Q   And then what was done with the body, John Ed?

A   It was put in a casket.

Q   Was the casket out on the bank?

A   Yes, Sir.

Q   And who was supervising that? Was it Chester Miller?

A   Chester Miller. He was the one that handled him.

Q   And he was the undertaker there?

A   That's right.

Q   Now, in the course of Chester and those who were assisting him in removing the body from the boat and putting it in the casket, do you recall seeing a ring on the deceased's finger and seeing that ring removed from his finger?

A   Yes, Sir.

Q   Do you remember generally what kind of ring it was, the general description of it?

A   Yes, Sir. It was a—it looked like a home-made ring.

Q   Was it silver or gold?

A   It was silver looking.

Q   Did it have any marks or identification on it that you remember?

A   Yes, Sir.

Q And what were they?

A 1943 was the date.

Q 1943? Did it have any other marks?

A Yes. It had May—I don't remember just what date was.

Q Did it have any initials on it?

A L. T.

Q Did you see that ring on the deceased's finger before it was taken off his finger?

A Yes, Sir.

Q And who took it off his finger?

A This Miller's helper.

Q Do you know whether that was Chester's boy or not?

A I think his name is Simon Garrett.

Q Did you see Simon when he took the ring off the deceased's finger?

A Yes, Sir.

Q What was done with that ring after Simon took it off the body?

A He gave it to Moses Wright.

Q Do you know what Moses did with it?

A Yes, Sir.

Q What did he do with it?

A He carried it to his house.

Q Did you see the ring at any time thereafter?

A Yes, Sir.

Q How long was it after that when you saw it again? When did you see it again?

A He gave it to me as soon as that boy looked at it.

Q How is that?

A He gave it back to me there at his house.

Q Did you go with him back to his home?

A   I carried him back down there.

Q   You didn't drop him out there at Money?

A   No. I carried him out there.

Q   And when you took him back home, he returned that same ring back to you?

A   Yes, Sir.

Q   And have you had that same ring in your possession since?

A   Yes, Sir.

Q   I will hand you this ring, Mr. Cothran, and I ask you if you can identify it as the same ring that was taken from the body there at that point on Tallahatchie River on the day that you went over there? (A ring is shown to the witness.)

A   It is.

Q   And have you given anybody else possession of that ring since you have had it?

A   Nobody but you.

Q   Nobody else except me?

A   That's right.

Q   Now, you were speaking from your recollection a few minutes ago when I asked you what marks of identification were on the ring. And for the purposes of the record now, and for the benefit of the jury, I would like for you to read what marks, or initials, or figures are on that ring.

A   (Reading) "May 25, 1943." And then right under that it has got "L. T."

Q   The initials "L. T."?

A   Yes, Sir.

MR. CHATHAM: If the Court please, we at this time will offer this ring in evidence as Exhibit 1 to the testimony of Mr. John Ed Cothran.

THE COURT: It will be received in evidence.

(A ring was tagged and marked as Exhibit 1 to the testimony of Mr. John Ed Cothran by the reporter.)

Q Now, John Ed, I wish you would step down off the witness stand and look at this object lying on the floor here in front of the jury, and if you can, I wish you would tell the jury when was the first time you saw that object? And will you tell what it is and the first time you saw it?

A Well, the first time I saw it was out there at that river that morning, laying in a boat there.

Q Was it in the boat with the body at the same time you testified of your seeing the body?

A That's right.

Q And on that same day?

A Yes, Sir.

Q Was it in the same boat with the body or was it in a separate boat?

A It was in the same boat.

Q At the time you saw the fan and the body, was the wire still attached to the fan and to the body or not?

A No, Sir, it wasn't.

Q The wire was not attached to the body when you saw it?

A The wire was still on the body but it was not on the fan.

Q Can you tell the court and jury where that fan has been since that day?

A It has been in the Sheriff's office down in Greenwood.

Q Who carried it there?

A I did.

Q And could you say that the object there on the floor is the same fan and that it is the same piece of wire that you took from the boat that was at the river that day?

A Yes, Sir.

Q And it has been in your possession since then?

A Yes, Sir.

Q Mr. Cothran, you are familiar with the area around Money where Uncle Moses Wright's house is situated or where the house is that he was living in on August 28th of this year, are you?

A   Yes, Sir.

Q   And is that house in Leflore County, Mississippi?

A   Yes, Sir.

Q   Now, John Ed, how long have you been a peace officer?

A   Almost eight years.

Q   And during that time I want you to tell the court and jury whether or not you have had numerous occasions to see bodies that have been maimed and beaten and shot or wounded?

A   Yes, Sir, I have.

Q   And since you have, I would like for you to describe for the court and jury the condition of this boy's body that you saw there in the boat that you have testified to and about, with reference to any wounds or abrasions on or about his head or body? And describe them, if you can, please, Sir?

A   Well, his head was torn up pretty bad. And his left eye was about out, it was all gouged out in there, you know. And right up in the top of his head, well, there was a hole knocked in the front of it there. And then right over his right ear—well, I wouldn't say it was a bullet hole, but some of them said it was . . .

MR. BRELAND: We object to what they said it was.

THE COURT: The objection is sustained.

Q   But there was a hole there on that side of his head . . . ?

MR. BRELAND: We object to the leading form of the question.

THE COURT: I believe he said there was a hole in his head there.

Q   And I believe you said there was a hole there, and you indicated with your finger that it was about one inch above the right ear, is that right?

A   Yes, Sir.

Q   And could you describe the dimensions of that hole by an illustration with a dime or a penny, or anything of that sort?

A   No—it wasn't anything like that big. It was just a small hole.

Q Could you tell whether or not that hole penetrated the skull?

A No, Sir.

Q What portion of the left side of his head was caved in?

A Right above his ear, on that side (indicating with his hand).

Q Do you mean at a point next to the left temple?

(At this point, one of the jurors stated that he could not hear the witness's answer.)

THE WITNESS: I said it was on the left side of his head, right alongside his left ear and above his ear.

Q From the way you indicated with your finger, you began at a point on the left temple, about an inch above the left eye and his left ear, and extending back to a point about an inch or an inch and a half behind the left ear, is that correct?

MR. BRELAND: I think we should let the witness make his own statement about that, Your Honor.

THE COURT: Was that right, Mr. Cothran? Did Mr. Chatham state it correctly?

THE WITNESS: I think I have got confused myself, Judge.

THE COURT: Then suppose you tell it to the jury, yourself, Mr. Cothran. Just state it to them in your own words, and show on your head, as best you can where it was, and just what the condition looked to you.

THE WITNESS: There was a small hole in his head right above the ear over on the right side of his head, over here—and that was all tore up. (The witness hesitated in his answer at this point.) Now the reason I hesitated there, I wanted to be sure I was getting it on the right side.

Q And what about the front part of his head, and on his forehead?

A There was a place knocked in on his forehead.

Q Did that seem to penetrate the skull?

A Well, it looked like it did.

Q With reference to other parts of his body being maimed or mutilated, did you notice that?

A There wasn't any.

Q Did you notice anything at all other than about the head?

A No, Sir.

MR. CHATHAM: Take the witness.

CROSS EXAMINATION BY
MR. CARLTON:

Q Mr. Cothran, I believe you ran for Sheriff of Leflore County this last summer, is that right?

A Yes, Sir.

Q That is, this summer?

A That's right.

Q And in that campaign, I believe that Mr. Milam's brother-in-law over at Minter City, Mr. Campbell, supported you in that race, is that right?

A Yes, Sir.

Q And Mr. Milam supported you in that race?

A Yes, Sir.

Q And Mr. Roy Bryant, from Money, supported you, is that right?

A Yes, Sir.

Q And Mr. Beaner (?), a full brother of Mr. J. W. Milam, also supported you, I believe?

A Yes, Sir.

Q And the entire family, generally, have been friendly with you over a period of years, is that right?

A That's right.

Q And you have confidence in that family, and the family has confidence in you?

A Yes, Sir.

Q And you have known J. W. Milam for several years, have you?

A For about two years.

Q   And he was friendly with you and you were friendly with him?

A   Yes, Sir.

Q   And they were right in treating you as a friend, isn't that right?

A   Yes, Sir.

Q   And they were right in feeling that you would treat them fairly and properly?

A   That's right.

Q   Now, when this statement that Mr. Milam was supposed to have made to you there in the courthouse in Greenwood on Monday, the 28th . . .

MR. CHATHAM: We object to that statement that it was supposed to have been made. He had already testified that he unequivocally made a statement.

Q   Mr. Cothran, this statement to which you testified that Mr. Milam made to you on Monday, the 28th—or I believe it was the 29th—of August, was anyone present when that conversation was had between you all?

A   No, Sir.

Q   And where was it made?

A   Up in the jail there.

Q   Was Mr. Roy Bryant present at that time?

A   No, Sir.

Q   Was there anyone else there at all?

A   There was no one but J. W. and myself.

Q   Was he in a cell at the time?

A   We were going in a cell.

Q   And he made this statement to you right after you arrested him?

A   Well, he stopped there and talked to me after we got to the jail.

Q   And that is when he made the statement to you?

A   Yes, Sir.

Q And had you told him anything that he might say there would be used against him?

A No, Sir.

Q Had you told him that he was under arrest?

A Well, no, Sir, I hadn't.

Q Had you given him any reason to think that you were asking that question for the purpose of incriminating him?

A Well, I just asked the question.

Q And you talked to him and asked him that just as one friend would ask another friend, is that right?

A Yes, that's right.

Q And just what was the exact question which you asked him, John Ed?

A I asked him if they had carried that boy off.

Q You asked him if they had carried that boy off?

A That's right.

Q And you used the term or words, "If they had carried the boy off"?

A Yes, Sir.

Q And just what was his answer?

A He said that they carried him up to Roy Bryant's store, and they talked to him, and then they let him go.

Q Now, let's get over here and look at this gin fan or this object on the floor here, John Ed. Will you tell the jury just how that fan is made, and for the purpose of the record, will you describe it so that the reporter can get it down here? Will you give us a description of that fan?

A What do you mean?

Q Well, how many blades are in it?

A I don't know.

Q Count them there, please, Sir.

A Eighteen.

Q   It has eighteen blades?

A   That's right.

Q   Are those blades flat or cupped?

A   They are cupped on the bottom and kind of flat at the top.

Q   And they are set in there between the metal sides, I believe, is that right?

A   That's right.

Q   Are the sides circular?

A   Yes, Sir.

Q   And of course, the fan is lying flat on the floor now, is that right?

A   Yes, Sir.

Q   And one side is lying flat on the floor, and then come these eighteen blades, and then the next side is on top of that, is that correct

A   That's right.

Q   And there is a big, heavy hub in the center there is that right?

A   That's right.

Q   And those blades are sharp on the end, is that correct?

A   Yes, Sir.

Q   Now, how wide is this hub across here?

A   About three inches.

Q   Is that made out of heavy metal or light metal?

A   Heavy.

Q   And is it round or square?

A   Round.

Q   How long are those blades, Mr. Cothran? That is, from the inside edge to the outside edge, what is your best judgement as to the length of the blades?

A   Six or eight inches, I imagine, something like that.

Q   And how wide across is the fan? What is the diameter, approximately?

A   About—almost three feet.

Q Have you had occasion to weigh that fan?

A I did.

Q And how much does it weigh?

A Seventy pounds.

Q When you took the fan out of the boat up there at the river, was it muddy or clean like it is now?

A It was full of mud.

Q Who took it away from the scene there?

A Two colored boys put it in my car.

Q Did it still have mud on it when they put it in your car?

A Yes, Sir.

Q Did it get your car muddy?

A Yes, Sir, it sure did.

Q And of course, it weighed considerably more when you took it out of the river there than it does now, is that right

A Almost twice.

Q Then you would say that the weight was somewhere around one hundred and forty pounds when it came out of the river, is that right?

A Yes, Sir, I sure would.

Q Now, how long was this barbed wire that was wrapped around the neck of this body in the boat? How long was that wire, the length of it, from his neck?

A They had the wire off the fan when I got up there. I don't know how much of it they had off. But it was tied around the fan before, and I would judge from the length of it now—well, I would say the length—well, it looked to me like it would have been a width of about that long (indicating with his hands).

Q Would you say that is about eighteen inches?

A Something like that.

Q Then about eighteen inches would have been the distance the body was from the fan, is that right?

A   Yes, Sir.

Q   Now, this wound over his right ear, the small wound, was it round or what kind of a wound was it?

A   It wouldn't say because I don't know.

Q   Was it just a hole there?

A   It was just a little hole.

Q   And as I understood from your testimony, there were some gashes or cuts over his left ear?

A   That's right.

Q   And these gashes over his left ear, what did they look like?

A   They was just gashes, is all I know.

Q   And how many were there?

A   I know there was two.

Q   And how close together were they?

A   Oh, they were pretty close together.

Q   Was it possible for those gashes to have been made by this fan dropping on that head, in your best judgement?

A   You mean if they dropped that on his head?

Q   Well, the body was found in the river, I believe, is that right?

A   Yes, Sir.

Q   Do you think the body went in the river under its own power?

A   I don't know.

MR. SMITH: Your Honor, we object to what he thinks, even if it is cross examination.

THE COURT: Yes—don't ask the witness that.

Q   Of course, you don't know, Mr. Cothran, whether the body went in the river first or whether the fan went in the river first, do you?

A   No, Sir.

Q   But those wounds on the left-hand side of his head were such that they could have been made by this fan dropping on the head, isn't that right?

A   Yes, Sir. If it had hit him, it would have.

Q   And the depressed place in the forehead of that body, the gash there, that could have been made by the fan blades or by the hub, too, couldn't it?

A   Yes, Sir.

Q   In your best judgement, was it possible for that place, the wound over his right ear, was it possible for that to have been made by a snag in the river?

A   Yes, it could have been.

Q   John Ed, when you arrested Mr. Milam, did he ask you to be allowed to talk to counsel or to an attorney?

A   Yes, Sir.

Q   And what did you answer him?

A   I told him he could call in the office.

Q   And did you allow him to call his counsel or his attorney?

A   I don't know whether he did or not.

Q   Was that before the statement which you testified about was made or after?

A   It was before. We went in the office there, but I don't know whether he called or not.

Q   All right. Now, John Ed, I believe you testified on direct examination that there was no mutilation of this body except around the head?

A   That's right. If there was, I didn't see any.

Q   Had the boy's privates been mutilated?

A   No, Sir.

Q   Did his back show any signs of any bruises or any wounds at all on the back?

A   Now you are asking me a pretty hard question there. That body was in pretty bad shape, and I couldn't hardly tell. And I wouldn't want to answer that "Yes" or "No." At least, you couldn't see any.

Q Then you couldn't see any signs of that?

A You couldn't see any.

Q Now, let's go down to the morning of Wednesday, the 31st of August, when you left Greenwood—I believe you said that Deputy Sheriff Weber, from Itta Bena, Leflore County, was with you?

A Yes, Sir.

Q Was anybody else in the car with you?

A No, Sir.

Q And after you left there, where did you first stop?

A At Moses Wright's.

Q And did you pick up anybody there at Moses Wright's?

A We picked up Moses Wright.

Q Did you pick up anybody else there at Moses Wright's?

A No, Sir.

Q And as I understand, you stopped again between there and the river, is that right?

A I did.

Q And where did you stop?

A We stopped at Ray's Service Station in Philipp.

Q Did you pick up anybody there?

A Yes, Sir.

Q Who did you pick up there?

A I never did ask the man his name.

Q Did you at any time pick up Deputy Smith of Tallahatchie County?

A Not then.

Q Not on that trip?

A I don't remember ever picking him up.

Q When you got up there to the river, and after you parked your car, could you see the body in the boat in the river down there?

A Not from where we parked the car.

Q   And why couldn't you see it?

A   There was some bushes and trees between me and where the boat was.

Q   After you stopped and parked the car there, did Moses Wright get out of the car with you?

A   Yes, Sir.

Q   And then you walked down towards the river, I believe?

A   That's right.

Q   And when you were about fifteen or twenty yards away from the boat, did Moses make any statement about whether the body in the boat was that of Emmett Till or not?

A   Yes, Sir. He said, "I believe that's him."

Q   And when he made that statement to you, where was the body at the time?

A   It was in the boat.

Q   And where was the boat then?

A   It was setting on the river bank about—I would say, about twenty feet from us.

Q   The boat was about fifteen or twenty feet from you or would you say it was fifteen or twenty yards away?

A   Feet.

Q   And was the body lying on its back or was the body on its stomach?

A   It was on its stomach.

Q   And which end of the body was towards you and Moses?

A   The head.

Q   Now there at the boat, was Moses's attention directed to the ring that was on this boy's hand?

A   Well, I don't know just how—I don't know who first saw that ring.

Q   But was Moses asked any questions there about the ring?

A   That's right.

Q And what did Moses say there about the ring?

A He said he didn't know about the ring at the time, but he said he would carry it out to his house and ask his boy about it, that he would know.

Q And Moses said at that time that he didn't know anything about the ring?

A That's right.

Q What hand of the body was the ring on?

A It was on his right hand.

Q Do you know which finger it was on?

A I think it was on his middle finger.

Q Was there any tape wrapped around the ring?

A I didn't see any.

Q Did the ring come off the hand or finger easily or was it hard to get off?

A It wasn't any trouble to get off.

Q Beg pardon?

A The ring didn't seem any trouble to get off, or it didn't look like it was. I think the undertaker took it off.

Q Now, when Moses got up close to the boat and saw the body there, did he make any statement to you such as, "I could be mistaken that it might could not be him"?

A He did.

Q At the time this ring was taken off his finger, did the skin come off with the ring?

A Yes, Sir.

Q And how about the finger nails?

A I didn't notice about that.

Q Did you examine his left hand?

A No, Sir.

Q   Was the skin slipped badly all over his body?

A   I didn't notice that, but when they pulled that ring off, it slipped off.

Q   And you didn't look at the left hand at all?

A   No, Sir.

Q   What was the position of his tongue there at the scene?

A   It was swelled out of his mouth.

Q   And what was the condition of the body all over as regards swelling?

A   It was bad.

Q   And was he a well-developed body?

A   Yes, Sir.

Q   And what was the condition of his privates there when he was turned over?

A   It was in bad shape.

Q   Were they swelled or stiff?

A   Well, swelled or stiff.

Q   And were they well developed privates?

A   Yes, Sir.

Q   How old would you estimate this body to be?

A   I wouldn't.

MR. CARLTON: That is all, Your Honor.

THE COURT: Any further questions, Mr. Chatham?

MR. CHATHAM: Just one minute, Your Honor, please. We want to offer—well, I am not in a condition right now—or I can't lift this object here, this gin fan, but we want to offer it as Exhibit 2 to Mr. Cothran's testimony.

THE COURT: All right, sir—I think we will just let the Court Reporter take care of that.

REDIRECT EXAMINATION BY
THE DISTRICT ATTORNEY:

Q   John Ed [Cothran], during the cross examination by Mr. Carlton, at one point there with reference to Uncle Moses Wright's statement, I believe he asked you if Uncle Moses at that time expressed any doubt that his identification of the body, and I believe you answered at that time that Uncle Moses said he might be mistaken; is that right?

A   Yes, Sir.

Q   And at that particular time, I want you to tell the court and jury whether the corpse was lying on its stomach or on its back?

A   Mr. Chatham, as well as I remember it was still on its stomach. Now I wouldn't say for sure whether it had been turned over or not. But I think it was on its stomach.

MR. CHATHAM: We would like to now introduce these photographs, if we may. The writing has been covered up now.

THE COURT: I think the picture of the body was received in evidence this morning as an exhibit concerning Mr. Strickland's testimony. But the other ones had not been properly identified at the time, as I recall.

MR. CHATHAM: Then can we introduce both of these photographs now? We have had the testimony about the fan now.

MR. CARLTON: We have no objection.

THE COURT: All right. There has been no objection, and the picture of this wheel or fan will be received as Exhibit 2 to the testimony of Mr. Strickland.

(A photograph was then marked as Exhibit 2 to the testimony of Mr. Strickland by the reporter.)

(WITNESS EXCUSED.)

THE COURT: We will now recess until ten o'clock tomorrow morning. . . .

For the State:

Hon. Gerald Chatham, District Attorney;

Hon. Robert B. Smith, III, Special Assistant to the District Attorney;

Hon. Hamilton Caldwell, County Attorney.

For the Defendants:

Hon. J. J. Breland, of Sumner, Mississippi;

Hon. C. Sidney Carlton, of Sumner, Mississippi;

Hon. J. W. Kellum, of Sumner, Mississippi;

Hon. John W. Whitten, Jr., of Sumner, Miss.;

Hon. Harvey Henderson, of Sumner, Mississippi.

* * * *

FOURTH DAY

This day, this cause having been continued for further hearing; on this the 22nd day of September 1955, comes the District Attorney, came also the defendants, each in his own proper person and represented by counsel and announced ready to proceed herein. Whereupon, came the same jury, composed of J. A. Shaw, Jr.,[21] and eleven others, being specially sworn to try the issue.

Thereupon, the cause proceeded to further trial before the Judge aforesaid and the jury, when and where the following proceedings were had, as follows:

C. F. (CHICK) NELSON,[22]

A witness introduced for and on behalf of the State, being first duly sworn, upon his oath testified as follows:

---

21. James "J. A." Shaw Jr. (1924–1979) "was a farmer living in Webb, Tallahatchie County, Mississippi." Anderson, "Who's Who in the Emmett Till Case."

22. Chester F. "Chick" Nelson (1903–1978) "was the mayor of Tutwiler, Tallahatchie County, Mississippi, whose funeral home embalmed and prepared . . . Till's body for shipment back to Chicago. . . ." Anderson, "Who's Who in the Emmett Till Case."

DIRECT EXAMINATION BY
MR. SMITH:

Q Will you state your name, please, sir?

A C. F. Nelson.

Q And I believe they call you "Chick," is that right?

A Yes, Sir.

Q Mr. Nelson, what is your occupation?

A I have a furniture store for one thing.

Q And are you also manager and operator of a funeral home?

A That's right.

Q Where is the funeral home?

A At Tutwiler, Mississippi.

Q Do you hold any official position in the town of Tutwiler?

A Yes, Sir. I am Mayor.

Q You are the Mayor of the town?

A Yes, Sir.

Q Mr. Nelson, directing your attention to the last part of August, were you called upon or requested to come to Greenwood to pick up a body?

A Yes, Sir.

Q And who were you advised that the person would be that you were to pick up? What was the name?

MR. BRELAND: We object to that, Your Honor.

THE COURT: The objection is overruled.

THE WITNESS: Emmett Till.

Q And did you go or send someone to Greenwood to pick up that body?

A Yes, Sir, I did.

Q And to what funeral home did they go to pick up that body?

A The Century Funeral Hone [sic], I think they call it. Let's see— that was Chester . . .

Q   Do you mean the funeral home of Chester Miller?

A   Yes, Sir.

Q   He was the operator of that funeral home?

A   That's right.

Q   And did they bring a body back?

A   They did, yes, Sir.

Q   And after the body was brought back, what was done with it?

A   We prepared it the best we could and shipped it to Chicago.

MR. BRELAND: We object to that, Your Honor.

THE COURT: The objection is overruled.

Q   And you say it was shipped to Chicago?

A   Yes, Sir.

Q   And to which funeral home in Chicago was it shipped? To which person or individual was it shipped, do you know?

A   Rainer [sic] and Sons.[23]

Q   Rainer [sic] and Sons?

A   Yes, Sir.

MR. SMITH: Your witness.

CROSS EXAMINATION BY
MR. BRELAND:

Q   To your own personal knowledge, you didn't know the identity of the body that was brought to your funeral home, do you?

A   No, Sir.

MR. BRELAND: That is all.

(WITNESS EXCUSED.)

* * * *

---

23. Ahmed A. Rayner Sr. (1893–1989) "was the funeral director who received Emmett Till's body after its arrival in Chicago on September 2, 1955. He defied orders from Mississippi to keep the casket sealed and allowed Mamie Bradley to examine the remains of her son." Anderson, "Who's Who in the Emmett Till Case."

Chapter 3

THE STATE'S CASE AND THE DEFENSE'S ATTACK

NOT EVEN THE MOTHER COULD IDENTIFY HER SON?

The prosecution continued to introduce evidence to establish the identity of the body as that of Emmett Till. Thus, yet more evidence was presented by those who knew Emmett and by way of his father's "L. T. May 25, 1943" inscribed ring, the one Emmett was wearing when his body was found. In both respects, Mamie Till-Bradley, who had been flown into Mississippi by the prosecution, was the State's best witness. Ms. Bradley also corroborated with certainty that the badly disfigured body was that of her son. Her testimony was essential in helping the prosecution counter the corpus delicti defense that there was no identifying evidence of the actual death of her son.

The defense, by way of J. J. Breland, continued to object to the admission of the ring into evidence on the ground that no foundation for its admissibility had been legally established. Furthermore, Breland made a three-pronged attack on Bradley's testimony for the prosecution:

1. *The Profit Motive Argument*: He questioned Bradley about life insurance policies she and her mother had on Emmett (admitted into evidence over the prosecution's objection). The inference, of course, was that there was some scheme afoot to collect insurance money—a theory the defense lawyers continued to advance later in the trial;

2. *The Before and After Argument*: In an attempt to prove the impossibility of identifying the corpse, Breland sought to introduce evidence of photos that appeared in the *Memphis Press-Scimitar* and in the *Chicago Defender*, photos taken of the corpse. He asked that these photos be contrasted with other photos Bradley had introduced of Emmett taken the year before he came to Mississippi. Here again, this "before and after" approach was designed to establish the impossibility of identifying the badly disfigured face–such that not even his mother could recognize it as that of her son. Judge Swango allowed the "before and after" evidence to be admitted, though he ruled that the death photos be limited to one and with no reference to the newspapers in which they appeared. He also allowed the pre-death photos to be admitted into evidence. The preliminary cross-examination of this line of questioning was conducted outside the presence of the jury.

3. *The Blame the Victim Argument*: Finally, Breland cross-examined Bradley as to whether and how she instructed Emmett to conduct himself when in the presence of whites during his stay in Mississippi. Judge Swango sustained the prosecution's objection to this line of questioning. Thus, this evidence, offered outside the presence of the jury, was not admitted.

MAMIE BRADLEY,[1]

A witness introduced for and on behalf of the State,[2] being first duly sworn, upon her oath testified as follows:

------

1. Upon arriving in Mississippi, Mamie requested police protection, which purportedly irritated the prosecutor, Gerald Chatham. See Houck & Grindy, *Emmett Till*, p. 59. When Mamie first entered the courtroom, Sheriff Strider "marched up to her, issued her a subpoena, and loudly announced, 'You are now in the state of Mississippi. You will come under all rules of the state of Mississippi.'" *Ibid.*, p. 78. As to her appearance, she was "[d]ressed stylishly in a grey dress with a white collar and a small black hat [and] was given a seat at the Negro press table" before she took the witness stand. "Arrival of Victim's Mother Causes Stir," *Jackson State Times*, September 20, 1955, sect. A, p. 2.

2. "As she sat down, 270-pound Sheriff H. C. Strider pushed his way through the crowd and handed her a subpoena as a witness." *Greenwood Commonwealth*, "District

DIRECT EXAMINATION BY
MR. SMITH:

Q   Your name is Mamie Bradley?

A   Yes, Sir.

Q   Where do you live, Mamie?[3]

A   Chicago, Illinois.

Q   Mamie, did you have a son, who, in his lifetime was known as Emmett Till?

A   Yes, Sir.

Q   How old was Emmett?

A   Fourteen years of age.

Q   Is his Father[4] living today?

A   No Sir. He died in the service.

Q   He died in service?

A   Yes, Sir.

Q   Do you remember the date of his death?

A   Yes, Sir; the 2nd of July, 1945.

Q   Where was he when he died?

A   In the European Theatre.

Q   Mamie, in the first part of September, 1955, or the last part of August, were you advised that your son, Emmett Till, had been in some difficulty or trouble down here?

A   Yes, Sir.

Q   And who advised you of that?

A   The Mother of Curtis Jones, Mrs. Willa Mae Jones.[5]

Attorney Seeks More Time," p. 1.

   3. Note that even the prosecution did not use the term "Mrs." or "Miss" in addressing Mamie Bradley.

   4. Louis Till (1922–1945).

   5. Willie Mae Wright Jones (1917–?) was "the oldest child of Moses and Lucinda Larry Wright. She was the mother of Curtis Jones, a cousin of Emmett Till who traveled from Chicago to Mississippi shortly after Emmett and Wheeler Parker left, and was in the

Q And how did she advise you? Was it by telephone?

A Yes, Sir.

Q Where was your son at that time?

A He was visiting my Uncle, Moses Wright, in Money, Mississippi.

Q And when did he come down here?

A He left Chicago, Illinois, on the 20th of August.

Q And I believe he was supposed to come home shortly thereafter, is that right?

A Yes, Sir. He was going to stay two weeks.

Q Now, later, after you got that information, was a body sent to Chicago that was supposed to be the body of your son, Emmett Till?

A Yes, Sir.

Q And where was that body first seen by you?

A At the Rainer [sic] Funeral Home.

Q Did you observe the body there?

A Yes, I did.

Q And where was the body when you saw it there at the funeral home?

A The first time I saw it, it was still in the casket.

Q Did you see it later on?

A Yes, Sir. I saw it later on after it was removed from the casket and placed on a slab.

Q At the time it was still in the casket, had anything been done to the body then, if you know?

A No, Sir. The seal had never been broken the first time I saw the body.

Wright home the night Emmett was abducted. It was Willie Mae's phone call on Sunday morning, August 28, 1955, that notified Mamie that Emmett had been kidnapped. . . . As of 2008, she [was still] living in Chicago, and [was then] the oldest living direct link to the Emmett Till case." Anderson, "Who's Who in the Emmett Till Case."

Q   When the body was placed on the slab, was anything done then? Had anything been done to the body after it was removed from the casket?

A   The only change was that the body had been clothed.

Q   It had some clothes on then?

A   Yes, Sir.

Q   Mamie, I wish you would state to the court and jury whether you could identify the body you saw there at the funeral home as that of your son, Emmett Till?

A   I positively identified the body in the casket and later on when it was on the slab as being that of my son, Emmett Louis Till.

Q   Will you please tell the court and jury how you looked at it and what you did in identifying it?

A   I looked at the face very carefully. I looked at the ears, and the forehead, and the hairline, and also the hair; and I looked at the nose and the lips, and the chin. I just looked at it all over very thoroughly. And I was able to find out that it was my boy. And I knew definitely that it was my boy beyond a shadow of a doubt.[6]

Q   Mamie, when your husband, the father of Emmett Till, was killed overseas, were his effects sent to you?

A   Yes, Sir, they were.

Q   I will ask you if in those effects there was a ring?

A   Yes, Sir, there was a ring.

Q   What kind of a ring was it? What color was it?

A   The ring was white, or it looked like some kind of white metal.

MR. BRELAND: Now, Your Honor, we now object to the testimony of this witness with reference to the effects, or what is purported to be the effects of her dead husband being sent to her, without showing just who, when, and how those effects were sent.

---

6. "Fifteen feet away at the defendants' table, Bryant stared at Bradley without emotion, while Milam sat in his chair reading letters, simultaneously chewing gum and smoking cigars." Ethan Michaeli, *The Defender: How the Legendary Black Newspaper Changed America*, Boston: Mariner Books (2018), pp. 331, 581 n. 29.

THE COURT: Yes, I believe there would have to be a prior connection on the identification of the ring, I think.

MR. SMITH: All we are trying to do, Your Honor, is to identify the ring that the boy had on.

THE COURT: You can proceed a little differently, I believe.

MR. SMITH: Yes, Sir.

Q Mamie, I will ask you if your son had a ring and frequently wore a ring that was sent along in the effects of your husband that you got?

A Yes, Sir.

MR. BRELAND: We object to that, Your Honor, for the reason that she said that the effects were sent to her that were supposed to belong to her dead husband. But it hasn't been shown in evidence anything about the identity of those effects.

THE COURT: The objection is overruled.

Q I now hand you a ring, Mamie, that has engraved on it "May 25, 1943," with the large initials "L. T.," and I ask you if that was among the effects that were sent to you which were purported to be the effects of your dead husband?

A Yes, Sir.

Q What was your husband's name?

A Louis Till.

Q In other words, his initials were "L. T."?

A Yes, Sir.

Q And after you got this ring along with his effects, what happened to it?

A I kept the ring in a jewelry box, but it was much too large for the boy to wear. But since his twelfth birthday, he has worn it occasionally with the aid of scotch tape or string. He had to have something else on with it to make it fit his hand tightly enough. But usually though it was kept in his personal jewelry box. And on the morning of September—or of August 20th when he got ready to board the train, he was looking in his jewelry box to get some cuff links, I think it was, and when he looked in the box there, he saw this ring, and he put it on his hand, or on his finger, and he shook his hand, to make sure that it would stay on there and not fall off. And I remember that I casually remarked to him I said, "Gee, you are getting to be quite a grown man." And then he said to me . . .

Q   Now don't tell what he said. But did he then put the ring on his finger?

A   Yes, Sir.

Q   And he left Chicago with it, did he?

A   Yes, Sir.

Q   And you definitely say that was the ring that he left there with?

A   Yes, Sir.

Q   And that was the ring he had when he came down here to Mississippi?

A   Yes, Sir.

Q   Now Mamie, I have here a picture which has been introduced in evidence as Exhibit 1 to the testimony of Mr. Strickland here in this trial. And I hand you that picture and ask you if that is a picture of your son, Emmett Till?

A   Yes, Sir.

Q   That is him, isn't it?

A   Yes, Sir.

MR. SMITH: If the Court please, just one minute . . . these pictures have never been shown to the jury, and I wonder at this point if you might let the jury look at them.

THE COURT: They can have them. They have been introduced in evidence.

(The two exhibits, Exhibits 1 and 2 to the testimony of Mr. Strickland are given to the members of the jury for examination.)

MR. SMITH: You may take the witness.

CROSS EXAMINATION BY
MR. BRELAND:

Q Mamie, where were you born?

A I was born in Webb, Mississippi.

Q You were born in Webb, Mississippi?

A Yes, Sir.

Q That is a little town just two miles south of here, is that right?

A I can't tell you the location.

Q But it is about two miles south of Sumner, isn't it?

A I don't know.

Q When did you leave Mississippi?

A At the age of two.

Q Then you have just been told that you were born in Webb, Mississippi? You don't remember, is that right?

A Yes, Sir.

Q What was your mother's name?

A Alma Carthan.[7]

Q Was she born in Mississippi?

MR. CHATHAM: We are going to object to this, if Your Honor please. This is highly immaterial in this case, and I am sure we want to get through with this trial some time.

THE COURT: I think we are going a little far afield. But I will let the witness answer that question.

---

7. Alma Smith Carthan Gaines Spearman (1902–1981) "was the mother of Mamie Bradley and grandmother of Emmett Till. She helped her daughter in the days after Emmett was kidnapped and murdered, and it was at her home that Chicago reporters first congregated. She was born in Mississippi and married Wiley Nash Carthan in 1919. She lived in Mississippi until moving to Argo, Illinois, with her husband and daughter in 1924, where she was a founder of the Argo Temple Church of God in Christ. In the early 1930s she and Nash separated and divorced, after which she married Tom Gaines. He died in 1944, and she married Henry Spearman in 1947. After his death in 1967, she moved in with Mamie and Gene Mobley, where she lived until her death." Anderson, "Who's Who in the Emmett Till Case."

THE WITNESS: Yes, Sir.

Q Do you know who left with you when you left Mississippi?

MR. SMITH: We object to that, Your Honor. That has nothing to do with this case at all.

THE COURT: The objection is sustained.

Q When you can first remember, where were you living?

A In Argo, Illinois.

Q How far is that from Chicago?

A Approximately thirteen miles.

Q And how long did you live there at Argo, Illinois?

MR. SMITH: If the Court please, we are going to object to this line of questioning. It is highly immaterial and has nothing at all to do with this case.

THE COURT: The objection is sustained.

Q When did you move to Chicago?

MR. SMITH: We object to that, Your Honor.

THE COURT: The objection is sustained.

Q What is your age, Mamie?

A Thirty-three.

Q When your son, Emmett, left home with the intention of coming to Mississippi, when was his mind made up to come to Mississippi?

A One week previous to the day he left.

Q Did you and him talk about it?

A Yes, Sir.

Q And you discussed it together between you, did you?

A Yes, Sir.

Q And how many times did you discuss it with him?

A I probably wouldn't be able to tell you that.

Q   Well, about how many times?

A   Several times at least.

Q   Did you go with him to the train when he left Chicago?

A   Yes, Sir.

MR. SMITH: We object to that, Your Honor. That has nothing to do with this.

THE COURT: The objection is sustained.

Q   Mamie, did Emmett ever have any trouble up there in Chicago? Was he ever in any trouble up in Chicago?

A   No, Sir.

MR. SMITH: We object to that, Your Honor.

THE COURT: The object is sustained.

Q   By the way, did you have any insurance on Emmett Till?[8]

A   Yes, Sir.

MR. SMITH: We object to that, Your Honor.

THE COURT: I am going to overrule your objection to that question.

Q   Did you have any life insurance on him?

A   Yes, Sir.

Q   How much did you have?

A   About four hundred dollars straight life.

Q   You had about four hundred dollars insurance on him?

A   I had a ten-cent policy and a fifteen-cent policy, two weekly policies, and they equalled [*sic*] four hundred dollars.

Q   You had two policies that equalled [*sic*] four hundred dollars?

A   Yes, Sir.

Q   How long had you had those policies out on him?

---

8. Discussed by Mamie Bradley (Till-Mobley) in Till-Mobley & Benson, *Death of Innocence*, pp. 179–80.

A   Almost from his birth.

Q   With what companies were they?

A   Well, Metropolitan. . . .

MR. SMITH: We object to that, Your Honor.

THE COURT: The objection is sustained.

Q   To whom were those policies payable?

MR. SMITH: We object to that, Your, Honor.

THE COURT: The object is overruled.

THE WITNESS: Will you repeat the question, please?

Q   To whom were those policies made payable? Who was the beneficiary in those policies?

A   I was the beneficiary on one and my Mother was on the other.

Q   Were they both for four hundred dollars each?

A   Well, one was for a hundred and ninety-three dollars, I think, and one was a little bit more. It was approximately four hundred dollars on the two of them.

Q   And have you collected on those policies?

A   No, Sir.

Q   Have you tried to collect on them?

MR. SMITH: We object to that, Your Honor. That is highly irrelevant.

THE COURT: The objection is overruled.

Q   Have you tried to collect on those policies?

A   I have been waiting to receive a death certificate.

Q   Have you contacted the insurance companies about the policies?

A   Yes, Sir.

Q   And you and your mother, both, have done that?

A   Yes, Sir, together.

Q   Now, Mamie, what newspapers do you subscribe to in Chicago?

MR. SMITH: We object to that, Your Honor.

THE COURT: The objection is sustained.

Q Do you read the *CHICAGO DEFENDER*?

MR. SMITH: We object to that, Your Honor.

THE COURT: The objection is sustained.

MR. BRELAND: Your Honor, I think this is important because I have some exhibits that I want the witness to identify.

MR. CHATHAM: If the Court please, I think it is perfectly obvious what he is trying to get at. And I think counsel should be counseled not to ask any more questions like that.

THE COURT: The objection is sustained. Now, will you gentlemen of the jury step back in the jury room a moment, please.

(The jury retired to the jury room, and the proceedings continued in the absence of the jury.)

Q Do you subscribe to the *CHICAGO DEFENDER*?

A No Sir, I don't subscribe to the paper, but I do buy it and read it.

Q You buy it and read it?

MR. SMITH: If the Court please, we want the record to show that we object to all this line of questioning.

THE COURT: The jury is out of the room, and the Court has already sustained your objection.

Q Have you been reading the *CHICAGO DEFENDER* since the trial of this cause?

A Yes, Sir.

Q And also since the incident happened that has been referred to here?

A Yes, Sir.

Q And you have been getting it, have you?

A Yes, Sir. I read it every week, anyway.

Q And you read everything in it, do you?

A I wouldn't say the entire thing.

Q I mean, you read everything in it referring to this incident, do you?

A No, Sir. I haven't read the paper all through since I found out the child had been found dead.

Q Did you read the paper of Saturday, September 17th?

A I would have to look at it to see.

Q I will hand it to you, the paper of that edition. (A paper is shown to the witness.)

A I haven't even seen this one, I don't think. This is the national. I might have seen the other one. You see there are two DEFENDERS. But the national, I haven't seen.

Q These papers are edited by colored people, is that right?

A Yes, Sir.

Q I will hand you a portion of that particular paper, that edition of that particular paper, and ask you to look at the photograph and see if you have seen that?

A I have seen this picture but not in this paper. I saw a much smaller picture in another copy of the DEFENDER.

Q But is that a likeness of the picture you did see?

A Yes, Sir.

Q Have you a photograph of your son, Emmett Till, with you?

A Yes, Sir, I have.

Q And have you got it on your person?

A It is with my Father in the witness chambers

Q When was that photograph made?

A Two days after Christmas, 1954.

Q 1954?

A Yes, Sir.

Q Did you have several of those photographs made?

A Yes, Sir.

Q   And did you furnish any of those photographs to members of the press?

A   Yes, Sir.

Q   And that was for photographic purposes to put in the papers, is that right?

A   Yes, Sir.

Q   Now I hand you a paper—this is not a Chicago paper; this is the *MEMPHIS PRESS-SCIMITAR*—and I will ask you to look at that photograph in the upper left part of the paper and state whether that is a copy of that photograph you furnished the press?

A   Yes, Sir. I have a copy of it with me if you would like to see it.

Q   And you don't have more than one photograph of that picture with you?

A   I have one copy of three different pictures.

Q   You have three different pictures with you?

A   Yes, Sir.

Q   Have you got any more of those at home?

A   Yes, Sir.

Q   In other words, you could use one copy here, and you wouldn't be deprived of anything by having one copy in the record? You would still have a copy for yourself?

A   Yes, Sir.

Q   And you could have more copies made of those if you wanted them, is that right?

A   Yes, Sir.

MR. BRELAND: If the Court please, we would like for those to be produced here at this particular hearing so that she might identify those photographs she might have with her.

MR. SMITH: We object to that, Your Honor.

THE COURT: Can you get the photographs?

THE WITNESS: Yes, Sir. My Father has them in the witness room.

MR. SMITH: What is your Father's name?

THE WITNESS: John Carthan. And he has the pictures with him. They are in this coat.

MR. BRELAND: Tell them to bring John Carthan to the courtroom and to bring his coat with him.

(After a short period, an envelope is produced and handed to the witness on the stand.)

  Q Mamie, will you take out those photographs that are in that envelope?

  A Yes, Sir.

(Three photographs are given to Mr. Breland by the witness.)

  Q Mamie, you have presented to counsel for the defendants what purports to be three separate photographs of your son, one of which has a woman in it taken with him. Is that you?

  A Yes, Sir.

  Q Can you tell the court and jury the last one of the photographs made, if they were made at different times?

  A All of these pictures were made on the very same day.

  Q They were all made on the same day?

  A Yes, Sir. As a matter of fact, there was one more picture made at the time, and I believe it is one where a picture was taken where he was lying across the bed and looking this way, but unfortunately, I do not have one of those with me.

  Q Mamie, I hand you now what purports to be a photograph of some person. Will you state whose photograph that is?

  A That is a photograph of Emmett Louis Till.

  Q That is your son?

  A Yes, Sir.

MR. BRELAND: We would like to have that marked as an exhibit for identification, please.

THE COURT: All right.

(A photograph is marked as Exhibit I to the testimony of Mamie Bradley for identification by the reporter.)

> Q Mamie, I believe you stated that the photograph on the front page of that *Press-Scimitar*, in the upper-left-hand corner of those photographs, of the group of photographs there, that it is a photograph of your son?
>
> A Yes, Sir.
>
> Q Was that a picture that as made from one of the photographs that you have testified about?
>
> A Not one of these three that I have shown you.
>
> Q But it was one taken at the same time?
>
> A Yes, Sir.

MR. BRELAND: This is on the front page of the edition of the *Memphis Press-Scimitar* of Thursday, September 15th, 1955; and we offer that photograph in the upper left-hand corner on that front page of that paper as Exhibit 2, for purposes of identification by this witness.

THE COURT: All right.

(A photograph is marked as Exhibit 2 to the testimony of Mamie Bradley for identification by the reporter.)

> Q Mamie, I hand you a paper, being page 19 of the *Chicago Defender*, on the date of September 17th, 1955, which purports to be a photograph of some person. Will you look at that and state whether or not that is also a photograph of Emmett Till or the person who was shipped back to Chicago that you saw at the funeral home there?
>
> A This is a picture of Emmett Louis Till as I saw it at the funeral home.
>
> Q That is a picture of the body as you saw it in the funeral home in Chicago, Illinois?
>
> A Yes, Sir.
>
> Q And being the picture of the same body which you then identified as Emmett Till?

A   Yes, Sir.

Q   And which you now identify as that of Emmett Till, is that right?

A   Yes, Sir.

MR. BRELAND: Now, if Your Honor please, we ask that this be marked as Exhibit 3 to the testimony of this witness for the purposes of identification.

THE COURT: All right.

(A photograph is marked as Exhibit 3 to the testimony of Mamie Bradley for identification by the reporter.)

Q   Mamie, do you state to the Court that the photographs which you now have identified as Exhibit 1 to your testimony for purposes of identification, and the photograph which you identified in the *PRESS-SCIMITAR* as Exhibit 2 to your testimony for purposes of identification, and the photograph in the *CHICAGO DEFENDER*, under date of September 17th, 1955, as Exhibit 3 to your testimony for purposes of identification, are a likeness of those photographs of those scenes? And do you state that they are true pictures of the scenes you saw?

A   Yes, Sir.

THE COURT: Have you finished with your examinations?

MR. BRELAND: I believe we have, Your Honor. And we submit that these are proper at this time.

THE COURT: Have you finished with your examination of this witness outside the hearing of the jury?

MR. BRELAND: Yes, Sir.

MR. SMITH: Your Honor, we think this is highly incompetent, this whole part of the case. And as far as the pictures being introduced here, nothing has been shown as to the way they were taken or the manner in which they were taken, and nothing of that kind has been shown or proved. No one has testified to the competency of the photographs. And we say that they are highly incompetent.

THE COURT: With reference to that, I believe the witness testified that the pictures taken—that one of them is a picture of her son that was taken shortly after Christmas, and I believe the witness testified that it is a true likeness of her son during his lifetime. And she also testified that the picture taken in Chicago after his death portrays a true picture of what she saw there at that time.

Now, the Court is going to admit these pictures in evidence—that is, one picture there that she produced, so that the jury may see the likeness of Emmett Till during his lifetime.

And the Court is going to let be introduced in evidence the picture made in Chicago after his death. It will be cut from the paper, and the paper itself will not be any part of the exhibit.

And another thing, there will be no reference to any newspapers to which this witness may subscribe in Chicago, or any reference to what she may read. And there will be no reference or anything said about any newspapers or pictures other than this picture which she has identified as being a picture of her son taken after his death as she saw it there in Chicago. That picture will be permitted.

And there will be no reference to any other pictures or newspapers, or any reference as to what this witness may have read or subscribed to whatsoever. These pictures that the Court is permitting to be introduced in evidence are for the benefit of the jury, so that they may see a likeness of Emmett Till during this lifetime, and also a likeness of his body, as the witness stated, as she saw it in Chicago after the body was returned to Chicago.

MR. BRELAND: There is one other thing, Your Honor, that I think we ought to go into before the jury returns, and I think possibly there might be some objection to it.

THE COURT: Well, whatever you have for this witness of that nature, then let's get it out while the jury is still out.

MR. BRELAND: All right. Sir.

Q   Mamie, you said that you discussed your son's trip down to Mississippi several times with him before he left your home in Chicago, is that correct?

A   Yes, Sir.

Q Did you caution him how to conduct himself and behave himself while he was down here in Mississippi before he left there?

A Yes, Sir.

Q Now, you have quoted in the press—I don't know whether you said it or not, but the press report shows it in quotations that you are supposed to have made, in these words, now listen carefully, and says: "I told him several times before he left for Mississippi that he should kneel in the street and beg forgiveness if he ever insulted a white man or white woman." Now, did you tell him that?

A Not those exact words.

Q Well, what did you tell him?[9]

A I will give you a liberal description of what I told him. I told him when he was coming down here that he would have to adapt himself to a new way of life. And I told him to be very careful about how he spoke and to whom he spoke, and to always remember to say "Yes, Sir" and "No, Ma'am" at all times.

And I told him that if ever an incident should arise where there would be any trouble of any kind with white people, then if it got to a point where he even had to get down on his knees before them, well, I told him not to hesitate to do so. Like, if he bumped into somebody on the street, well, and then they might get belligerent or something, well, I told him to go ahead and humble himself so as not to get into any trouble of any kind. And I told him to be very careful how he walked in the streets at all times.

Q And did you direct his attention as to how to act around white people, and how to conduct himself about a white man? The paper says that you cautioned him about his behaviour [*sic*] before any white men. Did you call his attention to that?

A Yes, Sir.

Q And did you specifically indicate to him and caution him not to do anything to any white man so as not to bring on any trouble?

A Yes, Sir.

---

9. She discusses her instructions to Emmett in Till-Mobley & Benson, *Death of Innocence*, pp. 100–01 ("Every generation has its cautionary tale.").

Q And from the newspaper quotation, the newspaper report says that you did that several times, is that true?

A I did. I impressed it on him very carefully as to how he should act while he was down here.

Q He had been in Mississippi before, had he?

A Yes, Sir.

Q And he had visited here close to Sumner before?

A Yes, Sir, with that same uncle.

Q And that was after he got to be a big boy, was it?

A I think he was about nine years old then.

Q And those are the only two times that he has been in Mississippi, so far as you know?

A No, Sir. He came down here once when an infant, about fifteen months old, maybe something like that. I know he was a small baby. And then I think he came down here again while he was very small, maybe four or five years old. And then he was down here when he was about nine, and then this last trip.

Q And did you caution him in those conversations you had with him not to insult any white women?

A I didn't specifically say white women. But I said about the white people. And I cautioned him not to get in a fight with any white boys. And I told him that, because, naturally living in Chicago, he wouldn't know just how to act maybe.

Q Prior to his coming down to Mississippi, and prior to his leaving Chicago, while he was living there in Chicago, had he been doing anything to cause you to give him that special instruction?

A No, Sir. Emmett has never been in any trouble at any time.

Q And he has never been in a reform school?

A No Sir.

Q And he never had any trouble in any way with any white people?

A No, Sir.

Q I believe you live on the south side in Chicago, is that right?

A   Yes, Sir, on the south side.

Q   And that is the part of Chicago referred to as the black belt, is that right?

A   Yes, Sir.

Q   And the people in the community, are they all colored people or white people?

A   There are a few white people living there.

Q   And they have their homes there, is that right?

A   Yes, Sir.

THE COURT: Now is that all?

MR. BRELAND: Yes, Sir.

THE COURT: Now the objections to all that testimony will be sustained, and there will be no questions along that line whatsoever. And since the Court has ruled on the pictures, the objection to all the testimony is sustained. And there will be no further reference to it, and there will be no questions asked concerning that after the jury comes in.

(The jury returned to the courtroom, and the proceedings continued with the jury present.)

Q   This is Mamie Bradley, is that right?

A   Yes, Sir.

Q   And you are the Mother of Emmett Till?

A   Yes, Sir.

Q   And you live at Chicago, Illinois, is that right?

A   Yes, Sir.

Q   And you live on the south side of Chicago, is that right?

A   Yes, Sir.

Q   And did your son, Emmett Till, leave your home there in Chicago at any time to come to Mississippi in the month of August?

A   Yes, Sir.

THE COURT: I think all that was in, Mr. Breland, before the jury retired. But you may proceed with the examination.

Q   And your son did leave your home in Chicago with the expectation of coming to Mississippi, is that right?

A   Yes, Sir.

Q   And you didn't come with him?

A   No, Sir.

Q   Now, I hand you what purports to be a photograph of your son. Is that a photograph of your son?

A   Yes, Sir.

Q   And that is a true and correct photograph of your son at the time it was taken?

A   Yes, Sir.

Q   And when was that picture taken?

A   This was made in my home two days after Christmas of 1954.

Q   Right after Christmas of 1954?

A   Yes, Sir. It was on about the 27th of December.

MR. BRELAND: We now ask that this photograph be identified which has already been marked as Exhibit 1 to the testimony of this witness for the purpose of identification.

Q   Now I will hand you what purports to be another photograph. Will you look at it and tell the court and jury what this is?

A   This is a picture of my son after he was sent back to Chicago dead. This is the way I saw him the second time. He had his clothes put on his body then. When I saw him the first time, he didn't have any clothes.

Q   And how much time elapsed from the time you first saw him without clothes until you saw him in the likeness of that photograph there?

A   I saw the one with his clothes on and without the clothes on the same day. Perhaps a half an hour or an hour had elapsed. I am not clear on that.

Q   And was the first view you had of your son there before the clothes were put on the body a likeness of the photograph shown here? That is, was it like the picture shown in that photograph?

A   The face, yes, Sir.

Q   And everything was the same except that clothes had been put on the body the second time you saw him, is that right? That is, it was the same as it was when you saw him the first time when he had no clothes on, is that right?

A   No, Sir. The first time I saw him, he had a hole in his head up here (indicating with her hand), and that was open. And he had another scar. I can't tell you exactly where it was. It was either over the right eye or the left eye. I can't remember just now. And he had a gash in his jaw, and his mouth was open and the tongue was out. That is the first time when I saw him without his clothes on. But from this picture here, it seems like his mouth has been closed, and that gash was sewn up, and that place in his forehead up there has been closed up. That is the way it looks to me.

Q   Then the photograph there is a better picture of him than the way it was when you first saw him, is that right?

A   Yes, Sir.

MR. BRELAND: This is the photograph that we asked to be marked as Exhibit 1 to the testimony of this witness for purposes of identification. You may take the witness.

MR. SMITH: That is all, if the Court please.

(WITNESS EXCUSED.)

Chapter 4

THE STATE'S CASE
"I HEARD SOMEBODY HOLLERING"

The prosecution closed its case by calling the last three of its twelve witnesses. These witnesses were presented to testify to the murder itself and those involved in it. To that end, prosecutor Chatham called Willie Reed, Add Reed (Willie's grandfather), and Amandy Bradley, all of whom lived near the shed where the beatings (and presumably the murder) occurred. All three were surprise witnesses called by the prosecution.[1]

Dr. T.R.M. Howard (aided by NAACP field representatives Medgar Evers, Ruby Hurley, and the Black press) was the driving force behind the discovery of these witnesses and the one responsible for bringing them to court to testify. Howard "claimed that the murder likely took place on the Sheridan plantation in Sunflower County, which was managed by J.W. Milam's brother, Leslie Milam. District Attorney Stanny Sanders called it a 'startling development,' one that might move into his jurisdiction." He also claimed "that two Negroes who worked on the plantation 'have not been seen or heard of since.'"[2] As it turned out, the jurisdiction was not changed, and the two missing men (Levi

---

1. See *Greenwood Commonwealth*, "District Attorney Seeks More Time," p. 1; James L. Kilgallen, "Slain Boy's Uncle Identifies 2 Men Who Abducted Youth," *Atlanta Daily World*, September 22, 1955, p. 1.

2. Houck & Grindy, *Emmett Till*, p. 85, citing "New Witnesses May Take Till Murder Trial to Sunflower," *Delta Democrat-Times*, September 21, 1955, p. 1. See Beito & Beito, *T.R.M. Howard*, pp. 135–37, 166–70. See also, Wright Thompson, "His Name was Emmett: What We Still Don't Know About Emmett Till's Murder," *The Atlantic* (Sept. 2021).

Collins and Henry Lee Loggins) were not located in time to testify. Even so, the three witnesses Dr. Howard helped to locate did testify.

Willie Reed, then eighteen, was the prosecution's star witness insofar as the murder was concerned. He knew both defendants and testified that he saw J. W. at the scene of the crime, namely, at Leslie Milam's barn, and that he heard "hollering" and "licks." He also testified that he saw four white men in the cab of a 1955 Chevrolet pickup "and three colored men" in the back of the pickup along with someone who "favored" a photo of Emmett.

At one point in Willie Reed's testimony, and amid protests by Breland, Judge Swango granted one of Breland's objections and stated, "As far as I can see, these defendants have not [yet] been connected with the incident in any way." But thereafter, when Breland made a motion to exclude all of Willie Reed's testimony—and tendered three reasons for doing so—Judge Swango declared, "That motion will be overruled."

The defense, this time headed by Joseph Kellum, therefore had to cross-examine Reed, who had been deposed by the five defense lawyers the day before. The main part of Kellum's argument was to challenge what exactly Reed saw, whom exactly he saw, and at what precise distance he was when he claimed to see J. W. Milam and those in the cab and in the back of the Chevrolet pickup truck. Note that Reed did not testify against Roy Bryant. When Kellum concluded, Breland moved once more that Reed's testimony be excluded. Again, Judge Swango denied the motion.

Amandy Bradley testified at the murder trial that she saw four white men entering and exiting a barn on the plantation the morning after Emmett was abducted. She also saw a truck outside of the barn. In some of the African American newspaper accounts from the time, as well as in the FBI's 2006 report, much of what Willie Reed and Amandy Bradley testified to was corroborated.

WILLIE REED[3]

A witness introduced for and on behalf of the State,[4] being first duly sworn, upon his oath testified as follows:

DIRECT EXAMINATION BY
MR. SMITH:

Q   Your name is Willie Reed?

A   Yes, Sir.

Q   Where do you live, Willie?

A   I live on Mr. Clint Sheridan's[5] [*sic*]. . .

Q   You live on Mr. Clint Sheridan's [*sic*] place?

A   Yes, Sir.

Q   How old are you, Willie?[6]

A   Eighteen.

Q   Do you know Mr. Leslie Milam?[7]

---

3. Willie Reed (1937–2013) ". . . lived next door to the Sturdivant plantation managed by Leslie Milam and testified that he heard beating and yelling coming from a tool shed near the barn on the plantation. He also saw J. W. Milam leave the shed and get a drink of water. After the acquittal, he moved to Chicago, where, upon his arrival, he suffered a nervous breakdown due to the stress built up over the trial. He worked as a surgical orderly for forty-eight years at Jackson Park Hospital in Chicago. It was there that he met his wife, Juliet Mendenhall, who was then a nurse's aide, [and later] a registered nurse. They married in 1976. After years of declining health, he died of [gastrointestinal] bleeding at age seventy-six." Anderson, "Who's Who in the Emmett Till Case."

4. Since he was a surprise witness, Reed had to appear in the judge's chambers *before* testifying, to inform the court and defense of the nature of his testimony. "There, seated with their feet up on Judge Swango's desk, were Roy Bryant and J. W. Milam. Their lawyers were there, too. . . . Willie didn't take a seat. He didn't even think about that. He just stood there and answered the questions about the testimony he would give." Till-Mobley & Benson, *Death of Innocence*, p. 176. See also, Wright Thompson, "His Name was Emmett Till: What We Still Don't Know About Emmett Till's Murder," *The Atlantic* (Sept. 2021).

5. Willie Reed lived on Shurden plantation; Leslie Milam managed the Sturdivant plantation where the shed is. These were two separate plantations. The Sturdivant plantation is also where Amandy Bradley lived.

6. Reed "spoke softly, so the judge had to ask him to speak up several times." Till-Mobley & Benson, *Death of Innocence*, p. 182.

7. Leslie Field Milam (1925–1974) "was born in Tallahatchie County, Mississippi, to William Leslie and Eula Morgan Milam. He was the brother of J. W. Milam and half-

A Yes, Sir.

Q Do you know Mr. J. W. Milam when you see him?

A Yes, Sir.

Q Do you see him here in the courtroom?

A Yes, Sir.

Q Will you point him out, please, Sir?

A He is sitting right over there (pointing with his hand).

Q The man, I believe, that you pointed out, is the bald-headed man, is that right?

A Yes, Sir.

Q Now, Willie, going back to Sunday, the 28th of August of this year, did you see Mr. J. W. Milam at any time during that day?

A Yes, Sir.

Q Where did you see Mr. Milam?

A I seen him—when I seen him he was coming to the well.

Q What well?

A The well from the barn over on Mr. Milam's place.

Q You saw him coming to a well, is that right?

A Yes, Sir.

Q And on whose place was that well?

A It was on the place that Mr. Milam owned.

Q Do you mean Mr. Leslie Milam?

A Yes, Sir.

Q Does Mr. Leslie Milam operate the place that the well is on where you saw Mr. J. W. Milam that morning?

A Yes, Sir.

---

brother to Roy Bryant. . . . He married Francis Moody Waldrup in 1949. According to witnesses, Emmett Till was beaten and shot in a tool shed at the Sturdivant plantation that Leslie Milam managed, and that they saw Milam present. According to the 2004–2006 FBI investigation, Milam confessed to a local minister shortly before his death that he had been involved in Till's murder and that he had been troubled by that involvement." Anderson, "Who's Who in the Emmett Till Case."

Q What is the relationship between Mr. Leslie Milam and Mr. J. W. Milam?

A Well, I heard some say he was a brother.

MR. BRELAND: We object to what he heard.

THE COURT: If he knows he can testify to that.

Q Do you know whether they are—well, do you know what relation they are to each other, whether they are cousins or brothers? That is, if you know?

A No, Sir, I don't know.

Q Where do you live, Willie? Who do you live with?

A Mr. Clint Sheridan [*sic*].

Q I mean who is in your home there with you?

A My grandfather.

Q What is his name?

A Add Reed.

Q On that particular Sunday morning, did you leave your home there where you are living?

A Yes, Sir.

Q And about—approximately what time did you leave?

A Between six and seven.

Q And where were you going?

A To the store.

Q To what store?

A Mr. Glenn Patterson's.

Q You were going to Mr. Glenn Patterson's store?

A Yes, Sir.

Q Which direction is that store from where you live?

A North.

Q And in going to that store, state whether or not it is necessary for you to pass by Mr. Leslie Milam's house?

MR. BRELAND: We object to the leading form of the questions.

THE COURT: The question is leading. See if you can ask him without leading the witness.

Q   In going from your house to the store, what place do you have to pass by?

A   I pass by Mr. Milam's.

Q   Then Mr. Milam lives out there, does he?

A   Yes, Sir.

Q   That is Mr. Leslie Milam, is that right?

A   Yes, Sir.

Q   And not Mr. J. W. Milam?

A   No, Sir.

Q   Is there any shed, or barn, or other building on the place there?

A   Yes, Sir.

Q   What kind of a building was that?

A   Green.

Q   Well, what kind of a building was it? Will you tell the jury what kind of a building it was?

A   It was a barn.

Q   A barn?

A   Yes, Sir.

Q   Did it have any open sheds, or was there a door, or what?

A   Yes, Sir, it had some doors there.

Q   Now, Willie, as you went from your house to the store that morning, did you see anyone in or around or about Mr. Leslie Milam's house, or in the road going towards the house?

A   No, Sir.

Q   As you came up towards Mr. Milam's house, did you see anyone out there?

A   I didn't see anyone out around the barn. But I seen the truck when it passed by me.

Q A truck passed by you?

A Yes, Sir.

Q What kind of a truck was it?

A Green and white.

Q It was green where and white where? How was it colored?

A The top was white.

Q And what was green?

A The body was green.

Q It was a truck with the body green and a top white, is that it?

A Yes, Sir.

Q And what kind of truck was that?

A It was a '55 Chevrolet.

Q And who, if anyone, was in that truck that you saw?

A Well, when the truck passed by me I seen four white men in the cab and three colored mens in the back. And I seen somebody sitting down in the truck back there.[8]

Q You say you saw some white men in the cab?

A Yes, Sir.

Q And you also saw three colored men in the back there, in the back end?

A Yes, Sir.

Q And you say there was somebody down in the back end of the truck?

A Yes, Sir. I seen another colored boy.

Q There was one colored fellow sitting down on the bottom of the truck in the back, is that right?

A Yes, Sir.

---

8. The FBI's 2006 report on the Till murder confirmed that there were *multiple* parties involved in the kidnapping and murder, and not simply the two defendants as suggested after the trial by William Bradford Huie in his *Look* magazine articles and in his 1959 book (see Chapter 15, *infra*). See also Tell, *Confessional Crises and Cultural Politics*, pp. 80–83.

Q   And how were those colored men sitting in the truck?

A   Well, they was—they had the back turned to me, sitting up in the truck there. And the other one was down in the truck.

Q   Were they sitting up on the sides in the back?

A   Yes, Sir.

Q   And the other one was sitting down in the bottom of the truck, is that right?

A   Yes, Sir.

Q   How close did you get to that truck?

A   I was about as far as from here to the door back there (pointing with his hand).

Q   Well, how far would you say that was? Would that be fifty feet?

A   It may be. I don't know.

Q   Did you have an opportunity there when you saw this truck to look at these people and see their features and so forth?

A   No, Sir. I wasn't thinking nothing like that was going to happen.

Q   You did see the people there, though, did you?

A   No, Sir.

Q   Well, I believe you said you saw the people in the truck, didn't you?

A   Yes, Sir.

Q   Now, later on did you recognize a photograph or anything that indicated to you who the one sitting down in the back end of that truck was?

A   Well, when I looked at this paper, I was sure—well, I seen it, and it seemed like I seen this boy someplace else before. And I looked at it and tried to remember, and then it come back to my memory that this was the same one I seen in the paper.

Q   And was that Emmett Till?

A   I don't know if that was him, but the picture favored him.

MR. BRELAND: We object to that, Your Honor.

THE COURT: The objection is sustained unless it is connected, of course.

Q   Now, did the picture you saw in the paper of Emmett Till . . .

MR. BRELAND: We object, Your Honor. That is certainly leading the witness.

THE COURT: It is highly leading.

Q   Do you know who that was in the back end of the truck sitting down back there?

A   No, Sir. But the boy that was sitting in the back of the truck favored the boy that I seen in the paper.

MR. BRELAND: We object to that, Your Honor.

THE COURT: The objection is sustained.

MR. SMITH: I think it is highly competent.

THE COURT: There are a lot of things I think is wrong with that identification. And I think we are delving in the realm of hearsay there.

Q   What did you do after you saw that truck come in there?

A   Well, I come on by the barn.

Q   When you came by the barn, did you hear or see anything there at that time?

A   I heard something.

Q   And what did you hear?

A   It was like somebody shipping somebody.

MR. BRELAND: We object to that.

THE COURT: The objection is sustained.

Q   Willie, I have a picture here that has been offered as Exhibit 1 to the testimony of Mrs. Mamie Bradley for purposes of identification. . . .

MR. BRELAND: We object, Your Honor. That is not in evidence here.

THE COURT: It has been offered or introduced for purposes of identification, and it may be used as such.

Q   Now I ask you to look at that picture, and I ask you whether or not, does that or does that not resemble the person you saw sitting there in the back of that truck on that particular day?

MR. BRELAND: We object, Your Honor.

THE COURT: The objection is sustained.

Q   Is that the boy you saw in the back of that truck?

MR. BRELAND: We object.

THE COURT: The objection is sustained. But you can [ask] him if he had ever seen that boy before.

Q   Have you ever seen that boy before?

A   It is a picture of the boy I seen on the back of the truck.

MR. BRELAND: If the Court please, we object to that because he hasn't identified the person he saw, and he didn't even know him. And we don't think the witness has been qualified to answer that particular question.

THE COURT: I believe the witness has stated that the picture here which has been offered for identification purposes as a picture of Emmett Till during his lifetime is the boy that he saw in the back of the truck that morning.

Q   Now what happened with that truck? What did they do with the truck, Willie?

A   The truck was setting in front of the barn there when I went on up to the next house, up to Miss Mandy's house. And I asked her . . .

MR. BRELAND: We object to that, Your Honor.

THE COURT: Don't repeat anything you said to anybody or anything that was said to you by anybody.

Q   As you passed the barn, I believe you said the truck was setting out in front of the barn, is that right?

A   Yes, Sir.

Q   Was anyone in the truck then?

A   No, Sir.

Q   Did you see anyone in or about the barn?

A   No, Sir.

Q   Did you hear or see anything as you went by the barn?

A   Yes, Sir. I heard.

MR. BRELAND: We object to what he heard.

THE COURT: The objection is sustained.

MR. SMITH: Just for my guidance, Your Honor, I would like to know the ground for his objection.

THE COURT: As far as I can see, these defendants have not been connected with the incident in any way.

Q   Now, later on in the morning, did you see Mr. J. W. Milam out there?

A   Yes, Sir.

Q   Where did you see him?

A   Well, when I passed by he came out by the barn to the well.

Q   And was that Mr. J. W. Milam, the man who is sitting over there (pointing to the defendant, Mr. Milam)?

A   Yes, Sir.

Q   Will you state whether he had anything unusual about his person?

A   Yes, Sir.

Q   What did he have?

A   He had on a gun.

Q   Was it a pistol, a rifle, or a shotgun?

A   He had on a pistol. He had it on his belt.

Q   And what did Mr. J. W. Milam do when you saw him?

A   He just came to the well and got a drink of water.

Q   What did he do then?

A   Then he went back to the barn.

Q   And as you passed the barn, did you hear or see anything?

MR. BRELAND: We object, Your Honor.

MR. SMITH: If Your Honor please, I believe we have got the defendant right there, going in and out of the barn.

THE COURT: I don't think it has been connected sufficiently, Mr. Smith.

Q   Just where did Mr. Milam come from when you saw him that morning?

A   He came from the barn.

Q   And where did he go when he left there? After he got a drink of water and left the well, where did he go then?

A   He went back to the barn.

Q   Did you hear or see anything as you passed the barn?

MR. CARLTON: We object, Your Honor.

THE COURT: I think he has got it straight now. I will overrule the objection.

Q   Did you see or hear anything as you passed the barn?

A   I heard somebody hollering, and I heard some licks like somebody was whipping somebody.

Q   You heard some licks, and you also heard somebody hollering, is that right?

A   Yes, Sir.

Q   What was that person hollering?

A   He was just hollering, "Oh."

Q   You heard someone hollering "Oh," is that right?

A   Yes, Sir.

Q   Did they holler once or was it more than once, or was it two or three times, or what?

A   They hollered more than once.

Q   And what about the licks? Was it just one lick you heard, or was it two, or were there several licks?

A   There was a whole lot of them.

Q   You heard a whole lot of licks?

A   Yes, Sir.

Q   And was that a human being you heard or was it some kind of animal?

A   Well, it sounded like a human being.

Q   When you went on down the road, then where did you go, Willie?

A   Well, I went on down and stopped there at Miss Mandy's home.

Q   And that was Mandy who?

A   [Amandy] Bradley.[9]

Q   What did you do then?

A   Well, she told me to come back to the well.

MR. BRELAND: We object to any conversation there, Your Honor.

THE COURT: Don't state what anybody said.

Q   All right, Willie, where did you go then?

A   To the store.

Q   And after you left Mandy's house the first time where did you go?

A   I came to the well.

Q   You came to the well?

A   Yes, Sir.

Q   And what did you come to the well for?

---

9. Amandy Bradley (c. 1905–?) "lived on the Sturdivant plantation near Drew, Sunflower County, Mississippi, at the time of the . . . murder. This plantation was managed by Leslie Milam, brother of J. W. Milam and half-brother to Roy Bryant.. . . . After the trial she, like most of the other black witnesses, moved from Mississippi to Chicago. She is rumored to have moved back to Mississippi before her death, but her whereabouts after 1956 remain unknown. A granddaughter believes she died sometime in the 1960s." Anderson, "Who's Who in the Emmett Till Case."

A   I came to get her a bucket of water.

Q   And did you hear or see anything while you were down there at the well?

A   I could still hear somebody hollering.

MR. CARLTON: We object to that, Your Honor.

THE COURT: I think the objection is well taken.

Q   Where did the hollering apparently come from?

A   From the barn.

Q   And where did you go after you left the well?

A   I went to the store.

Q   And then what did you do?

A   I don't understand what you are talking about now.

Q   I said, what did you do after you went to the store?

A   I came back home and got ready and then I went to Sunday School.

Q   And on your way back from the store, did you see or hear anything then?

A   No, Sir.

MR. BRELAND: We object to this repetition. He has asked that one time before.

THE COURT: I will let him answer the question.

Q   On the way back, did you hear or see anything, or hear or see anybody?

A   No, Sir, I didn't see anything. They were gone.

Q   Was the truck gone?

A   Yes, Sir.

MR. SMITH: Take the witness.

MR. BRELAND: I want to make a motion, Your Honor. And we don't ask that the jury retire at this time. But the defendants move to exclude the testimony offered by this witness, for the first reason that there is no sufficient connection between what he relates from the witness stand and these two defendants. And second, that there has been no sufficient identification by this witness of Emmett Till, the party named in the indictment. And third, there is no sufficient connection between the happenings or occurences [sic] related by the witness and the body of the person that was taken from the Tallahatchie River which was alleged to be that of Emmett Till.

THE COURT: That motion will be overruled.

MR. SMITH: One further question, if the Court please.

Q Willie, do you remember what Sunday that was?

A Yes, Sir.

Q What was it?

A Do I remember what Sunday it was?

Q Yes.

A It was on the fourth Sunday.

Q On the fourth Sunday of what month?

A Of August.

Q August of this year?

A Yes, Sir.

MR. SMITH: Take the witness.

CROSS EXAMINATION BY
MR. KELLUM:[10]

Q I believe you stated your name is Willie Reed?

A Yes, Sir.

_____

10. Joseph W. Kellum (1911–1996) "was one of five defense attorneys representing J. W. Milam and Roy Bryant in their murder trial. He had lived in Tallahatchie County since 1920 and was admitted to the bar in 1939. In 1955 he ran for district attorney and lost that race just a week before Emmett Till was murdered." Anderson, "Who's Who in the Emmett Till Case."

Q How old are you, Willie?

A Eighteen.

Q Are you going to school now, Willie?

A Yes, Sir.

Q What grade are you in?

A Ninth.

Q You are in the ninth grade?

A Yes, Sir.

Q On August 28th, when you say you saw this truck, was that the first time you had ever seen this truck?

A Yes, Sir, it was the first time I ever seen it.

Q That was the first time you ever seen it?

A Yes, Sir.

Q How far do you live from Glendora and Money?

A I wouldn't know, Sir. I live a good ways.

Q Do you know Mr. Leslie Milam?

A Yes, Sir.

Q And do you know Mr. J. W. Milam?

A Yes, Sir, I know him.

Q How many times have you seen Mr. J. W. Milam before Sunday, that last Sunday in August, of this year?

A I seen him about three or four times.

Q You saw Mr. J. W. Milam about three or four times before that?

A Yes, Sir.

Q And where did you see him?

A Well, I seen him once when he came over to Mr. Milam's.

Q When you first saw the truck on that Sunday morning, which direction was the truck going in?

A It was coming south, and then it turned and went north.

Q Which direction were you going?

A   I was going east, and then I turned and went north.

Q   When the truck passed you, how far were you from the truck?

A   About as far as from here to the door (pointing with his hand).

Q   You say you were as far as from here to that door?

A   Yes, Sir.

Q   Was the side of the truck that has the driver in it the side that was close to you?

A   Yes, Sir.

Q   And who was driving the truck?

A   I didn't pay much attention who was driving the truck.

Q   Was Mr. J. W. Milam driving the truck?

A   I didn't notice who was driving. I didn't pay attention.

Q   Did you see Mr. Milam there in the truck?

A   I didn't see him in the truck but I seen him over by the barn.

Q   But you didn't see him in the truck?

A   No, Sir.

Q   Have you ever seen Emmett Till in his lifetime?

A   Well, Sunday morning was the first time I seen him.

Q   But you never had seen him prior to that time?

A   No, Sir.

Q   And you don't know whether that was Emmett Till or not, do you?

A   Well, he favored the picture I just looked at.

Q   When was the first time that picture was shown to you?

A   The first time the picture was showed to me?

Q   Yes.

A   Well, I seen it in the paper.

MR. BRELAND: We object to any picture he saw in the paper.

THE COURT: The witness is answering in response to the gentleman's question.

Q   And you say you had never seen this boy before?

A   No, Sir.

Q   How far were you from the truck when the truck passed by?

A   About as far as from here to the door (pointing with his hand).

Q   And that truck was coming from what direction?

A   It was coming from the east, headed towards the south, and then it turned.

Q   Is that a straight road there?

A   Yes, Sir.

Q   There is no bend in the road at all?

A   Yes, Sir, there is a bend in the road, and when the truck got to the bend, then it turned off on that little old hill and went north.

Q   Is that a paved road or dirt road?

A   It was a gravel road.

Q   How fast would you say the truck was going?

A   I wouldn't know, Sir.

Q   Was it going fast enough to stir up any dust?

A   It had dust, but I don't know how fast he was driving.

Q   And you were walking in the same direction that the truck was going?

A   I was meeting the truck and then it turned right off there at the hill where I was supposed to go down the hill, too.

Q   When the truck turned, it was going in which direction then?

A   North.

Q   And on what side of that road were you walking?

A   I was on the right-hand side.

Q   You were on the right-hand side?

A   I was going down the hill.

Q   And you were on the same side that the driver of the truck was on?

A   Yes, Sir.

Q And how many men were in that truck?

A Four.

Q Four men?

A Yes, Sir.

Q And did you recognize that Mr. Milam was in the truck there as one of the four men you saw?

A I didn't pay too much attention to them inside the truck. I just looked at the ones in the back.

Q But you didn't pay any attention to the men who were inside the truck?

A No, Sir.

Q Then you wouldn't say that Mr. Milam was inside the truck?

A No, Sir, I wouldn't say that.

Q And on the back of the truck, you remember seeing one person that you say was Emmett Till?

A Yes, Sir.

Q And who was the other person on the back of the truck with Emmett Till?

A I never had seen them before.

Q Do you know who the third party was in the back of the truck?

A No, Sir.

Q Where they about the same size as Emmett Till?

A No, Sir.

Q Well, were they larger or smaller?

A Larger than he was.

Q Were these three parties sitting on the back of the truck there, were they on the side of the truck or down on the floor of the truck?

A They was sitting up on the side of the truck.

Q All three of them?

A Three of them was and one was sitting in the floor of the truck.

Q   One was sitting in the floor of the truck?

A   Yes, Sir.

Q   Now, on which side of the truck were those three sitting who you say were on the side of the truck? Were they on the right-hand side or the left-hand side of the truck?

A   They was sitting on the driver's side.

Q   Were they on the same side that you were on, since you say you were walking on the driver's side when the truck passed you?

A   Yes, Sir.

Q   Were they sitting close together?

A   Yes, Sir, sitting pretty close together.

Q   They were pretty close together, were they?

A   Yes, Sir.

Q   But Till was on the floor, or the third party you thought was Till was on the floor, is that right?

A   Yes, Sir.

Q   Now, the side of that truck is about a foot or eighteen inches high from the floor, is it not?

A   I wouldn't know how high.

Q   You wouldn't know how high the side of the truck is?

A   No, Sir.

Q   And yet when the truck passed by you, and you say there were two men sitting on the side of it, you were able to notice the third party that was sitting in the floor of the truck?

A   There were three men sitting up on the side of the truck.

Q   How many men were sitting on the side?

A   Three.

Q   Then you saw three men on the side of the truck, and there was one on the floor, which makes four men in the back of the truck is that right?

A   Yes, Sir.

Q   This fourth person you say you saw there, have you been able to recognize him since that day?

A   I don't understand.

Q   The fourth man you mentioned there, have you seen him since that time?

MR. SMITH: If the Court please, any one of them could be the fourth man. I wish you would have him identify him.

THE COURT: Yes—will you have him identify any one of them Mr. Kellum.

Q   Willie, how far do you live from this barn or shed that you mentioned?

A   I don't know, but I don't live too far down.

Q   Would you say you lived a quarter of a mile away or a half a mile?

A   I just wouldn't know how far.

Q   When you passed by this shed or barn, how far were you from the barn?

A   Well, I wouldn't know, Sir, just how far I was from the barn. But I wasn't too far from it.

Q   Well, how many steps would it be from this spot where you passed by the barn over to the barn?

A   I wouldn't know, Sir.

Q   Well, would you say it was a hundred yards?

A   I just wouldn't know how far it was.

Q   You don't know how far it was?

A   No, Sir.

Q   When you first saw this person that you thought was Mr. Milam, then how far from him were you?

MR. CHATHAM: We object to the use of the word "thought."

THE COURT: I think it would be better to ask the question about the person that he testified to was Mr. Milam.

Q This person that you testified to was Mr. Milam, he was how far from you when you first saw him?

A I wouldn't say how far because I wouldn't know.

Q Then you don't know whether you were one hundred yards away, or two hundred yards, or five hundred yards away from him?

A No, Sir.

Q Just what attracted your attention there for you to notice him at all?

A Sir?

Q What made you notice him at all?

A Well, I don't understand what you are talking about.

Q Was it a usual thing for people to go out to the well and get water to drink?

A Yes, Sir.

Q And was this person you identified as Mr. Milam at the well?

A Yes, Sir.

Q And at that time you were on the road, is that right?

A Yes, Sir.

Q How far is that well from the road?

A Oh, it is just—you see, I had passed the well. The road is right by the well, but I was going down the road then.

Q You had already passed the well?

A Yes, Sir.

Q And then, I suppose, you turned around and looked to see this person that you identified as Mr. Milam going to the well, is that it?

A Yes, Sir.

Q How far were you beyond the well when you turned around?

A I wouldn't know, Sir.

Q Well, what caused you to turn around and look towards the well?

A Well, I just looked back there, and I seen him when he came to the well.

Q Now, Willie, you discussed this matter with two or three lawyers over across the street in the law office over there yesterday or two days before, isn't that right?

A Yesterday.

Q And did you tell the lawyers at that time that it was at least three hundred yards away?

MR. SMITH: We object to that unless you state who it was.

Q Do you remember that I was in the room at the time?

A Yes, Sir.

Q And do you remember that this gentleman here was in the room (indicating one of the defense counsels)?

A Yes, Sir.

Q And do you recall that this gentleman here was in the room then (indicating another defense counsel)?

A Yes, Sir.

Q And do you remember these two gentlemen here (indicating two other defense counsel)?

A Yes, Sir.

Q And you were there talking to all of us, were you not?

A Yes, Sir.

Q And do you remember when this gentleman here (indicating one of the counsel) asked you how far it was from the well to where you were, and you replied that it was at least four hundred yards?

A Yes, Sir, I said that.

Q You said that, did you?

A Yes, Sir.

Q Well, then how far was it to the well from the barn?

A The well wasn't too far from the barn.

Q Was the well as far from the barn as you were from the well?

A Yes, Sir.

Q And I believe you stated you heard something that sounded like licks there in the barn?

A Yes, Sir.

Q But you didn't see anybody in the barn at all, did you?

A No, Sir.

Q And you don't know whether that was somebody hammering there, trying to fix a wagon or a car, or something like that, do you?

A It was somebody whipping somebody.

MR. BRELAND: We object to the conclusion of the witness.

THE COURT: The objection is sustained. But you will have to be careful in objecting to answers to your own counsel's questions.

Q And you don't know what caused the noise there, and you couldn't see, could you?

A No, sir.

Q And you don't know who was in the barn because you never did look into the barn, did you?

A No, Sir.

Q And you don't know whether Mr. Milam was in the barn or not, do you?

A I seen Mr. "J. W." when he left the barn.

Q But you didn't see him in the barn, did you?

A No, Sir. But I seen him when he left the barn and went to the well, and then I seen him when he went back towards it.

Q But you don't know whether he went in the barn or behind the barn, do you?

A No, Sir. He was headed straight to the front of the barn.

Q And also, if all of the people on the truck were in the barn, then that would make eight, is that right?

A Yes, Sir.

Q That is, four white men and four colored men?

A   Yes, Sir.

Q   And you weren't able to understand anything that was said in the barn at all?

A   No, Sir.

Q   Did you report this to anybody after you left there that day?

A   Well, I was talking with the grandfather.

Q   You talked to your grandfather about it?

A   Yes, Sir.

Q   But you had never seen either of the men other than Till and Mr. J. W. Milam before?

A   No, Sir.

Q   And even though the truck passed you, and you were on the right side of the truck, facing the truck you say you saw three men sitting up on the side of the truck in the back of it, is that right?

A   Yes, Sir.

Q   And you were still able to recognize a person sitting down in the bottom of the truck?

A   Yes, Sir, because he was sitting with his back to the cab and his face was facing me because he passed right by me. And I could see his face.

Q   Willie, when this truck passed you, it was going in one direction and you were going in the opposite direction, isn't that correct?

A   Yes, Sir.

Q   In other words, you were meeting the truck as it was coming towards you, is that right?

A   Yes, Sir.

Q   Did you not make the statement in this law office the day before yesterday, or yesterday, that when the truck passed you, it was going real fast?

A   It was going real fast when I first seen it. It was coming down the main road then. But when he got to the hill, there where he was supposed to turn off, then he checked up on the speed.

Q How far were you from the hill?

A I wouldn't know, but about as far as from here to the door.

MR. KELLUM: That is all.

REDIRECT EXAMINATION BY MR. SMITH:

Q Willie, you testified that these five lawyers had you over here in the office across the street yesterday, and that you made the statement to them that you saw Mr. J. W. Milam come out to the well, and that you were about three hundred or four hundred yards away. Now, did you put that estimate on the distance, or did these lawyers ask you if it was three or four hundred yards away?

A Well, they asked me how far it was, and I told them that I didn't know, but I reckon it was about four hundred yards maybe.

Q Have you ever been in the barn or shed there?

A Yes, Sir. I once been in there.

Q You have?

A Yes, Sir.

Q Who has control of that barn or shed? Whose place is it on?

A I wouldn't know, Sir.

Q Well, who operates the place there? Who lives there next to the barn?

A Mr. Leslie Milam.

Q How far is it from the barn or shed—whichever one it is—to Mr. Leslie Milam's house?

A Well, I really wouldn't know.

Q Can you point out something, anything here that you can point out, to show us the distance from the house to the barn?

A Well, about as far as from here to the outside there (pointing with his hand).

Q As far as from here to the outside over there?

A Yes, Sir.

Q And what would you say that is? Would you say that is fifty, sixty, or seventy yards?

MR. BRELAND: We object to his leading the witness.

THE COURT: The objection is overruled. The witness may answer if he knows.

Q Well, is it fifty, sixty, or seventy yards? Would you say it was something like that?

MR. BRELAND: We object to the leading form of the question.

THE COURT: The objection is overruled.

Q Willie, will you tell us, was it fifty, sixty, or seventy yards away, or just how far was it? That is, what distance is it that you have pointed out to us there?

A I just really wouldn't know.

Q In other words, you wouldn't know how to put the yardage on it, is that right?

A Yes, Sir.

Q Now, I want to ask you, as you testified a while ago that you saw a man that you identified as Mr. J. W. Milam come out of the barn and go to the well, and then go back towards the barn, did you see him before you heard some noise in the barn and some hollering in there, or was it after you heard that?

A After I heard it.

Q You saw him there after you heard it, is that right?

A Yes, Sir.

MR. SMITH: That is all.

MR. BRELAND: That is all, Your Honor. But I would like to ask that the jury be retired as we would like to make a motion.

THE COURT: All right, Sir. The jury will step back into the jury room.

(The jury retired to the jury room, and the proceedings continued in the absence of the jury.)

(WITNESS EXCUSED.)

MR. BRELAND: The defendants move the Court to exclude all evidence offered by this witness and to direct the jury to wholly disregard it as to both defendants, J. W. Milam and Roy Bryant. That is our first motion. And we ask that for the reason that the testimony of this witness is not shown to have had any relation to the disappearance of Emmett Till or the identification of the body located and removed from the Tallahatchie River. That is our first motion.

THE COURT: Go ahead.

MR. BRELAND: And now comes the defendant, Roy Bryant, and moves the Court to exclude all evidence introduced by this witness and direct the jury to wholly disregard it as to the defendant Roy Bryant; because Roy Bryant has not been identified in any way or in any respect as being any person present on the occasion testified on by this witness.

THE COURT: Do you gentlemen have anything you want to say on that?

MR. SMITH: Yes, Sir, just a couple of remarks, Your Honor. In the first place, as we all know, the defendants had the right of severance, and they had a right to be tried separately at any time up to when the jury was empaneled. But they chose to stand trial together.

But we can't put on proof for just one defendant and exclude it as to the other. We have to put on any proof that implicates either one of them. And since they made their own decision to be tried together, we feel that it is wholly competent.

THE COURT: I think the motion will be overruled.

(At this point in the proceedings, eleven forty-five a.m., the Court took a recess until one thirty-five p.m., this date, at which time the proceedings were resumed.)

Emmett Louis Till lying on his bed in Chicago home in 1955.
— PHOTO BY EVERETT/SHUTTERSTOCK (10308259A)

September 1, 1955: Moses Wright (Emmett's great uncle: (1892–1977), right, and his son Simeon Brown Wright (1942–2017), sit in their home in Money, Miss., near Greenwood. — AP PHOTO

1955: Greenwood, Mississippi: George Wilson Smith (1902-1975), Sheriff of Leflore County, standing with leg up on car. He arrested and booked Roy Bryant and J.W. Milam on kidnapping charges and was the one who received the initial confession of Bryant that he had kidnapped Emmett Till.

Mississippi murder trial of Emmett Till scene in Sumner, Miss., during the trial of Roy Bryant and J.W. Milam for the murder of Emmett Till.

General view of the courtroom in Sumner, Miss. on Sept. 19, 1955, during the first-degree murder trial of Roy Bryant and J.W. Milam. Prospective jurors are seated in the jury box at upper left. Circuit Court Judge Curtis Swango, Jr., presiding. Bryant, elbows on railing, his wife, and Milam are in the center. Members of the defense, prosecution and newsmen crowd the area beyond the railing. Spectators are seen in the foreground —AP PHOTO

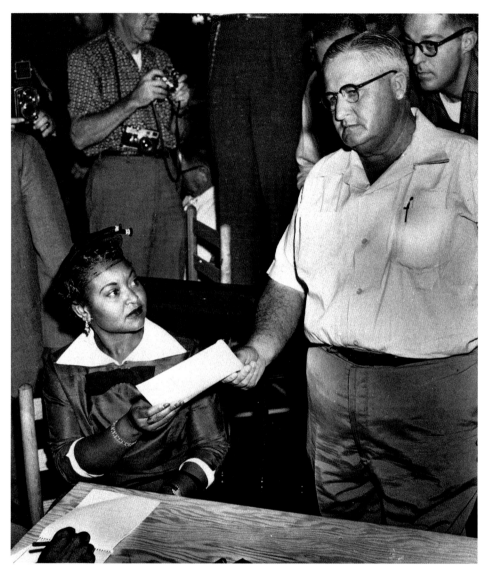

Sept. 20, 1955: Mamie Till-Bradley (1921–2003), Emmett Till's mother, receives
a subpoena from Tallahatchie County Sheriff H.C. Strider (1904–1994), right, in a courtroom
in Tallahatchie, Miss. to appear as a witness in the murder trial. — AP PHOTO/FILE

Circuit Judge Curtis M. Swango, Jr. (1908–1968). Presided over the murder trial.

PHOTO BY ED CLARK/THE *LIFE* PICTURE COLLECTION/SHUTTERSTOCK (12056317A)

Sept. 20, 1955: Jurors sit in a courtroom in Summer, Miss. for the trial of Roy Bryant and J.W. Milam who are charged with the murder of 14-year-old Emmett Till. Acquitted by the all-white jury, the two confessed to the killing of the black teenager in a 1956 *Look* magazine article. From left in the front row are Gus Ramsey, James Toole, E.L. Price, J.A. Shaw Jr., Ray Tribble, and Ed Devaney. In the second row are Travis Thomas, George Holland, Jim Pennington, Davis Newton, Howard Armstrong, and Bishop Matthews. —AP PHOTO/FILE

African American press reporters sitting at separate card table during the murder trial.

PHOTO BY ED CLARK/THE *LIFE* PICTURE COLLECTION/SHUTTERSTOCK (12475080A)

Defendants J.W. Milam (1919–1980) and Roy Bryant (1931–1994) sitting with wife,
Carolyn Bryant (1934–2023), and children during murder trial.

Prosecuting attorneys sit at a table in the Tallahatchie County Courthouse during the murder trial of J.W. Milam and Roy Bryant, Sumner, Mississippi, September 1955. From left, District Attorney Gerald Chatham (1906–1956), assistant attorney general Robert B. Smith III (1914–1967), and Tallahatchie County prosecuting attorney James Hamilton Caldwell (1898–1962).

Leflore County Deputy Sheriff John Ed Cothran (1914–2008) examines the cotton gin fan used to weigh down the body of 14-year-old Emmett Till in the Tallahatchie River, about 25 miles north of Greenwood, Miss., Sept. 1, 1955. The boy's body was found with barbed wire used to tie the body to the weight.

AP PHOTO/GENE HERRICK

Ink and wash illustration shows Mose Wright (also known as Moses Wright, 1892-1977) (standing, left) as he points to the accused in open court during the trial of J.W. Milam and Roy Bryant in the Tallahatchie County Courthouse, Sumner, Mississippi, September 19, 1955. At left is Circuit Judge Curtis M. Swango. Jr. (1908-1968).

Initialed ring presented as evidence as that taken from the body of Emmett Till at the murder trial in Sumner, Miss., September 22, 1955. — AP PHOTO

Pencil sketch of defense attorney Jesse Josiah "J.J." Breland (1888-1969),
lead defense counsel during the trial of J.W. Milam and Roy Bryant in the Tallahatchie
County Courthouse, Sumner, Mississippi, week of September 19, 1955.

J.W. Milam, 36, and half-brother Roy Bryant, 24, confer with one of their lawyers,
Joseph W. Kellum (1911–1996), right, just before pleading innocent to murdering Emmett Till.

Sketch of Mrs. Carolyn Bryant testifying in Emmett Till murder trial

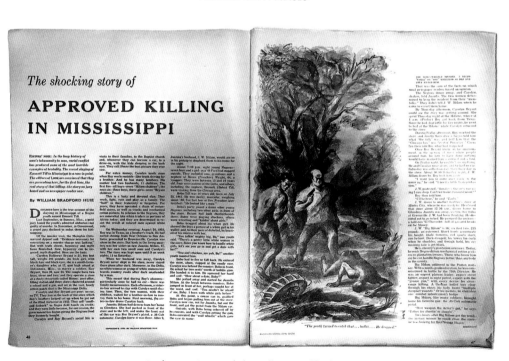

Look magazine article by William Bradford Huie.

Washington, D.C., March 29, 2022: Biden Antilynching Act Signing. President Joe Biden signs the Emmett Till Antilynching Act in the Rose Garden of the White House.

ADD REED,[11]

A witness introduced for and on behalf of the State, being first duly sworn, upon his oath testified as follows:

DIRECT EXAMINATION BY
MR. SMITH:

Q   Your name is Add Reed, is that right?

A   Yes, Sir.

Q   How old are you, Add?

A   I am sixty-five.

Q   You are sixty-five years old?

A   Yes, Sir.

Q   Where do you live, Add?

A   I live over on Clint Sheridan's [sic] place.

Q   You live on Clint Sheridan's [sic] place?

A   Yes, Sir.

Q   And what county in Mississippi is that in?

A   Sunflower.

Q   Then you live in Sunflower County?

A   Yes, Sir.

Q   Do you know Mr. Leslie Milam?

A   Yes, Sir.

Q   How far does he live from you?

A   Well, he don't live very far, right across the bayou. He is on one side and I am on the other.

---

11. Add Reed (1879–1977) ". . . testified that the morning after Emmett was abducted, he walked past the barn at the Shurden plantation and saw Leslie Milam and another white man. He was the grandfather of Willie Reed. . . ." Anderson, "Who's Who in the Emmett Till Case."

Q Then that is only a short distance or so, is that right? You are on one side of the bayou and he is over on the other side, on the other land there, is that right?

A Yes, Sir.

Q Now, Add, you are the grandfather of Willie Reed who testified this morning, is that right?

A Yes, Sir.

Q And does he live there at your place?

A Yes, Sir, he lives with me.

Q He lives with you?

A Yes, Sir.

Q Now, on the morning of August 28th, Sunday morning, did you go anywhere that morning?

A Yes, Sir. I left my place and went across the bayou to get some slop to feed my hogs.

Q Which direction did you go from your house that morning when you left?

A Well, we started east, and then we crossed Mr. Milam's place over there. I was going for some slop.

Q Did you pass by any building or anything there on Mr. Milam's place?

A Yes, Sir.

Q First, let me ask you that, Uncle Add: Did you see anybody after you left your place? Did you see anybody around Mr. Milam's place?

A Before I got up the hill. I seen two men.

Q Did you recognize either one of those men?

A Well, I recognized one of them.

Q And who was that?

A I knowed Mr. Milam, but I didn't know the other man.

Q And which Mr. Milam do you mean? Was that Mr. Leslie Milam or Mr. J. W. Milam?

A   Mr. Leslie Milam.

Q   Now, as you went along the road and you passed the place, did you pass any building there on Mr. Milam's place?

A   Yes, Sir.

Q   Was there any vehicle parked around that building?

A   I remember seeing one truck.

Q   What kind of a truck was it?

A   It was a white truck. That was all I paid attention.

Q   Was it a big truck or a pickup?

A   It was a pickup.

Q   And what time of the morning was that?

A   Well, it was around eight o'clock, I reckon.

Q   Do you know whether or not your grandson, Willie, had left home prior to your leaving that morning?

A   He left before I did.

Q   Had he gotten back home before you left? Did he get back or was he there when you left home?

A   No, Sir.

Q   What kind of buildings did you pass there?

A   Well, I think it was a kind of a shed. There was a shed right here (indicating with his hand), and right over here was an oat bin (indicating with his other hand). It used to be called an oat bin.

Q   As you passed there, Uncle Add, will you tell the jury and the court if you heard anything out of the ordinary?

MR. BRELAND: We object to that, Your Honor.

THE COURT: The objection is sustained.

THE WITNESS: Yes, Sir.

THE COURT: Don't answer the question. Don't state anything until you are told to do so.

MR. SMITH: Take the witness.

CROSS EXAMINATION BY
MR. CARLTON:

Q Uncle Add, this place where you live, what direction is it from Drew?

A It is about three-and-a-half miles west of Drew.

Q Is it due west of Drew?

A Yes, Sir.

MR. CARLTON: That is all.

(WITNESS EXCUSED.)

(At this point in the proceedings, the Court took a recess, and shortly thereafter the proceedings were resumed.)

* * * *

AMANDY BRADLEY,[12]

A witness introduced for and on behalf of the State, being first duly sworn, upon her oath testified as follows:

DIRECT EXAMINATION BY
MR. SMITH:

Q Your name is Amandy Bradley?

A Yes, Sir.

Q I believe it is really Mary Bradley, but they call you Amandy, is that right?

A Yes, Sir.

Q How old are you, Amandy?

A Fifty.

Q Where do you live?

A I live out there on Mr. Leslie Milam's place.

Q You live on Mr. Leslie Milam's place?

A Yes, Sir.

---

12. See note 9, *supra.*

Q   About how far do you live from Mr. Leslie Milam's house?

A   Well, not so far, but I don't know just how many yards.

Q   Can you point out something here in the courtroom or something outside here that will show us just about how far you live from his house?

A   I don't know. It might be a little further down than this hotel up here, I reckon; a little further.

Q   Can you see Mr. Leslie Milam's house from where you live?

A   Yes, Sir.

Q   Does he have any barn or shed around there reasonably close to his house?

A   Yes, Sir.

Q   And in which direction is that shed from his house?

A   I think it is setting kind of west, back of his house.

Q   Now I direct your attention to the last Sunday in August, the 28th day of August, 1955. Did you see Willie Reed that day?

A   Yes, Sir.

Q   You know Willie Reed?

A   Yes, Sir.

Q   And does he live down there close to you?

A   He lives on Mr. Clint Sheridan's [sic] side, south of Mr. Milam.

Q   Then he lives south of where you live?

A   Yes, Sir.

Q   What time of the morning was it when you saw him, Amandy?

A   Well, as near as I can come to it—I didn't pay particular attention—but it was along about—between six thirty and seven o'clock.

Q   And where did you see him?

A   He came to my house.

Q   When he came to your house—now don't tell what he told you—but did he mention any unusual thing that he had seen or heard that morning?

A   Yes, Sir, he sure did.

Q   Did you look out the window or go out the door and look down towards Mr. Milam's place?

A   No, Sir, I didn't go out the door. I looked out the window.

Q   Did you see anybody out there around that shed down there on Mr. Leslie Milam's place?

A   Yes, Sir. I saw . . .

MR. CARLTON: If the Court please, unless he can connect it up, we are going to object to any testimony about the witness seeing anybody there.

THE COURT: You may proceed.

Q   Did you see anybody down there that morning?

A   Up there around the barn?

Q   Yes.

A   Yes, Sir.

Q   And who did you see there or what did you see?

A   I saw four white men, but I didn't know who they were.

Q   Did you see any kind of a truck or anything up there?

A   Yes, Sir.

Q   What happened down there while you were looking down towards the shed? What did the four white men do and what happened?

A   Well, they was just coming in and out from around the barn there, just going back and forth there in and out around the barn. But I don't know what they was doing.

Q   Did you recognize any of those men?

A   I sure did.

Q   Could you identify any of those men if you saw them again?

A   Well, I know the one they said it was. But it was at some distance there. But they said it was . . .

Q   Now don't say what they said. Just tell what you saw and what you know.

A   Well, at such a distance I just wouldn't know.

MR. CARLTON: We object, if Your Honor please, to the testimony about what she saw down there. She has not connected this up with anything that has to do with this case.

THE COURT: The objection is sustained.

Q   While you were looking down there, what did those men do?

A   Well, I didn't see there doing anything but going in and coming out of the shed there. And then one went to the well and got a drink of water and then went back to the shed.

Q   Would you recognize that man if you saw him again?

A   This man that come to the well for a drink of water, he was kind of a tall man and bald headed.

Q   What did these men do relative to the truck? What did they do with the truck?

A   Well, you see, I didn't see the truck when it come up there. But I saw it when they left. I seen it when they drove away. But what was in the truck, I wasn't close enough to see.

Q   Did they do anything with the truck at all, or did they move it before they left?

A   Yes, Sir. They backed it up under the shed.

Q   They backed the truck up under the shed?

A   Yes, Sir.

Q   And was that the same shed they had been going back and forth from?

A   Yes, Sir.

Q   And then I believe you testified they drove off, is that right?

A   Yes, Sir.

Q   And that shed is on Mr. Leslie Milam's place, isn't it?

A   Yes, Sir.

MR. SMITH: Take the witness.

MR. CARLTON: If Your Honor please, we move that the testimony of this witness be excluded and the jury be instructed to disregard it because of the disconnection as far as this case is concerned, and there is no relativeness as far as the defendants are concerned.

THE COURT: That motion will be overruled.

MR. CARLTON: We have no questions.

(WITNESS EXCUSED.)

MR. SMITH: If the Court please, the State rests. [Thursday, 11:55 a.m.]

MR. BRELAND: We would like to ask time for a conference, Your Honor.

THE COURT: How much time do you want?

MR. BRELAND: Well, Your Honor, we have two witnesses—one is here but the other one is in Greenwood. One is Dr. Otken.[13] And he is a busy man, and we will have to get in touch with him so that he can come over here.

THE COURT: I will give you whatever reasonable time you need.

MR. BRELAND: I would say about fifteen minutes will be sufficient.

THE COURT: All right, Sir. We will now take a short recess.

(At this point in the proceedings, one fifty-five p.m., the Court took a recess until two thirty five p.m., this date, at which time the proceedings were resumed.)

---

13. Luther "L. B." Otken (1889–1969) "was a physician living in Greenwood, Leflore County, Mississippi, who testified at the Milam–Bryant murder trial on behalf of the defense. Although he only viewed the body briefly, he never physically examined it. His testimony as to the condition of the body aided the defense in their argument that the body had been in the river longer than Emmett Till had been missing. He also testified at the grand jury hearing that handed down the murder indictment against J. W. Milam and Roy Bryant. He began practicing medicine in Greenwood in 1915." Anderson, "Who's Who in the Emmett Till Case."

MR. BRELAND: If the Court please, we would like to present motions at this time.

(The jury retired to the jury room, and the proceedings continued in the absence of the jury.)

MR. BRELAND: Now comes the defendants, Roy Bryant and J. W. Milam, and now move the Court to exclude all the evidence offered by and on behalf of the State of Mississippi, and direct the jury to return a verdict of Not Guilty.

Now comes the defendant Roy Bryant, and moves the Court to exclude all evidence introduced for and on behalf of the State as against him, and direct the jury to return a verdict of Not Guilty as to this defendant, Roy Bryant.

And now comes the defendant J. W. Milam, and moves the Court to exclude all evidence introduced for and on behalf of the State as against him, and direct the jury to return a verdict of Not Guilty on his behalf.

THE COURT: Those motions will be overruled for the reason that the Court is of the opinion that the evidence offered on behalf of the State of Mississippi, that that evidence as a whole presents issues for the determination of the jury. So the motions are therefore overruled.

(The jury returned to the courtroom, and the proceedings continued with the jury present.)

MR. BRELAND: The defendants now offer in evidence the photograph identified by Mamie Bradley as being the photograph taken of her son, Emmett Till, on the day—or a couple of days—after Christmas of 1954.

THE COURT: That will be received in evidence as an exhibit to the witness' testimony in the defendants' case.

(The photograph so marked was then shown to the jury.)

MR. BRELAND: The defense now offers in evidence a photograph that was identified by Mamie Bradley as a picture taken of the body shipped from Tallahatchie County, Mississippi, to Chicago, Illinois, as being a true likeness of the body which she examined and testified that she identified as that of Emmett Till.

THE COURT: That will be received as Exhibit 2 in the defendants' case.

(The photograph so marked was shown to the jury.)

Chapter 5

THE DEFENSE'S CASE
THE WHITE WOMAN, THE BLACK BOY,
AND THE WHISTLE

Carolyn Bryant, Roy Bryant's wife, was the first witness called by the defense. In some respects, it was odd that Ms. Bryant, the object of the "wolf whistle," was called as a witness for the defense. If anything, she might seem to be a likely candidate for the prosecution to call as a witness for the State to establish a *motive* for the kidnapping and murder.

Though a warrant had initially been issued for Carolyn Bryant's arrest, authorities later changed their minds and never executed the warrant: "We aren't going to bother the woman," Sheriff George Smith said. "She's got two small boys to take care of."[1]

---

1. "Officer Fears Actions Build Up Resentment," *Jackson Daily News*, September 5, 1955, p. 1; "Officers Hunt for Evidence to Support Charges of Murder," *Meridian Star*, September 8, 1955, p. 1; "Halt Hunt for Woman in Slaying," *Biloxi Daily Signal*, September 3, 1955, p. 1; Houck & Grindy, *Emmett Till*, pp. 22, 30.

In June 2022, a copy of the unserved warrant (dated August 29, 1955) was discovered, which prompted calls to execute it. See Jay Reeves & Emily Wagster Pettus, "1955 Unserved Warrant for Woman in Emmett Till Case Found in Mississippi Courthouse Basement; Relatives Seek Arrest," *USA Today*, June 30, 2022, https://www.usatoday.com/story/news/nation/2022/06/29/emmett-till-arrest-warrant-mississippi-carolyn-bryant-donham/7773367001/: "The search group [that helped to discover the unserved warrant] included members of the Emmett Till Legacy Foundation and two Till relatives: cousin Deborah Watts, head of the foundation, and her daughter, Teri Watts. Relatives want authorities to use the warrant to arrest [Carolyn Bryant] Donham. . . ." Subsequently, "Till's cousin, Patricia Sterling, filed a federal lawsuit against Ricky Banks, the sheriff of Leflore County, Mississippi, seeking to compel the elected official to serve a 1955 arrest warrant against Carolyn Bryant Donham. . . ." Maya Yang, "Emmett Till Relative's Lawsuit Seeks to Serve White Woman's Arrest Warrant," *The Guardian*, Feb. 11, 2023, https://www.theguardian.com/us-news/2023/feb/11/emmett-till-lawsuit-serve-arrest

At the trial, Ms. Bryant ("Mrs. Roy Bryant") was asked nineteen questions by defense counsel Sidney Carlton before there was a serious objection raised by Robert B. Smith III, special assistant to the district attorney: "[W]e object to anything that happened on Wednesday evening unless it is connected up," is how he couched his first objection to the events that allegedly occurred when Till went into Bryant's market. Carlton countered that what happened in the market with Carolyn was all part of the sequence of events (the *res gestae*) related to the alleged crime, and thus her testimony should be admissible. In response, Judge Swango instructed the jurors to return to the jury room while the questioning of Ms. Bryant continued outside their presence, this to determine its relevance and prejudicial nature. If, after hearing Carolyn Bryant's testimony, the judge was satisfied with its merit, then the jury would be recalled and the questioning would resume; otherwise, the jurors would not hear the evidence, though many probably had heard much of it before the trial. Since her trial testimony was published the next day in, among other places, the *Jackson State Times*,[2] the jurors may well have heard it in any event.

Later in an exchange with Carlton, Smith added, "[A]nything whatsoever that happened down there on Wednesday is no justification for murder anyway. And we feel that [it is] wholly incompetent and irrelevant in this case. Anything that happened before those men going down to Moses Wright's house is certainly not competent to bring in here." J. J. Breland for the defense countered, arguing the evidence should be admissible. When her testimony was completed, Judge

---

-warrant-carolyn-bryant-donham. See *Sterling v. Banks* (N.D. Miss., Feb. 7, 2023) (In an action based on 42 U.S.C. 1983 and the Fourteenth Amendment, the plaintiff asked the court, per Trent Walker and Malik Shabazz, Esqs., to "[g]rant Plaintiff preliminary and/or permanent injunctive relief by ordering the Defendant, his employees, agents, officers, servants, and successors to serve the arrest warrant issued against Carolyn Bryant, now Carolyn Donham and not engage in any act which obstructs justice pertaining to the proceedings of Carolyn Donham."), https://www.documentcloud.org/documents/2360 7994-emmett-till-federal-lawsuit.

2. "Judge Sends Jury Out of Courtroom During Testimony of Defendant Roy Bryant's Wife," *Jackson State Times*, September 23, 1955, sect. A, p. 2. See also "Mrs. Bryant Tells How Northern Negro Grabbed Her, 'Wolf-Whistled' in Store," *Jackson Daily News*, September 23, 1955, p. 9; "Mrs. Bryant Testifies Youth Grabbed Her," *Richmond Times Dispatch*, September 23, 1955, p. 1.

Swango ruled that "it is the opinion of the Court that this evidence is not admissible," whereupon the jurors were recalled to the courtroom.

To return to the issue raised above, why did the defense lawyers feel the need to present the testimony of a witness that could be detrimental to their case? One answer has to do with what happened seventeen days *before* the trial began, when Carolyn met with the defense lawyers and declared, "The boy came to the candy counter, and I waited on him, and when I went to take the money he grabbed my hand and said, 'How about a date?' And I walked away from him, and he said, 'What's the matter, baby, can't you take it?' He went out the door and said, 'Good-bye,' and I went out to the car and got a pistol, and when I came back he whistled at me—this whistle while I was going after a pistol—he didn't do anything further after he saw the pistol."[3] (As pointed out by Timothy Tyson, it is "critical to note that this account does not include the physical assault she testified to in court twenty days later."[4] That alleged assault was repeated in a 1956 *Look* magazine story written by William Bradford Huie: "Bobo jumped in front of her, perhaps caught her at the waist" (see Part V for a more extended account).

Hence, Carolyn's testimony, even more so than what she first told her husband's lawyers, was highly inflammatory. By that measure, this was exactly what the defense lawyers wanted her to say on the stand; they wanted the all-white male jury to hear about this purported sexual assault on white womanhood by a Black fourteen-year-old boy. In doing so, they planned to turn Emmett into the villain and Carolyn into the victim. And her testimony—though ultimately excluded—did just that in the minds of many who were in the courtroom or who read the news accounts the next day.[5] But such a tactic also had a real downside for the defense: if indeed it was Emmett who was the offender, then that would mean that Roy Bryant and J. W. Milam had lied when they said they released Till after Carolyn said he was not the one who whistled. Recall that when Roy was arrested by Sheriff Smith, Bryant stated,

---

3. Anderson, *Emmett Till,* p. 30.

4. Tyson, *The Blood of Emmett Till,* p. 53.

5. See, e.g., "Judge Sends Jury Out of Courtroom During Testimony of Defendant Roy Bryant's Wife," *Jackson State Times,* September 23, 1955; "Woman in Lynching Case Weaves Fantastic Story," *Washington Afro-American* September 24, 1955, cited in Metress, *The Lynching of Emmett Till,* pp. 89–97.

"My wife [Carolyn] said he [Emmett] wasn't the right one, and I turned him loose at the store."[6] He also confessed to kidnapping Till. Such facts presented a problem for Carolyn and the defense. If her testimony confirmed what her husband had said earlier, then she would have to deny that Emmett had accosted her since Roy said they had released Emmett. If she were to state otherwise, as she did at trial, then either she or her husband would be lying. Legally speaking, this is all the more important since Sheriff Smith's testimony as to Bryant's kidnapping confession was deemed admissible (see Chapter 2).

Four other twists: First, mindful of what was just noted, "over the years [Carolyn] always maintained that she told her husband the boy they brought to the store for her to identify was not Emmett Till."[7] Second, it is noteworthy that nowhere in the direct-examination exchange[8] between Carlton and Carolyn Bryant is the name Emmett Till ever mentioned. Third, bear in mind that the defense lawyers had argued strenuously that there was no way to establish that the body found in the river was that of Emmett Till (see Chapters 6, 7, and 10). If that were the case, why would Carolyn Bryant's testimony be relevant at all, especially given her claim that Emmett was not the one who whistled at her? One answer is that the defense's plan was not to establish relevance but rather to generate animus against Emmett Till. As we will see from the summation of the defense's closing arguments (Chapter 10), Sidney Carlton will refer back to Ms. Bryant's (inadmissible) testimony, concerning the "Negro" who "molested" her.[9] Finally, there is this statement by Carolyn Bryant Donham contained in a memoir that was to remain sealed until 2036 but which was made public without her authorization in July 2022, some eight months before she died:

> August 23, 1955—a date that is engraved in my memory.
> A fourteen-year-old young man walked into our store in

---

6. "Sheriff Smith said Bryant admitted taking the boy from his uncle's home but said the youth was released when Mrs. Bryant said he was not the boy who made the remarks to her." *Jackson Daily News*, September 1, 1955; Anderson, *Emmett Till*, p. 42.

7. Tyson, *The Blood of Emmett Till*, p. 203.

8. There was no cross-examination by the prosecution since, after hearing the defense's direct-examination, Judge Swango ruled that the testimony was inadmissible.

9. Tyson, *The Blood of Emmett Till*, p. 171.

Money, Mississippi, early evening as I worked alone. That night, I was frightened beyond words. Three nights later, my husband, Roy Bryant, his brother, J. W. Milam, and *a group of other men tortured and killed* that young man. The horror that played out that night changed both my life and my country forever. I never asked for nor wanted any of this to happen. . . .No one was ever held responsible for Emmett Till's death. The people that were involved in the unjust and gruesome murder should have been held accountable, but they walked free. (Emphasis added.)[10]

MRS. ROY BRYANT,[11]

A witness introduced for and on behalf of the defendants, being first duly sworn, upon her oath testified as follows:

---

10. Excerpted from "I Am More than a Wolf Whistle" by Carolyn Bryant Donham (made public July 2022, though originally to remain sealed in the Southern Historical Collection at the University of North Carolina at Chapel Hill until 2036).

11. Carolyn Bryant (1934–2023) "was born in Indianola, Sunflower County, Mississippi. She won two beauty contests in two different high schools, and at age seventeen, left school to marry Roy Bryant on April 25, 1951. She was the target of the 'wolf whistle' by Emmett Till while she was running the counter at the Bryant Grocery and Meat Market on August 24, 1955, in Money, Leflore County, Mississippi. She testified during the murder trial that on the occasion of the whistle, 'a Negro man' entered the store, grabbed her, asked her for a date, and used various obscenities. Judge Curtis Swango decided that her court testimony of the incident inside the store was not admissible before the jury and so they never heard it. She admitted in 2008 that this part of her testimony (that Till grabbed her) was not true. She had already borne two sons with Roy Bryant by the time of the trial, and later bore a third son and a daughter. The store in Money closed soon after the murder trial, and the family later moved to East Texas and then to Vinton, Louisiana. They returned to Mississippi in 1973. She and Roy Bryant divorced in 1975. She married Griffin Chandler in 1984, and after his death in 1988, she [married] David Donham. She lived for several years in Greenville, Mississippi. She was a major focus of the 2004–2005 investigation by the FBI as a possible accomplice in the kidnapping and murder of Emmett Till, but there was no evidence to support that and in February 2007 a grand jury failed to indict her. After the death of her son Frank in 2010, she left Mississippi. She suffers from rheumatoid arthritis and lives with her son, Thomas Lamar, in Raleigh, North Carolina." Anderson, "Who's Who in the Emmett Till Case." She died in late April 2023. See Margalit Fox, "Carolyn Bryant Donham Dies at 88; Her Words Doomed Emmett Till," *New York Times*, April 27, 2023, https://www.nytimes.com/2023/04/27/us/carolyn-bryant-donham-dead.html.

DIRECT EXAMINATION BY
MR. CARLTON:

Q What is your name, please, ma'am?

A Mrs. Roy Bryant.

Q You are the wife of one of the defendants in this case, the defendant Roy Bryant, is that right?

A Yes, Sir.

Q How old are you, Mrs. Bryant?[12]

A Twenty-one.

Q And how tall are you?

A Five feet, two inches.

Q How much do you weigh, Mrs. Bryant?

A One hundred and three pounds.[13]

Q Do you have any children?

A Yes.

Q What are those children's names?

A Roy Bryant, Jr., and Thomas Lamar Bryant.

Q And they are both boys, I believe?

A Yes.

Q What is Roy Jr's age?

A He is three.

Q And how old is Thomas Lamar?

A Two.

Q How old is your husband, Mrs. Bryant?

A Twenty-four.

Q When were you all married?

---

12. Notice the difference in how the white witnesses are addressed.

13. "Almost universally the white Mississippi press described Carolyn Bryant as 'a pretty twenty-one-year-old married mother of two.'" Houck & Grindy, *Emmett Till*, pp. 9, 60, 79.

A   April 25th, 1951.

Q   Did Roy serve in the Armed Forces?

A   Yes.

Q   When did he enlist in the Armed Forces?

MR. SMITH: We object, Your Honor. That is incompetent, immaterial, and irrelevant.

THE COURT: The objection is overruled.

Q   When did he enlist in the Armed Forces?

A   In June of 1950.

Q   That was about ten months, I believe, before you married?

A   Yes.

Q   How long did he stay in the service?

A   Three years.

Q   Did he get out in about June of 1953 then?

A   Yes.

Q   Now Mrs. Bryant, I direct your attention to Wednesday night, on the 24th day of August, on that evening, who was in the store with you?

MR. SMITH: If the Court please, we object to anything that happened on Wednesday evening unless it is connected up.

MR. BRELAND: We will connect it.

THE COURT: Will the jury please retire to the jury room.

(The jury retired to the jury room, and the proceedings continued in the absence of the jury.)

MR. CARLTON: If the Court please, it is the position of the defendants in this case that on the direct examination of Moses Wright by the State, the State showed that one of the men who came to the home of Moses Wright on the night of Wednesday, the 24th day of August, testified that one of these men wanted to see the boy that did the talking down at Money.

The State having introduced that testimony has raised inferences which the defendants believe they are entitled to explain and to show what happened.

And the State having opened the inquiry as to the occurences [*sic*] on that occasion has given the defendants the right to explain those occurences [*sic*].

And further the defendants believe that these occurences [*sic*] are a part of what the State alleges is one entire transaction, the beginning and inception of the incident. And as much, the occurances [*sic*] there on that occasion are a part of the res gestae of the case. And as such the defendants should be permitted to offer testimony in that particular.

MR. SMITH: If the Court please, I don't know on what statement Mr. Carlton bases his idea or his statement that we opened the thing up for anything that happened on Wednesday prior to that particular Sunday morning. Our proof started with the occurance [*sic*] on Sunday morning at two o'clock when two or more persons came to Moses Wright's house for the boy. And we went from there on with our evidence and proof.

We have offered no proof whatsoever of anything that happened prior to that time. And Mrs. Bryant has not been brought into this thing whatsoever. And I think I am safe in saying that her name has not even been mentioned in this case.

The Supreme Court of Mississippi has many times held that former difficulties where not a part of the res gestae cannot be brought in as evidence. In other words, in a series of occurances [*sic*] which might chronologically follow one another in a short space of time, the Supreme Court has ruled that those things are not competent if they are not a part of the res gestae. And I am sure Your Honor is familiar with that more than I am.

And there have been numerous cases of homicide and assault, where parties would have some difficulty one day and then the next day they might meet up and some other trouble or altercation take place between them.

And we contend that anything whatsoever that happened down there on Wednesday is no justification for murder anyway. And we feel that [is] wholly incompetent and irrelevant in this case. Anything that happened prior to those men going down to Moses Wright's house is certainly not competent to bring in here.

MR. BRELAND: If the Court please, I believe the prosecution has looked at these things and the Supreme Court rulings in a different light than ___. And I would like to call the attention of the Court to the fact that the Supreme Court[14] has ruled that an incident may be separated by days, and by weeks even, but if they can be connected as part or partial of a man's transaction, then it doesn't mean that these things must all happen right together.

If any of the happenings can be connected up and it forms a background for a later happening, then that can be considered as part of an entire transaction. And I believe the Supreme Court has ruled on that several times in the past.

THE COURT: Gentlemen, as the Court understands our Supreme Court decisions relating to such evidence, evidence of prior difficulties may be introduced providing that it can be considered a part of the res gestae, and particularly where there has been any altercation, or a difference, or an incident between parties, and the deceased is shown to be the aggressor, or when there is any question of doubt as to who might have been the aggressor, then such evidence would be admissable [*sic*]. But without such a showing it would not be admissable [*sic*].

MR. WHITTEN: Excuse me, Your Honor, but I don't think that is our strongest point in our argument. In the first place, the State, by its own witness, has raised in the minds of this jury some question as to whether what happened down there at the store in Money was just mere talk.

But it was not only stated just one time to the jury, but it was repeated two other times, as I recall, that the reason these men were down there was because they wanted to see the boy that had done the talking down at Money.

---

14. Presumably, the reference is to a ruling or rulings by the Mississippi Supreme Court, as suggested by Judge Swango's comments immediately below.

And we believe that where the State raises or puts in evidence any testimony, even though it might be immaterial to the issues, we say that the accused must have an opportunity to explain it or develop it further to show the jury all the facts.

THE COURT: The Court is of the opinion that any accused in any criminal case can bring out anything relating to a continuation of any part of an alleged crime. But the testimony that is being offered here of details of a prior incident, I do not believe that is admissable [*sic*].

And the Court's recollection of the testimony was that Moses Wright testified that the defendant, J. W. Milam, stated that he wanted the boy that did the talking over at Money. And I believe there was another reference in the testimony where they said something about the boy that did the talking over at Money or down at the store in Money. But the Court is of the opinion that evidence of the details of what occured [*sic*] there at the store on that particular evening is not permissable [*sic*] here.

MR. BRELAND: And another thing, Your Honor, we contend that whatever might be competent in evidence as to these defendants is also competent with reference to their families, because they have the same right to protect their families as they do themselves.

THE COURT: That would be perfectly true with reference to the statement I made in the beginning relating to prior incidents or conflicts between parties, and members of their immediate families would also be included in that. But that is admissable [*sic*] in evidence under our Supreme Court decisions only where some question as to who was the aggressor at the time the crime with which they might be charged was committed, or that some overt act was committed by the deceased at that time to make such evidence of prior conflicts, or prior difficulties, or prior relations between the parties, that can only be brought out and shown when such a question arises. And then such evidence where the immediate family is concerned would be admissable [*sic*] in evidence.

MR. BRELAND: We wish to develop the testimony for the sake of the record, Your Honor.

THE COURT: That is the Court's understanding under the rules and laws of evidence of the State of Mississippi in cases such as this. You may now proceed.

Q   Mrs. Bryant, on Wednesday evening or Wednesday night, the 24th day of August, 1955, did anyone—who was in the store with you that night?

A   No one.

Q   You were alone in the store at the time?

A   Yes.

Q   Was there anyone in the living quarters at the rear of the store?

A   Yes.

Q   Who was back there?

A   Mrs. Milam and her two children and also our two children.

Q   Did any incident occur in that store on that evening which made an impression on you?

A   Yes.

Q   And what time of the evening was that?

A   About eight o'clock.

Q   Was that before or after dark?

A   After dark.

Q   Just tell the Court what happened there at that time, please, ma'am.

A   This nigger man came in the store and he stopped there at the candy case.

Q   And in the store, where is the candy case located?

A   At the front of the store.

Q   And on which side is it?

A   It is on the left side as you go in.

Q   And that is the first counter there, is that right?

A   Yes, Sir.

Q   Now, is the store, with reference to that candy counter, is there anything back of the candy counter towards the wall of the store?

A   No.

Q   Is there any place to walk there or anything of that sort?

A   Yes, an aisle.

Q When this negro man came in the store, where were you in the store?

A I was farther back in the store, behind the counter.

Q Where were you in the store when this man came in?

A I was farther back behind the counter.

Q Were you on the same side or on the other side?

A The same side.

Q And when he came in, I believe you said he stopped in front of the candy counter, is that right?

A Yes.

Q And what did you do then?

A I walked up to the candy counter.

Q And what transpired up there at the candy counter?

A I asked him what he wanted.

Q And did he tell you?

A Yes.

Q Do you know what it was he asked for?

A No.

Q And did you then get the merchandise for him?

A Yes. I got it and put it on top of the candy case.

Q And what did you do then?

A I held my hand out for his money.

Q Which hand did you hold out?

A My right hand.

Q Will you show the Court how you held your hand out?

A I held out my hand like this (demonstrating by holding out her hand).

Q Which hand was that?

A My right hand.

Q And will you show the Court how you did that?

A   Like this (demonstrating by holding out her hand).

Q   And did he give you the money?

A   No.

Q   What did he do?

A   He caught my hand.

Q   Will you show the Court just how he grasped your hand?

A   Like this (demonstrating with her hand).

Q   By what you have shown us, he held your hand by grasping all the fingers in the palm of his hand, is that it?

A   Yes.

Q   And was that a strong grip or a light grip that he had when he held your hand?

A   A strong grip.

Q   And will you show the Court what you did? How did you get loose?

A   Well, I just jerked it loose, like this (demonstrating).

Q   It was about that difficult to get loose, was it?

A   Yes.

Q   And it was with that much difficulty that you got your hand loose?

A   Yes.

Q   Just what did he say when he grabbed your hand?

A   He said, "How about a date, baby?"

Q   When you freed yourself, what happened then?

A   I turned around and started back to the back of the store.

Q   You did what?

A   I turned to get to the back of the store.

Q   Did you do anything further then?

A   Yes. He came on down that way and he caught me at the cash register.

Q   You say he caught you?

A   Yes.

Q How did he catch you?

A Well, he put his left hand on my waist, and he put his other hand over on the other side.

Q How were you going down along the counter there? Did he approach you from the front, or from the rear or how?

A From the side.

Q Now, Mrs. Bryant, will you stand up and put my hands just where he grasped you? Will you show the Court and jury?

A It was like this (demonstrating by putting Mr. Carlton's hands on her body).

Q He grabbed you like that, did he?

A Yes.

Q In other words, with his left arm around your back?

A Yes.

Q And his left hand on your left hip?

A Yes.

Q And he had his right hand on your right hip?

A Yes.

Q Did he say anything to you then at the time he grabbed you there by the cash register?

A Yes.

Q What did he say?

A He said, "What's the matter, baby? Can't you take it?"

Q He said, "What's the matter, baby? Can't you take it?"

A Yes.

Q Did you then try to free yourself?

A Yes.

Q Was it difficult? Did you succeed in freeing yourself?

A Yes.

Q Did he say anything further to you at that time?

A Yes.

Q What did he say?

A He said, "You needn't be afraid of me."

Q And did he then use language that you don't use?

A Yes.

Q Can you tell the Court just what that word begins with, what letter it begins with?

(The witness did not answer verbally, but shook her head negatively.)

Q In other words, it is an unprintable word?

A Yes.

Q Did he say anything after that one unprintable word?

A Yes.

Q And what was that?

A Well, he said—well—"With white women before."

Q When you were able to free yourself from him, what did you do then?

A Then this other nigger came in the store and got him by the arm.

Q And what happened then?

A And then he told him to come on and let's go.

Q Did he leave the store willingly or unwillingly?

A Unwillingly.

Q How did the other negro get out of the store then? How did they leave?

A He had him by the arm and led him out.

Q Were there any white men in the store at the time this occurred?

A No.

Q Were there any other Negro men in the store at the time?

A No.

Q Were there any other persons outside the store?

A Yes.

Q Were they white men or colored men?

A　Colored.

Q　Were there a number of them out there? How many of them were out there?

A　Oh, about eight or nine.

Q　When he went out the door, did he say anything further after he had made these obscene remarks?

A　Yes. He turned around and said, "Good-by."

Q　And when he got out the door, what did you do?

A　I called to Mrs. Milam to watch me and then I ran out the door to go to the car.

Q　Which car did you go to?

A　Mrs. Milam's.

Q　What did you go to the car for?

A　For my pistol.

Q　Where was your pistol in the car?

A　Under the seat.

Q　It was under which seat?

A　The driver's seat.

Q　As you went out the door and went to the car, did you see this man again?

A　Yes.

Q　Where was he then? Where was he standing?

A　He was standing by one of the posts on the front porch.

Q　Your store has a front porch to it?

A　Yes.

Q　And these posts are on the front porch?

A　Yes.

Q　Did he say or do anything at that time?

A　He whistled and then came out in the road.

Q　Can you give a sound something like the whistle that he made there? Was it something like this? (Mr. Carlton demonstrated by giving two low whistles.)

A   Yes.

Q   When you got your pistol, Mrs. Bryant, where was this boy then? Or I should say where was this man?

A   When I turned around, he was getting in a car down the road.

Q   Did you rush back in the store then?

A   Yes.

Q   Had you ever seen that man before?

A   No.

Q   Have you ever seen him since?

A   No.

Q   Tell us what size man he was. Describe about how tall he was.

A   He was about five feet, six inches tall.

Q   And that is about four inches taller than you are, is that right?

A   Yes.

Q   And how much would you say that he weighed?

A   Around one hundred and fifty pounds.

Q   Did he walk with any defect?

A   No.

Q   Did he have any speech defect?

A   No.

Q   Did you have any trouble understanding him?

A   No.

Q   What sort of impression did this occurance [*sic*] make on you?

A   I was just scared to death.

Q   Mrs. Bryant, do you generally know the negroes in that community around Money?

A   Yes.

Q   What kind of store is it that you run there?

A   It is just a general store.

Q   Are most of your customers negroes or white people?

A   Most of them are negroes.

Q And of course, you come in contact with most of the negroes around there in that way?

A Yes.

Q And you know most of them around there, do you?

A Yes.

Q And was this man one of those?

A No.

Q Did he talk with a southern or northern brogue?

A The northern brogue.

Q Did you have any difficulty understanding him?

A No.

Q Did you have any white men anywhere around there to protect you that night?

A No.

Q Was your husband out of town?

A Yes.

Q Do you know where he was?

A He was in Brownsville.

Q What was his purpose in being away from home then?

A He had carried a load of shrimp there.

Q Where had he started out with that load of shrimp?

A From New Orleans.

Q When did you expect him home?

A I didn't know.

Q What was the reason for Mrs. Milam and the children being there with you?

A So that I wouldn't be alone.

MR. CARLTON: Now, we submit, Your Honor, that the testimony here is competent on the basis of the testimony which was introduced by the State to show that there was some talk in Money, and to remove from the minds of the jury the impression that nothing but talk had occurred there.

THE COURT: The Court has already ruled, and it is the opinion of the Court that this evidence is not admissible.[15]

(The jury returned to the courtroom, and the proceedings continued with the jury present.)

MR. CARLTON: We have no further questions, Your Honor.

MR. CHATHAM: No questions.

(WITNESS EXCUSED.)

* * * *

MRS. J. W. MILAM,[16]

A witness introduced for and on behalf of the defendants, being first duly sworn, upon her oath testified as follows:

DIRECT EXAMINATION BY
MR. CARLTON:

Q   What is your name, please, ma'am?

A   Mrs. J. W. Milam.

Q   How old are you, Mrs. Milam?

A   Twenty-seven.

Q   And you are the wife of one of the defendants here in the court-room, Mr. J. W. Milam, I believe?

A   Yes.

Q   When were you married, Mrs. Milam?

---

15. Generally speaking, the exclusion of such testimony would be significant. In this case, however, this "gesture was futile, of course, for every juror already knew of the occurrence." Whitaker, MA thesis, p. 151 (based on author's interview with jurors).

16. Mary Juanita Thompson Milam (1927–2014) "married John W. Milam on December 11, 1949, in Tallahatchie County, Mississippi. She was at the back of the Bryant Grocery and Meat Market, in the apartment, when the incident between Emmett Till and Carolyn Bryant occurred. . . . She and J. W. Milam were the parents of two sons and the family moved to east Texas in 1962. They later returned to Mississippi around 1965 and lived in Greenville, Washington County. She and J. W. were said to have later divorced, but she is listed as his wife in his obituary, and there is no divorce record for them in Greenville or Washington County. She moved to Ocean Springs, Mississippi, around 1994 and died there at age 87." Anderson, "Who's Who in the Emmett Till Case."

A In '49, December 10th.

Q Do you have any children?

A Two.

Q Will you give me their names, please, ma'am?

A Harvey and Billy.

Q How old is Billy?

A Four.

Q And how old is Harvey?

A Two.

Q And they are both boys, I believe?

A Yes.

Q Mrs. Milam, was your husband ever in the armed forces?

A Yes.

Q Do you know what Division he was in? What branch of service he was in?

MR. SMITH: If the Court please, we object to that as being immaterial and irrelevant to this case.

THE COURT: The objection is overruled.

Q Was he in the Army, or Navy, or Air Force?

A Army.

Q Do you know what rank he held when he first went in the Army, if any? Was he a private or an officer?

A Private.

Q And in what Theatre did he serve? Where was his service?

A In Germany.

Q In Germany?

A Yes.

Q While he was in service, was he ever wounded?

A Yes, Sir.

Q   Was he awarded any decorations as a result of that?

A   Yes.

Q   What decorations did he receive?

A   Purple Heart.

Q   Did he receive any citations for bravery?

A   I don't know.

Q   And what was his rank when he came out of the service?

A   A Lieutenant.

Q   Do you know the circumstances of his promotion to Lieutenant?

A   Well, it was a battlefield commission. I think that is what they call it.

MR. SMITH: We object to that, Your Honor. She wasn't there, and that would be strictly hearsay.

THE COURT: The objection is sustained.

Q   Where do you and Mr. Milam live, Mrs. Milam?

A   In Glendora.

Q   And is that in Tallahatchie County, Mississippi?

A   Yes.

Q   How long have you lived there?

A   Almost five years.

Q   What relation is J. W. Milam, your husband, to Roy Bryant?

A   A half-brother.

Q   Is it the same mother or the same father?

A   Their mother.

Q   That would then make you and Mrs. Roy Bryant sisters-in-law, I believe?

A   Yes.

MR. CARLTON: No further questions.

CROSS EXAMINATION BY
THE DISTRICT ATTORNEY:

Q   Just one question, Mrs. Milam: your husband is J. W. Milam, is that right?

A   Yes, Sir.

Q   And what relation is he to Leslie Milam?

A   A brother.

Q   He is a brother?

A   Yes, Sir.

MR. CHATHAM: That is all.

MR. CARLTON: That is all.

(WITNESS EXCUSED.)

Chapter 6

THE DEFENSE'S CASE
SHERIFF H. C. STRIDER—
THE FIXER

In his brief testimony, he became the defendants'
most important witness.

—ELLIOTT J. GORN[1]

It is somewhat unusual for a police officer to be called as a witness for the *defense*. The customary practice, as in the case of Sheriff George Smith, is for the prosecution to call such witnesses. Then again, when it came to Sheriff Henry Clarence "H. C." Strider, neither custom nor the rule of law stood in his way—he was, after all, *the Law* in Tallahatchie County.

Fifty-one at the time, Strider was an imposing figure, both in terms of his physical presence (somewhat short though weighing 270 pounds) and his local influence. His authority depended "upon the brutal armament of an oversized blackjack, sticking prominently out of the right-hand pocket of his trousers" and he personified "the type of law enforcement that caused so many Negroes to 'go North.'"[2] Strider was a man of immense political and personal power, someone who demanded submissiveness by everyone, from the Black families who worked on his large plantation to anyone subject to the authority of his badge—save for Roy Bryant and J. W. Milam, for whom he made a special exception when it came to their murder trial. From the outset, he

---

1. Gorn, *Let the People See,* p. 152 (note omitted).
2. Nichter, "'Did Emmett Till Die in Vain?,'" p. 28; Whitaker, "A Case Study of Southern Justice," p. 164.

asserted jurisdiction over the murder even though he had no such real jurisdiction, as the murder and kidnapping occurred in *another* jurisdiction.[3] Furthermore, Strider went to great lengths to assist the defendants and their lawyers. For example:

- He never interrogated the defendants;
- He never assisted, in any meaningful way, in the investigation of the kidnapping and murder;
- Even *before* the trial, he told the press that "[t]he whole thing looks like a deal made up by the National Association for the Advancement of Colored People";[4]
- Also *before* the trial, Strider denied that the body found was that of Till;[5]
- He ordered no autopsy;
- From the outset, he pushed for a speedy handling of the investigation,[6] which made gathering evidence and finding witnesses difficult for the prosecution;
- He attempted to have a quick burial of Till's body;
- Shortly after the body was discovered, Strider said that the body had "been in the water about two days," a claim he would later alter considerably during his trial testimony;
- He likely hid witnesses helpful to the prosecution;
- He went to great lengths to segregate the courtroom and attempted to exclude African American reporters; and
- On the first day of the trial he was overtly alarmist when he told reporters that he was on the lookout for suspicious Negroes who had fled after being seen lingering around the courthouse.[7]

---

3. See Tyson, *The Blood of Emmett Till*, p. 64; Tell, *Remembering Emmett Till*, pp. 40–41, 57, 58–59.

4. "Sheriff Says Body Found May Not Be Chicago Boy," *Richmond Times-Dispatch* (AP), September 3, 1955.

5. "Sheriff Believes Body Not Till's: Family Disagrees—Mother 'Positive' It Was Her Son," *Clarion Ledger*, September 4, 1955, p. 1.

6. *See* "Kidnap-Murder Case Will Be Transferred to Tallahatchie," *Greenwood Commonwealth*, September 1, 1955, p. 1 (Sheriff Strider said he "will seek speedy prosecution").

7. Regarding hiding witnesses, see Metress, *The Lynching of Emmett Till*, p. 163, 171, 173, 174, 178, 179, 197; regarding segregating courtroom and reporters, see *ibid.*, p. 44,

Eighteen days before the trial began, Strider had *signed* Emmett Till's death certificate, which named Till and described him as a "Negro . . . high school student" born in "1941." Cause of death: "murder." The death certificate also noted that the body, per the sheriff's request, had been sent to the "Avent Funeral Home," a Black funeral home. Even before that, when the body was first discovered, the sheriff summoned a Black undertaker to the scene.[8] "By the time of the burial, [even before the trial], Sheriff Strider had changed his mind. Suddenly he said he didn't even know if the body was that of a black person or a white person."[9] On September 3, 1955, Strider told reporters that owing to the condition of the body neither its identity nor its race could be established: "The body we took from the river," he stressed, "looked more like a grown man instead of a young boy. It was also more decomposed than it should have been after a short stay in the water."[10]

More than anything else, Strider's testimony, disingenuous as it was both times (see Chapter 7), served to raise the specter of doubt over one of the essential elements of murder: clear and concrete evidence of Till's death.

On cross-examination, Robert Smith challenged Sheriff Strider's claims on three grounds: (1) a police photograph taken at the time the body was discovered revealing the color of the body, (2) the Till death certificate Strider signed, and (3) the speed at which a badly beaten body decomposes. What is odd, however, is that Smith never questioned Strider about the ring found on Till's hand, the one that had Emmett's father's initials on it and about which Moses Wright testified earlier. That was, after all, strong proof of the identity of the body.

48, 58, 64, 176–77; regarding body in water for two days, see James Featherstone, "White Orders Investigation in Slaying of Delta Negro: White Deplores Slaying in a Note to NAACP Which Is Creating a National Issue," *Jackson Daily News*, September 1, 1955, cited in Tyson, *The Blood of Emmett Till*, pp. 63, 232 n. 23; regarding suspicious Negroes, see Gorn, *Let the People See*, p. 83.

8. Anderson, *Emmett Till*, pp. 45–46.

9. Crosby Kemper, interview with Devery Anderson, American History TV, C-SPAN.org (November 15, 2016) (20:06 through 20:52 minutes), https://www.c-span.org/video/?417900-2/1955-emmett-till-murder-case.

10. "Grand Jury Gets Case: Troops Posted in Delta as Mob Violence Feared in Aftermath to Slaying," *Jackson Daily News*, September 5, 1955, reproduced in Metress, *The Lynching of Emmett Till*, pp. 37, 38.

H. C. STRIDER,[11]

A witness introduced for and on behalf of the defendants, being first duly sworn, upon his oath testified as follows:

DIRECT EXAMINATION BY
MR. WHITTEN:

Q   This is Mr. H. C. Strider?

A   That's right.

Q   What official position do you have in Tallahatchie County, Mississippi?

MR. CHATHAM: We will admit that Mr. Strider is the Sheriff of Tallahatchie County, and a good one.

Q   Mr. Strider, did you have occasion on August 31st, I believe it was, to go down to a point on the Tallahatchie River to examine a body that had been found down there?

A   I did.

Q   What time did you get down there to the riverbank, Mr. Strider?

A   I would say around nine fifteen, something like that.

Q   Had the body been brought to shore at that time?

A   It had.

Q   Were you there when it arrived?

A   I was.

Q   Did you examine the body, observe it, and look at it after it was brought in?

A   The best I could, yes, Sir.

Q   Now tell the jury about the appearance and condition of that body as you saw it that morning.

A   Well, it was in mighty bad shape.

MR. CHATHAM: We object to that, Your Honor.

---

11. See Chapter 1 note 9, *supra*.

THE COURT: Just state the physical facts, not your own conclusions.

THE WITNESS: Well the skin had slipped—I would say it had slipped on the entire body. The fingernails were gone from the left hand. A ring on the right hand was holding the skin that held the fingernails on that hand. And the entire body, the skin was slipping or it had completely gone off it.

Q   What was the condition of the head? What did you observe there?

Q   [*sic*] [A] There was a small hole about one inch above the right ear. There was two—well, maybe two or three gashes on the head. And one was long—well, I would say about an inch above the right ear, extending around, about over the left eye. And then one was just a little above it, and then between there was a short one about an inch long.

Q   This hole you speak of that was over the right ear, did you determine whether it penetrated the skull?

A   I cut a stick about the size of a pencil and tried to find if it penetrated through the skull or not, and I was unable to find if it penetrated through the skull.

Q   Mr. Carlton has called my attention to the fact that you indicated the left side of your head and you stated that the gashes were on the right side. Is that correct? Will you explain that?

Q   [*sic*] [A] No—it is on the left side.

Q   The gashes were on the left side of the head?

A   The hole was above the right ear, and it was more to the front than to the back. And the gash was about along in here, and there was this cut place there (indicating his own head with his hand).

Q   Did you observe the tongue?

A   The tongue was extending, I would say, about two and a half or three inches. And the left eyeball was almost out, enough to almost fall out. And the right one was out, I would say, about three-quarters of an inch.

Q   Was there any odor about the body that indicated it was decomposed or that decomposition had set in?

A   It was so bad that we couldn't examine the body until the undertaker got there, and then he opened a deodorant bomb. And even
then we couldn't get too close, and he had to use a quart of some
kind of liquid. I didn't ask him just what it was.

And he covered the entire body with that then, and then we
were able to get up to where we could tell something about the
body.

Q   You live on the Tallahatchie River, I believe, is that right?

A   Well, about a quarter of a mile from the Tallahatchie River.

Q   And you know the river pretty well, do you?

A   I have known it since '35.

Q   And you know the approximate temperature of the water there at
that time of year, do you?

A   I do.

Q   And about what is it next to the surface of the river?

A   I would say the top of the water at this time of year it would run
around seventy degrees. And the deeper you go, well, the cooler
it will be.

Q   Do you know the approximate depth of the river?

A   Well, I would say from around twenty five to thirty five on the
average at the time when the body was found there. Of course,
you will find some places deeper, but on the average I would say
it is around thirty feet.

Q   Have you on other occasions taken bodies out of the river?

A   I have.

Q   Have you taken bodies out of the river during that time of the
year, during the summer period, just about the same time of the
year as it was then, in weather like we had here in August?

A   I have.

Q   Relate that circumstance to the jury, if you will, please.

MR. SMITH: We object to anything about taking any other body out
of the river. That has nothing to do with this case at all.

THE COURT: I think the circumstances would be inadmissible. The objection is sustained.

Q   Have you ever taken a body from the river that you knew had been there for a period of six days?

A   I have.

Q   Were the conditions under which that body was in that river about the same as the conditions under which this body was taken from the river?

MR. SMITH: We object to that, Your Honor.

THE COURT: The objection is sustained. But you can ask his opinion about the particular time that body was in the river, his opinion from his past experience.

Q   What then, Mr. Strider, is your opinion based on your past experience in taking bodies from the river, as to how long this particular body that was removed from the water on August 31st had been in the river?

MR. SMITH: We object to that, if Your Honor please. He is not a doctor, and he is not qualified to testify about that.

THE COURT: He is not qualified as a doctor, but he stated that he has had experience with other bodies taken from the river from time to time. And I think he is qualified.

Q   You may state your opinion on that, Mr. Strider.

A   I would say at least ten days, if not fifteen.

Q   Referring back to the condition of that particular body there, could you tell whether it was a white person or a colored person?

A   The only way you could tell it was a colored person—and I wouldn't swear to it then—was just his hair. And I have seen white people that have kinky hair. And the hair had slipped in some places on the head there, but some of it was there, and what I saw, it showed it to be sort of kinky, or that of a negro.

Q   Was that body recognizable to be that of any particular person?

A   Well, if one of my own boys had been missing, I couldn't really say if it was my own son or not, or anybody else's. I couldn't tell that. All I could tell, it was a human being.[12]

MR. WHITTEN: Your witness.

CROSS EXAMINATION BY
MR. SMITH:

Q   Mr. Strider, I just have two or three questions to ask you. I hand you here a photograph that is marked as Exhibit 1 to the testimony of Mr. Strickland, introduced here yesterday, and I ask you if that picture represents the condition of the body taken out of the river that you have referred to in your testimony?

A   That does.

Q   That is it?

A   Yes, Sir.

Q   I will ask you if that photograph shows that the skin or flesh is sluffed off at any place?

A   Well, you can't tell in several places. You see, the darkness of this picture shows that the entire skin on the body had slipped. This was made hours later, and it had begun to turn dark. At the time it was brought out of the water, he was just as white as I am except for a few places around that was just a little darker than other places. And except for that, he was just as white as I am.[13]

---

12. "When Sheriff Strider stated, on September 4 [before the trial], that he felt sure the body that had been found was not Till's and that Till was still alive, local press gave great prominence to the claim. This started rumors that the body had been placed there by the NAACP and that it was a cadaver from nearby Friendship Clinic in Mound Bayou, Mississippi. Dr. T.R.M. Howard, state NAACP leader, operated the clinic." Whitaker, "A Case Study in Southern Justice," p. 202 (notes omitted).

13. Sheriff Strider "confirmed that neither of them, nor really anyone involved with the case, had any doubts that the body was that of Emmett Till. It was unclear whether Strider or the defense attorneys came up with the idea to create a 'smoke screen' which would give the jurors an 'out.' Both the sheriff and the lawyers implied to me that the 'smoke screen' was their idea. The jurors selected were going to acquit. This 'smoke screen' gave the jurors an 'out' and kept them from receiving as much scorn as everyone involved felt would be coming at them. Not one juror stated to me that he had any doubt about the

Q   But this photograph does represent him as he was some hours later?

A   Only that there is some dark places on there that has developed.

Q   Now, Mr. Strider, either the same day or the day after you and the people got this body out of the river, there was a death certificate prepared for Emmett Till, was there not?

A   That's right.

Q   And I believe you signed that death certificate, did you not?

A   Yes, Sir.

Q   And that death certificate certified the fact that it was the body of Emmett Till, isn't that correct?

A   No, I didn't certify that body as Emmett Till. I said it was a dead body. I had never seen Emmett Till before, and I couldn't swear it was Emmett Till because I didn't know Emmett Till or what he looked like.[14]

And another thing, his body at that time was not identified at the scene, because I asked his uncle at the time there at the scene— could I just go ahead and tell what happened there?

Q   Yes, Sir.

A   Well, I called for his uncle. You see, I heard about this boy being gone or having disappeared there, and so I had the sheriff—well, I got the sheriff's office over at Greenwood, I got them to go by and pick up the uncle.

---

body's identity, or that the accused had actually murdered Till." "Emmett Louis 'Bobo' Till—Stories: Interview with Hugh Stephen Whitaker, Part 1," Fold3, https://www.fold3 .com/memorial/1480/emmett-louis-bobo-till/stories#ba3a0680-362f-11dc-130f-4e6c 1f5b1425; "Interview with Steven Whitaker," YouTube, uploaded by Interpore Society Time Capsule, April 20, 2018, https://www.youtube.com/watch?v=kM0HsdTS-Ug&list =PL8FApWLvLnHRuYl7EHKVd64lH60J5_nJV&index=7.

14. "Had Strider believed, [as he had also said before the trial], that the identification of the body sent up north [by Mamie Till-Bradley] was uncertain, he was duty bound to retain it. Certainly it was the body of *someone*, meaning an unsolved murder still lingered under his jurisdiction." Anderson, *Emmett Till*, p. 161. "Sidney Carlton in a nine-paragraph defense of the verdict published after the trial, said the prosecution never proved the body to be Emmett Till's. . . ." *Ibid.*, pp. 162, 432 n. 176, citing Sidney Carlton, "Defense Says Till Verdict Was Just," *Chicago Defender*, October 1, 1955.

And so then they went by and got the old man, and when he got there, he looked at this boy's body, and I said to him, "Moses, is this the boy that is missing from your home?"

And then he said, "I believe it is, but I couldn't say it is for sure."

And then I said to him, "What about this ring on his finger?" And then he said, "I don't know. I would have to ask my boys about that."

And then I said to him, "Do you mean to tell me, Moses, that he has been staying there at your home for a week with this ring on his finger, and eating there at the same table with you, and you don't even know this ring, or that you didn't notice he had a ring on his finger?"

And then he said, "No, Sir. I did not know about that ring. But my boys would know whether he was wearing that ring or not." That is what he said to me.

Q   Mr. Strider, do you know whether that death certificate had the name of Emmett Till on it or not?

A   No, I don't know.

Q   When you observed that body, were there any wounds on his body other than about the head?

A   There was no wounds at all that I could see. On his back it looked like probably it had just a little reddish cast to it. What could have caused that, I do not know. And I don't know whether it was bruised or not.

But there wasn't no broken places in the skin or anything like that. And his body wasn't bursted [*sic*] anywhere other than about his head.

Q   Mr. Strider, from your qualified experience in handling dead bodies brought out of the river, you know as a matter of fact, do you not, that a body that is wounded and beaten up and injured will decompose much quicker than a body that has not been? Isn't that true?

A   I would think so, yes, Sir.

Q   And you also know that conditions will vary in different bodies which will cause one body to decompose much quicker than another?

A   Well, I wouldn't say too much about that. But I have taken bodies out of the river that were in there much longer than this.

Q   But circumstances can make a difference, and circumstances can vary as far as a body is concerned, which might cause a body to decompose quicker or faster than another body?

A   Well, I thought it depended on the temperature.

Q   In your best judgment, Mr. Strider, was that not a bullet hole in his head?

A   I wouldn't say whether that was a bullet hole or not. I couldn't find where it penetrated into the skull. And I know that I cut a little stick and tried to find if it penetrated or not, but I never could locate where it penetrated into the skull.

MR. SMITH: I believe that is all.

REDIRECT EXAMINATION BY
MR. KELLUM:

Q   Mr. Strider, I would like to ask you this . . .

MR. CHATHAM: If Your Honor please, we object to more than one counsel examining the same witness.

THE COURT: I think the objection will have to be sustained. That will have to be done through the same counsel.

BY
MR. WHITTEN:

Q   Just one point of identification—the Moses that you spoke of was Moses Wright who testified here in this case, is that correct?

A   Yes, Sir; Moses Wright, who said he was the uncle of Emmett Till.

MR. WHITTEN: That is all.

(WITNESS EXCUSED.)

(At this point in the proceedings, 3:40 p.m., the Court took a recess until 4:05 p.m., this date, at which time the proceedings were resumed.)

Chapter 7

THE DEFENSE'S CASE "EXPERT" WITNESSES— THE BODY THAT WAS BEYOND RECOGNITION

The defense called three "experts" to testify as to the condition of the body found in the river and whether it was identifiable:

- Dr. L. B. Otken (a general practice medical doctor who only viewed the body but never touched it),

- H. D. Malone (an embalmer), and

- Sheriff Strider (who was recalled to offer his "expert" opinion).

Recall that at the time of the trial no autopsy had been conducted (that would not occur until 2005 when the FBI exhumed Till's body). Note also that none of these three witnesses was a pathologist.

The purpose of this segment of the defense's arguments was to raise doubt, yet again, as to whether there was sufficient evidence to establish that the body found in the river was that of Emmett Till. To that end, defense attorney Breland offered four kinds of arguments by way of the testimony of two medical "experts" and Sheriff Strider:

1. *The length of time the body had been dead argument*: Since Emmett had been missing for three days, any time much beyond that would indicate that the body retrieved could

not be that of Emmett Till. The defense's witnesses testified that in their "expert" opinions the body discovered was probably in the river for eight to ten days and perhaps as much as twenty-five days.

2. *The no bullet hole in the head argument*: Whatever the cause of death, the defense argued that the hole found in the head could not be proven to be that caused by a bullet. When on cross-examination Dr. Otken was asked whether "the round hole you described over the right ear . . . was that of a bullet hole," he replied, "I couldn't say."

3. *The pre- or post-death injuries argument*: During his testimony, Dr. Otken could not say for sure whether the injuries found on the body were caused before or after death. Thus, Breland asked, "Doctor, these wounds that you have described about this dead body's head, could you tell whether or not those wounds were made there before or after death from the condition that body was in?" To which Otken replied, "I couldn't." If that were so, then the cause of death might not have been murder.

4. *The long length of the corpse argument*: Dr. Malone testified that the body he placed in the casket nearly filled the six feet, three inches length of the coffin. But if Emmett was only five feet, four inches tall, then that body could not have been his, or so the argument went.

Such arguments were tendered to refute or at least cause confusion about testimony offered by Moses Wright and Mamie Till-Bradley and likewise to get around the "L. T." ring found on the body and the fact that Strider had signed the death certificate as being that of "Emmett Louis Till."

Finally, when Sheriff Strider returned to take the stand, Robert Smith grilled him as to "what efforts [he had] been making to find out whose body . . . was found" in the river. Smith: "You have not gotten any information about that as yet?" To which came the reply: "No, I have not."

DR. L. B. OTKEN,

A witness introduced for and on behalf of the defendants, being first duly sworn, upon his oath testified as follows:

DIRECT EXAMINATION BY
MR. BRELAND:

Q Give your name to the court reporter, Doctor.

A Dr. L. B. Otken. That is O-T-K-E-N, Otken.

Q Where do you live, Doctor?

A Greenwood, Mississippi.

Q How long have you lived in Greenwood, Mississippi?

A Since 1919.

Q Are you a regular, practicing, licensed physician in the State of Mississippi?

A I am.

Q Are you a member of the College of Surgeons?

A I am not.

Q You have been a regular, practicing physician and surgeon for how long, Doctor?

A Since 1917.

Q Where did you go to school and college?

A University of Texas.

Q Did you have any hospital training?

A Yes, Sir.

Q Where?

A Well, in Galveston, Texas; also in New York City; and two years in a Base Hospital with the U. S. Army.

Q And what war was that?

A World War I.

Q   Doctor, during that experience, in your hospital training, and in your regular practice, and also your service in the Army, did you ever have occasion to examine any dead bodies?

A   Yes, Sir, I did.

Q   And Doctor, have you ever had occasion to examine dead bodies that have been in the air and also those that have been in water?

A   I have.

Q   Would you please tell the jury or give the jury some kind of estimate as to the number of those dead bodies you have seen?

A   Oh, that would be hard for me to just say offhand, as to just how many of those bodies I have seen.

Q   Well, would it be a few or a large number?

A   What?

Q   Have you seen a few or a large number of those bodies?

A   I would say a large number.

MR. BRELAND: We submit, Your Honor, that he is an expert witness in his field.

THE COURT: I think the gentleman qualifies.

Q   Did you have occasion or did you on Wednesday, August 31st, 1955, did you examine and view a dead boy in the Miller Funeral Home, or the colored funeral home, over in Greenwood operated by one Miller?

A   I did.

Q   At whose request or suggestion was that examination made?

A   The sheriff's office of Leflore County.

Q   And is that the sheriff's office of Sheriff George Smith?

A   Yes.

Q   Did you know of the particular alleged crime that was being investigated at that time?

A   Well, I was told that this body was taken from the river.

Q   What river?

A   Tallahatchie.

Q   And you were called by the sheriff's office to come over there and make an examination of that body?

A   To view the body.

Q   Of course, you didn't make any pathological examination of the body?

A   I did not.

Q   Doctor, explain to the jury—and you may use medical or scientific terms, if you so desire—but will you please explain to the jury and describe the condition of that body to the jury as you saw it at that time?

A   This body was badly swollen; badly bloated. And I would estimate—now, as I previously stated, I did not touch this body. I want to make that plain to you—but I would estimate that this body would have weighed two hundred and seventy five pounds. It was that badly bloated.

   The skin and the flesh was beginning to slip on it. The head was badly mutilated. The right eye was protruding. And the tongue was protruding from the mouth.

Q   And what about the odor of the body?

A   Terrific.

Q   What was the state of putrefaction of that body at that time?

A   Well, I would say it was in an advanced state of decomposition— or putrefaction if you wish to call it that.

Q   Doctor, I want to ask this question: from the condition that you saw that body in, in your opinion, could anybody have identified any particular person as being that body?

MR. SMITH: If the Court please, we object to that question. We asked that same question, and it was objected to, and the objection was sustained.

THE COURT: The objection is overruled at this time.

THE WITNESS: I don't think you could. I don't think you could have identified that body.[1]

Q   Now suppose if the man had been another person's brother, could he have identified it, in your opinion?

A   I doubt it.

Q   Or if it had been a person's son, could a mother have identified that body, in your opinion?

A   I doubt it.

Q   Doctor, from your experience and study and your familiarity with the medical authorities, what, in your opinion, had been the length of time that the body had been dead, if it had been in the open air?

A   I would say eight to ten days.

Q   Well, if proof was shown that the body was taken from the Talla-hatchie River where the water was from twenty five to thirty feet deep, and the water at the top of the water—or the surface—was at a temperature of around seventy degrees, and that it was cooler, the deeper the water got—and that this particular body, when it was found, had a weight tied around its neck, weighing seventy-odd pounds—what then would be your opinion as to how long that body had been dead?

A   I would still say eight to ten days.

Q   Is that the minimum or the maximum?

A   That would have been a minimum.

---

1. "One of [Whitten's] responsibilities before the trial, he told [a *New York Times* reporter], was to go down to Greenwood and meet with Dr. L. B. Otken, who examined the body after it was pulled from the Tallahatchie River. Otken, he recalled, had told him, 'This is a dead body, but it doesn't belong to that young man that they're looking for.' Did he really believe that? 'I'm sure I did at one time,' Whitten said. 'I'm sure he convinced me of it.' Had his thinking since changed? 'Oh, yes,' he said. 'I believe that it was the body of Till.'" Richard Rubin, "The Ghosts of Emmett Till," *New York Times*, July 31, 2005, https://www.nytimes.com/2005/07/31/magazine/the-ghosts-of-emmett-till.html.

Q   And what would have been the probable maximum number of days?

A   Say two weeks.

MR. BRELAND: Take the witness.

CROSS EXAMINATION BY
MR. SMITH:

Q   Doctor, I just want to ask a few questions. It is true, is it not, that different conditions will cause a body to decompose at a different rate?

A   That is right.

Q   And of course, you don't have any knowledge whatsoever as to the condition which existed where this body was, do you?

A   I do not.

Q   Now, could you tell whether this was the body of a colored person or a white person?

A   I could not.

Q   There was nothing to indicate one or the other?

A   Not sufficiently for me to make a positive statement.

Q   But what, in your opinion, was it? Was it a colored person or a white person?

A   I just told you that I couldn't tell you whether it was a white person or a colored person.

Q   Doctor, had the skin all over the body slipped?

A   Not altogether, but it was slipping in various areas.

Q   I hand you here a photograph marked Exhibit 1 to the testimony of C. A. Strickland, and I ask you if that picture represents the body as it was at the time you saw it?

A   That is the body that I saw.

Q   Doctor, did you examine the body for wounds?

A   I merely viewed the body. I did not lay my hand upon it, and there were some things that I could see.

Q What did you see in the way of wounds or injuries to the body?

A There was a round hole just above and slightly behind the right ear. There was an opening in the forehead, I would say, more to the right center, that was triangular in shape.

A piece of bone was gone. And the skin flap was turned up rather than turned down. And behind the left ear, the head was badly crushed in as if by some blunt object.

Q Was there anything else that you observed?

A Well, there was mark around the neck as if something had been around the neck. But it was not there when I examined the body, so I can't state just what that was.

Q Was that mark around as much of the neck as you could see?

A It appeared to go all the way around.

Q And what about the rest of the body? Did you see any other injuries or wounds of any nature?

A That would be hard to say because of the decomposition. Your Honor, if you would allow me to say, those black splotches in that picture there, that was the areas of decomposition where the skin was beginning to come loose. Now what caused that, I don't know.

Q Doctor, in your opinion, was the round hole you described over the right ear, was that a bullet hole?

A I couldn't say.

Q What is your opinion as to whether it was or not?

A That would merely be a conjecture on my part. It was a round hole that went into the skull.

Q Doctor, in your opinion, did the injuries or wounds about the head look as if they might have been sufficient to cause his death?

A I would say so.

Q Doctor, did you sign a death certificate?

A I signed a death certificate in blank. I did not identify the body. As I remember, I stated that this was a body supposed to have been taken from the river and it had a hole above the right ear and the left side of the skull was crushed in.

MR. SMITH: I believe that is all.

REDIRECT EXAMINATION BY
MR. BRELAND:

Q   Doctor, do you know any of the parties involved in this particular controversy?

A   What do you mean by parties?

Q   I mean the Milam family, or the brothers, or half-brothers?

A   I do not.

Q   And Mr. Bryant and Mr. Milam, you do not know those two gentlemen?

A   I do not. You would have to point them out to me.

Q   Doctor, these wounds that you have described about this dead body's head, could you tell whether or not those wounds were made there before or after death from the condition that body was in?

A   I couldn't.

MR. BRELAND: I believe that is all.

RE-CROSS EXAMINATION BY
MR. SMITH:

Q   Doctor, is it true or not that a person who is fat and heavy and has a good deal of weight, fat weight, is it true that such a body will decompose faster than a body that is more slender and muscular?

A   That's right.

Q   And that would affect the rate of decomposition?

A   That is right.

MR. BRELAND: We object to that, Your Honor. I don't think it is relevant.

THE COURT: The objection is overruled.

Q   And Doctor, is it not also true that a body that has been badly beaten or injured will decompose faster than one that has not been?

A   That is right.

MR. SMITH: That is all.

REDIRECT EXAMINATION BY
MR. BRELAND:

Q   Doctor, observing that body as you saw it, and with the wounds that you saw on it, would that change your opinion on the length of time that the body had been dead, as you saw it?

A   No.

MR. BRELAND: That is all.

MR. SMITH: That is all.

(WITNESS EXCUSED.)

MR. SMITH: Before we proceed further, if the Court please, I would like to recall Mr. Strider to the stand.

THE COURT: All right, Sir.

* * * *

H. C. STRIDER,

Recalled as a witness for and on behalf of the State, having been duly sworn, upon his oath testified as follows:

RE-CROSS EXAMINATION BY
MR. SMITH:

Q   Mr. Strider, you are the same Sheriff Strider, who testified here a few minutes ago?

A   That's right.

Q   And you are the sheriff of Tallahatchie County?

A   That's right.

Q Sheriff, you testified that you went down to the river and found a dead body down there, is that correct?

A I didn't find it.

Q I mean, it was down there when you got there and you saw it?

A Yes, Sir.

Q And you had information that it was on your side of the river, did you not?

A Yes, Sir.

Q And I believe you testified that you couldn't tell whether it was a white man or a negro?

A That's right.

Q Sheriff, have you made any investigation to find out who that body was? Who that person was?

A Yes, Sir, I sure have.

Q And are you continuing your investigation?

A Yes, Sir.

Q And are you continuing your investigation at the present time?

A Not at the present time, no, Sir. I have been tied up here in Court.

Q I realize that, just the way we all have. But what efforts have you been making to find out whose body that was?

A Well, I have had several reports about a negro who disappeared over there at Lambert. And I went out there and investigated that, and one man would tell you that he saw him, or that he said somebody told him they saw him, and then someone else would tell me that someone else had told them something about it. And it would just carry you right around to where you started from.

Q But you got no information whatsoever to indicate whose body that was? You have not gotten any information about that as yet?

A No, I have not.

MR. SMITH: That is all

MR. BRELAND: No questions.

(WITNESS EXCUSED.)

* * * *

H. D. MALONE,[2]

A witness introduced for and on behalf of the defendants, being first duly sworn, upon his oath testified as follows:

DIRECT EXAMINATION BY
MR. BRELAND:

Q   This is Mr. H. D. Malone?

A   Yes, Sir.

Q   Where do you live, Mr. Malone?

A   Cleveland, Mississippi.

Q   How long have you lived at Cleveland?

A   Most of my life.

Q   What is your business, profession, or occupation?

A   I am an embalmer and a farmer.

Q   Oh—you own a farm also, do you?

A   Yes, Sir.

Q   What is your education, Mr. Malone? State what your education qualifications are that fits you for your profession of an embalmer.

---

2. Harry D. Malone (1920–1993) "worked for White and Black funeral homes in Tutwiler, Mississippi, at the time of the . . . Till murder. [He was] the embalmer of the body at the Avent Funeral Home in Tutwiler, MS. . . . His testimony stated that he believed the body had been in the river for at least ten days, aiding the defense argument that the body was not that of Emmett Till. Anderson, "Who's Who in the Emmett Till Case." There is some doubt, however, about who exactly was the main embalmer of Till. See Hendrickson, *Sons of Mississippi*, pp. 310–11; Anderson, *Emmett Till*, pp. 427–28 n. 83 (Woodrow Jackson claimed to be the main embalmer).

A I am a high school graduate, and I also had a year of college. And I am a graduate of a mortuary school, the John A. Gupton College of Nashville.

Q Is that an accredited college?

A Yes, Sir.

Q When did you graduate from that mortuary college?

A In 1952.

Q What experience have you had as an embalmer or mortician since that time?

A I have been steadily employed in the field since that time.

Q Do you mean in that character and kind of work?

A Yes, Sir.

Q And about how many dead bodies have you handled? What is your conservative estimate on that?

A Several hundred.

Q And have you ever had experience with bodies that have been dead for some length of time before you received them?

A Yes, Sir, I have.

Q And for what periods of time have they been dead? Just tell the jury generally.

A Well, anywhere from three days to ten days, or fifeen [sic] days; also some unknown.

Q Are you a licensed mortician or embalmer under the laws of Mississippi?

A Yes, Sir.

Q And in any other state?

A Yes, Sir.

Q What other state?

A Tennessee.

Q Have you ever been engaged in your profession in a funeral home over at Tutwiler?

A Yes, Sir.

Q And what is the name of the funeral home?

A Well, two. One of them is the Nelson Funeral Home, and another is the Avons (?)[3] Funeral Home.

Q And as I understand, the Nelson Funeral Home is a negro funeral home?

A Yes, Sir.

Q And Avons [*sic*] is for white people?

A Yes, Sir.

Q And you have done work at both of those places?

A Yes, Sir.

Q You work as a mortician at both of those institutions?

A Yes, Sir.

Q How long have you been such?

A Nearly three years.

Q Have you ever had experience with bodies taken out of the water?

A Yes, Sir, several times.

Q Did you have occasion to embalm this body that was taken from the Miller Funeral Home at Greenwood and brought to the Nelson Funeral Home at Tutwiler on the 31st day of August, 1955?

A Yes, Sir.

Q Did you do the work on that body?

A Yes, Sir.

Q Did you make an examination of that body?

A Yes, Sir.

Q State to the court and to the jury what the condition of that body was. Just give its general description, and then if there is any scientific or medical description, will you please explain such terms to the jury in layman's language.

   A The body was bloated, bloated and swollen so bad that it was beyond any possible recognition, I think.

---

3. Avent Funeral Home.

Q   Will you state that again?

A   The body was bloated, and it was so bloated that the features were not recognizable. There was a prevalent skin slip all over the body.

Q   Will you explain that to the jury?

A   Well, anywhere you touched it, the skin rolled up and slipped off. It just turned loose.

A   [*sic*] [Q] Go ahead.

A   And the entire skin on his left hand was off. How it got off, I don't know. But it was off when it came in, I guess.

And on the right hand, the fingernails were loose. It was just like the skin was loose, and it was just like they wasn't there at all. And the tongue was protruding from the mouth. His eyes were bulged up.

Q   Will you explain that to the jury as best you can?

A   Well, I mean bloated. And the hair came out easy. There were multiple lacerations about the head. The left eye was hanging from its socket. And the entire body was a bluish-green discoloration.

Q   And what did that indicate to you?

A   That indicated to me that the body had been dead possibly ten days or longer.

Q   Do you mean possibly? Is that what you mean, possibly?

A   Possibly; very likely that it had. It is very possible it had.

Q   And that means that the probability that it had, is that right?

A   Yes, Sir.

Q   And the greatest probability that it had?

A   Yes, Sir.

MR. SMITH: Your Honor, we object to counsel putting words in the witness's mouth.

THE COURT: The objection will be sustained. Counsel will please refrain from testifying.

Q   All right, go ahead.

A   There was a hole above the right ear in the skull.

Q   What was the color of the skin and flesh of the abdomen?

A   A bluish-green.

Q   And what did that indicate to you, if anything?

A   Advanced putrefaction.

Q   And you say the tongue was protruding from the mouth?

A   Yes, Sir.

Q   And about how far did it extend out of the mouth?

A   As far as it would go.

Q   And what did that indicate to you, if anything?

A   Nothing more than the presence of gas; tissue gas.

Q   Was that tissue gas you said?

A   Yes, Sir.

Q   Will you explain to the jury just what you mean by "tissue gas"?

A   Tissue gas is generated by all the tissues of the body after the body has reached an advanced stage of decomposition.

Q   And that gas you are talking about, is that gas coming off the stomach?

A   It is gas from every tissue in the body.

Q   Now, will you explain to the jury about rigor mortis, and tell what that is, and when it takes effect and when it leaves the body?

A   Rigor mortis is a stiffening of the body, the muscles and joints. And it is caused by a complex chemical reaction which generates lactic acid during its onset and throughout its duration.

   And this lactic acid retards putrefaction. The reason it does has to do with the pH of the body. And pH is the mathematical way of expressing the alkalinity or acidity of the body.

   The scale on that runs from zero to fourteen, seven being neutral. And during life, the normal body pH is 7.4, slightly alkaline. And if rigor mortis comes on in a body, this lactic acid runs your pH below seven, which is an acid condition. And putrefaction bacteria cannot live in there. And until the rigor mortis condition is gone, there can be no putrefaction.

Q About how long does rigor mortis last after time of death?

A Well, as a general rule, under normal conditions, it takes from four to six hours for it to reach its height. And its duration is from twelve to forty-eight hours.

Q Does any putrefaction or decomposition of the body take place during that period?

A No, Sir.

Q When does putrefaction or decomposition begin?

A At the time the body reaches seven, or neutral. That is the end of the rigor mortis, and that is when the body enzymes have overpowered this acid condition.

Q Does putrefaction or decomposition take place in a dead body of an able bodied person faster or quicker than it does in a body having a disease, like "T.B." or something like that?

A Will you state the question again.

Q I said, does putrefaction take place in a dead body quicker or later in an able bodied person than in a body of a person that has been sick with tuberculosis or any disease of that kind?

A That would be true with anything but tuberculosis.

Q Will you explain that?

A Well, in a person with tuberculosis, the body tissues are dried and emaciated, and there is not much muscle tissue there for generation.

Q Does putrefaction ordinarily take place earlier in a man that is well and able bodied than it does in one that has been sick, or one who dies from an illness?

Where would putrefaction take place first? Ordinarily would it be in the body of a well or able bodied person or one who has been sick?

A One that is highly active.

Q Now, you examined that body—and saw all the wounds on it, did you?

A I don't know if I saw them all or not. I saw some on the body, and what I saw I thought that was all.

Q   And you also saw those on the head?

A   Yes, Sir.

Q   And you saw the condition of the body, did you?

A   Yes, Sir.

Q   Now state to the court and jury whether or not putrefaction takes place quicker and becomes progressive faster in a body that has been in the air or in one that has been in water under the same atmospheric conditions?

A   Being in the water would retard putrefaction.

Q   And it would retard it to what extent?

A   Well, that would have to do with the temperature and also the physical state of the body.

Q   Now what you have testified to here is with reference to a body that has been in the air or in the water?

A   I have been telling you about a body under normal conditions. That would be in the open air.

Q   That is what you mean by "normal conditions"?

A   That's right.

Q   Now say a body is taken from the water, where the top of the water in a river would be around seventy degrees in temperature, and where the river would be twenty five to thirty feet deep, and where such a body had a seventy-pound weight tied to that body, and where the water would get colder the deeper it gets—what would be the difference in the rate of decomposition of a body that was in water such as I have described than a body out in the air?

A   I understood you to say a seventy-foot weight—do you mean a seventy-pound weight? Maybe I misunderstood you.

Q   Yes, a seventy-pound weight.

A   I would say it would be retarded considerably.

Q   What?

A   I would say it would be retarded considerably; putrefaction, that is.

Q   Then would you say that it would take longer or a shorter period of time for decomposition?

A   It would take longer for it to decompose.

Q   Well, having examined that body which you embalmed, and from your study and experience as a licensed mortician and embalmer, and having observed the number of bodies that you have, both those that have been in the air and also in the water, what would be your opinion as to the shortest length of time that this particular body had been dead that you embalmed?

A   About ten days.

Q   And what would be the probabilities of the length of time that it might have been dead? That is, as to the longest length of time it might have been dead?

A   I would say ten days.

Q   Do you mean the longest length of time it could have been dead?

A   No—not the longest; the shortest.

Q   I am asking you about the longest period of time it could have been dead.

A   That would be hard to say.

Q   What is your best judgment on that?

A   Somewhere between ten and twenty, or maybe ten and twenty five days, perhaps.

Q   Did that body come to that funeral home from Greenwood, from the funeral home at Greenwood, in any kind of a box or casket?

A   It came in a wooden, cloth-covered casket.

Q   What was the length of that casket, if you know, that it came in?

A   Six foot three.

Q   How did that body fit in that casket? How completely did it fill the casket end to end?

A   It filled it very near full.

Q   Do you mean from end to end?

A   Yes.

Q   Did you measure the length of that body?

A   No, I did not.

Q   What would be your estimate of the length of that body?

A   I would say the body was five feet, ten.

Q   Five feet, ten inches?

A   Yes.

Q   Could you tell from the condition that body was in, could you give the jury and the court a definite opinion as to how old the person was?

A   I wouldn't attempt to say at all.

Q   And was that because of the condition of the body?

A   That was because of the condition of the body.

Q   Is it possible for a mortician or a plastic surgeon expert to repair a body in the condition of the body that you saw there when it was embalmed, is it possible for such an expert to make it look more like its natural self?

A   Yes, Sir.

Q   And is that not the usual practice in a mortuary?

A   It is usually their practice to a certain extent.

Q   And is that more usually done in cities than it is in the country places?

A   I would say where the volume of the funeral business is, that is where you would find the experts qualified to do that work.

Q   And where do you usually find them, if you know? Would that be in country towns or in cities, if you know?

A   Well, I still say where the volume of the business is. And that would be in the cities, of course.

MR. BRELAND: That is all. Take the witness.

CROSS EXAMINATION BY
MR. SMITH:

Q   I want to see if I got your name right? Is your name Malone?

A   Malone, M-A-L-O-N-E.

Q Mr. Malone, you said there were some wounds or injuries about the body, did you not?

A About the head.

Q Would you please describe those to the jury? Tell what they were, and what they looked like?

A There was a wound in the crown of the head and also at the base of the skull. And there was a hole over the right ear. The left eye was hanging from its socket.

Q Did it look like it had been knocked out?

A I couldn't say.

Q Were there any other wounds about the head? Was there one over his left ear?

A There was one in the vicinity of that ear.

Q You say there was one in the vicinity of his ear?

A Somewhere in the vicinity of his ear. I don't know just exactly.

Q Did you see that ring or mark around the body's neck?

A I didn't notice any ring. I don't recall seeing any ring.

Q Now, it is true, Mr. Malone, is it not, that the conditions which exist at the place and where a body might be, those conditions would affect very greatly the rate of decomposition? Is that not true?

A Yes, Sir, they do.

Q And isn't it also true that a body that is wounded and beaten, and so forth, that such a body will decompose faster than one that is not?

A Under normal conditions, yes, Sir.

Q But of course, you have no knowledge of the conditions where this body had been, do you?

A No, Sir.

Q And what you are testifying to is what would happen under normal conditions, is it not?

A That's right.

Q And isn't it true that if a person is fat, or heavy, and has more fatty tissue than the average person, that such a body will decompose at a greater rate than one that is not so fat?

A Yes, Sir.

MR. BRELAND: We don't think that question is competent, Your Honor. It has not been shown that this body was fat.

THE COURT: The objection is overruled.

MR. SMITH: I think that is all.

(WITNESS EXCUSED.)

THE COURT: The Court will now recess until nine thirty in the morning. (At this point in the proceedings, 5:05 p.m., the Court took a recess until 9:30 a.m., the following day, at which time the proceedings were resumed.) . . .

Presiding:

Hon. Curtis M. Swango, Jr., Circuit Judge,

Seventeenth Judicial District of the State.

Appearances:

For the State:

Hon. Gerald Chatham, District Attorney;

Hon. Robert B. Smith, III, Special Assistant to the District Attorney;

For the Defendants:

Hon. J. J. Breland, of Sumner, Mississippi;

Hon. C. Sidney Carlton, of Sumner, Mississippi;

Hon. J. W. Kellum, of Sumner. Mississippi;

Hon. John W. Whitten, Jr., of Sumner, Mississippi;

Hon. Harvey Henderson, of Sumner, Mississippi.

* * * *

This day, this cause coming on to be heard, on this the 23rd day of September, 1955. Comes the District Attorney, came also the defendants, each in his own proper person and represented by counsel and announced ready to proceed herein. Whereupon, came the same jury, composed of J. A. Shaw, Jr., and eleven others, being specially sworn to try the issue. Thereupon, the cause proceeded to further trial before the Judge aforesaid, and the jury, when and where the following proceedings were had, as follows [*continued in next chapter*]:

Chapter 8

THE DEFENSE'S CASE
SEVEN CHARACTER WITNESSES

I've known [Roy and J. W.] for years.
They're men of good reputation, respected
businessmen in the community, what I'd call real
patriots . . . 100 percent real Americans.

—J. J. BRELAND[1] (press statement before the trial)

In less than an hour, the defense called seven character witnesses, three for defendant Milam (Lee Russell Allison, Lee McGarrh, and L. W. Boyce) and four for defendant Bryant (James Sanders, Harold Terry, Grover Duke, and Franklin Smith, a cousin of Sheriff George Smith).

J. W. Kellum took the lead in the direct examination for the defense, with J. J. Breland doing most of the evidentiary objections.

Gerald Chatham conducted the cross-examination for the state with Robert B. Smith doing many of the evidentiary objections.

For the most part, this segment of the trial was of little moment since the testimony of the seven character witnesses did little to help the defense and likewise little to harm the prosecution. "The only snag in the proceedings occurred when the prosecution cross-examined Allison: the defense objected vigorously when the state leadingly asked if it was true that Milam had 'been charged and pleaded guilty on quite a number of charges.' Indeed Milam was known in the area for bootlegging, among other things, but Judge Swango upheld the objection."[2]

---

1. *Jackson Daily News*, "Prosecution Doesn't Say if Death Penalty Sought," p. 1; Houck & Grindy, *Emmett Till*, p. 62.

2. Houck & Grindy, *Emmett Till*, p. 102.

LEE RUSSELL ALLISON,[3]

A witness introduced for and on behalf of the defendants, being first duly sworn, upon his oath testified as follows:

DIRECT EXAMINATION BY
MR. KELLUM:

Q   This is Mr. Lee Russell Allison?

A   It is.

Q   Where do you live, Mr. Allison?

A   About a mile south of Tippo.

Q   And how far is that from the little community of Glendora?

A   I would say around eight miles.

Q   How long have you lived in Tallahatchie County?

A   Practically all my life.

Q   What official position, if any, do you hold in Tallahatchie County?

A   Supervisor, Beat 4.

Q   And is Glendora in Beat 4?

A   It is.

Q   Do you know one of the defendants in this case, Mr. J. W. Milam?

A   I do.

Q   How long have you known him?

A   Some four years or probably a little over four years.

Q   Do you know in the community where he lives his general reputation for peace and violence?

A   It is good.

---

3. Lee Russell Allison (1915–1964) lived in Glendora. He was the Tallahatchie County supervisor. Anderson, "Who's Who in the Emmett Till Case." "[He] had just been reelected as a county supervisor over Beat 4, where Milam lived. Because Milam had supported Allison in this election, Chatham suggested that Allison's testimony was one way to reciprocate." Anderson, *Emmett Till*, Chapter 6.

MR. KELLUM: Take the witness.

CROSS EXAMINATION BY
THE DISTRICT ATTORNEY:

Q   Mr. Allison, were you a candidate in the recent August primaries for re-election?

A   I was.

Q   And you got elected, I hope?

A   I did.

Q   Did Mr. Milam support you in that election?

A   I believe he did. Most of them did.

Q   And any way that you could repay that favor, you would be glad to do it, and that is what you are doing now, is that right?

A   I don't know about repaying any favor.

Q   But that would be the natural thing to do, isn't that right?

A   Well, if I could return a favor, I would.

Q   Now, Mr. Allison, you weren't present with the defendant on August 24th—

MR. BRELAND: We object to that, Your Honor. That is previous to August 28th.

THE COURT: The objection is sustained.

Q   You have stated your opinion as to the general reputation of J. W. Milam?

A   I have.

Q   I want you to tell the jury if it is not an actual fact that he was convicted—or he was arrested and pleaded guilty to a charge . . .

MR. BRELAND: We object to that, Your Honor.

THE COURT: The objection is sustained. Will the jury please retire to the other room.

(The jury retired to the jury room, and the proceedings continued in the absence of the jury.)

MR. CHATHAM: I want to make this statement to the Court. We asked the question in perfectly good faith, and we are not intending to take any advantage of the witness or of the Court. And we asked the question for the simple reason that the witness testified to the good character and reputation of J. W. Milam as to peace and violence. And we want to interrogate him and ask him what he based that on.

THE COURT: But you didn't start your questions that way. You may ask your questions now in the absence of the jury, and we can perhaps let you finish the questions before we sustain any objection.

> Q   Mr. Allison, what you meant to tell the jury was that you don't know of any act of violence that was ever committed by J. W. Milam, so far as your personal knowledge is concerned? Isn't that right?
>
> A   That is all I can say. I can just say what I do know.

MR. BRELAND: If the Court please, that is going beyond the scope of our direct examination. And this is his cross examination of the witness.

THE COURT: Do you wish to withdraw your question? As the Court sees it, this examination is a cross examination, and it will have to be limited to the matters in issue in the charge here. And he has testified that the general reputation of the defendant, J. W. Milam, in the community in which J. W. Milam lives, that the general reputation for peace and violence is good.

Now, the cross examination will have to be limited to the reputation of the defendant, J. W. Milam, as to peace and violence. This is cross examination, you know.

> Q   Now, Mr. Allison, I believe you said that you have lived in that community practically all your life, is that right?
>
> A   I have.
>
> Q   And if you don't know everybody in your supervisor's district, it isn't because you didn't try to find them? You tried to find all of them, didn't you?
>
> A   I did, every one.

Q   And you wanted to make friends of every one of them, is that right?

A   Yes, Sir.

Q   Have you ever heard of Mr. J. W. Milam ever having been convicted of any criminal charge?

A   No, Sir.

MR. BRELAND: We object to that, Your Honor.

THE COURT: The objection is sustained, and the question is not to be asked in the presence of the jury. Let the jury come in, please.

(The jury returned to the courtroom; and the proceedings continued with the jury present.)

MR. CHATHAM: I don't believe I have anything further.

(WITNESS EXCUSED.)

* * * *

LEE McGARRH,[4]

A witness introduced for and on behalf of the defendants, being first duly sworn, upon his oath testified as follows:

DIRECT EXAMINATION BY
MR. KELLUM:

Q   You are Mr. Lee McGarrh?

A   Yes, Sir.

Q   How old are you, Mr. McGarrh?

A   Thirty-five.

---

4. Lee McGarrh (1920–2002) "lived in Glendora, Leflore County . . . A few months after the trial, his employee at his service station, a Black man named Clinton Melton, was murdered at the station by a white man, Elmer Kimbrell. The trial was held in Sumner, Mississippi, with several of the same cast of characters as the Milam–Bryant trial. This time, McGarrh, outraged at the murder, testified for the prosecution." Anderson, "Who's Who in the Emmett Till Case." As noted in the prologue, McGarrh retained a copy of the trial transcript, which his son turned over to the FBI after McGarrh's death.

Q   Where do you live?

A   At Glendora.

Q   Glendora, Mississippi?

A   That's right.

Q   How long have you lived at Glendora?

A   For the past ten years.

Q   Do you know Mr. J. W. Milam, one of the defendants in this case?

A   Yes, Sir, I do.

Q   How long have you known him?

A   Ten years.

Q   How far does he live from you there in the little community of Glendora?

A   Well, I would say, roughly, about three hundred yards.

Q   About three hundred yards?

A   Yes, Sir.

Q   Do you know there in this community where Mr. J. W. Milam lives his general reputation for peace and violence?

A   I do.

Q   Is that reputation good or bad?

A   Good.

MR. KELLUM: That is all.

CROSS EXAMINATION BY
THE DISTRICT ATTORNEY:

Q   Mr. McGarrh, what business are you in?

A   I operate a grocery store and service station.

Q   Were you qualified here at this term of Court as a juror? It seems that your name has been called out here before.

A   Well, I was called up but I was disqualified.

Q In other words, you were called up as a juror, and you disqualified yourself because—

MR. KELLUM: We object to that.

THE COURT: The objection is sustained.

Q Mr. McGarrh, you have known J. W. Milam for how long?

A Approximately ten years.

Q And have you lived close by him there in Glendora?

A Well, for about the past seven years, yes, Sir.

Q And during that time you have formed a warm friendship with him, is that right?

A We were close friends, yes, Sir.

Q And he has done business with you and you have done business with him?

A That's right, Sir.

Q And in your testimony here as to his good character, that is based on your own personal knowledge, and as far as you know, you have never heard of him being involved in any wrong doings?

A No, I have not; not to my knowledge.

Q And your testimony here this morning is based on your own knowledge?

A That's right, Sir.

Q And you, as a close friend of his, you want to help him out of his difficulty, is that right?

A Well, I didn't come up here to tell a lie. I came to tell the truth.

Q But that is the reason you are up here this morning, isn't it, because you are a friend of J. W. Milam?

A Yes, Sir.

MR. CHATHAM: That is all.

(WITNESS EXCUSED.)

* * * *

L. E. [*sic*] **BOYCE,**[5]

A witness introduced for and on behalf of the defendants, being first duly sworn, upon his oath testified as follows:

DIRECT EXAMINATION BY
MR. KELLUM:

Q   You're Mr. L. W. Boyce?

A   Yes, Sir.

Q   Where do you live, Mr. Boyce?

A   Three and a half miles out of Glendora.

Q   How long have you lived there?

A   Thirty years.

Q   Do you know Mr. J. W. Milam?

A   Yes, Sir.

Q   How long have you known him?

A   Nine years.

Q   Do you know there in the community where "J. W." lives in Glendora, do you know his general reputation for peace and violence?

A   It is good.

MR. SMITH: We object to that, Your Honor. He was not asked that question.

THE COURT: Just answer the question. Mr. Kellum, will you ask the question again?

---

5. Louis W. Boyce (1903–1956) "lived in Glendora, Tallahatchie County, Mississippi. . . . He was a local planter." Anderson, "Who's Who in the Emmett Till Case." As noted in William Bradford Huie's 1956 *Look* magazine account, an account later found to be quite suspect (see Part V, *infra*): "Bryant and Big Milam stood aside while Bobo loaded the fan. Weight: 74 pounds. The youth still thought they were bluffing. They drove back to Glendora, then north toward Swan Lake and crossed the 'new bridge' over the Tallahatchie. At the east end of this bridge, they turned right, along a dirt road which parallels the river. After about two miles, they crossed the property of L. W. Boyce, passing near his house. About 1.5 miles southeast of the Boyce home is a lonely spot where Big Milam has hunted squirrels. The river bank is steep. The truck stopped 30 yards from the water." "The Shocking Story of Approved Killing in Mississippi," *Look*, January 24, 1956.

Q In the community where "J. W." lives there in Glendora, do you know his general reputation for peace and violence?

A Yes, Sir, I know it.

Q And is that reputation good or bad?

A It is as good as anybody's.

MR. KELLUM: That is all.

CROSS EXAMINATION BY THE DISTRICT ATTORNEY:

Q Mr. Boyce, are you related to Mr. Milam or to any member of his family?

A No, Sir.

Q During the nine years that you have known him, have you formed a warm friendship with him?

A Not necessarily. I have done business with the man and have found him to be a good businessman, but we have had no close relations.

Q But your relations have been cordial and friendly?

A Well, there is no enemy to it.

Q And your relations with him have been cordial and . . .

A I found him a good man to do business with.

Q And he asked you to come up here and testify here in his behalf, and that is the reason you came here as a witness, is that right?

A No, Sir. He didn't ask me to come here at all.

Q Then how did you come here? Why did you come?

A I got notice from the lawyers to come up here.

Q And no one said anything to you about it?

A No.

Q And they didn't ask you what you were going to say?

A No.

Q   But you did come up here as a friend to tell about his reputation as a friend, and to help him out if you could, isn't that right?

A   I am up here to tell his reputation as I know it.

Q   But you are up here to help him out, isn't that true?

A   I am up here to tell about his reputation as I know it.

MR. CHATHAM: That is all.

(WITNESS EXCUSED.)

* * * *

JAMES SANDERS,[6]

A witness introduced for and on behalf of the defendants, being first duly sworn, upon his oath testified as follows:

DIRECT EXAMINATION BY
MR. KELLUM:

Q   You are Mr. James Sanders?

A   Yes, Sir.

Q   What age man are you, Mr. Sanders?

A   Forty-four.

Q   Where do you live?

A   I live three miles north of Money.

Q   How long have you lived there?

A   Well, this time I have lived there for about four and a half years.

Q   Do you know Mr. Roy Bryant?

A   Yes, Sir.

Q   Now long have you known him?

A   Nearly two years.

---

6. James Sanders (c. 1911–?) "lived in Money, Leflore County, Mississippi." Anderson, "Who's Who in the Emmett Till Case."

Q Do you know, there in the community where Mr. Roy Bryant lives in Money, do you know his general reputation for peace and violence?

A It is good.

MR. SMITH: We object, Your Honor. He wasn't asked that.

THE COURT: The objection is sustained. Just answer the gentleman's question.

THE WITNESS: Yes, Sir.

Q Is that reputation, Mr. Sanders, good or bad?

A It is good.

MR. KELLUM: Take the witness.

CROSS EXAMINATION BY
THE DISTRICT ATTORNEY:

Q Mr. Sanders, who asked you to come up here and testify for Mr. Roy Bryant?

A I volunteered to come up here.

Q And you are basing your statement of his good reputation on your friendship for him, and you are up here trying to help him out of his difficulty more than anything else, isn't that true?

A I am just up here to state the truth.

Q And you just heard somebody else say that, didn't you?

A No.

Q Well, I haven't accused you of not telling the truth, have I?

A No, you haven't.

Q And you are up here as his friend, to try and help him out in any way that you can in this difficulty, isn't that right? You are not here trying to hurt him, are you?

A No, Sir, I am not trying to hurt him.

Q And your statement to the jury about his good reputation in the community where he lives is made because of your desire to help him out more than your knowledge of his reputation, isn't that right?

A   No.

Q   Well, he hasn't been there more than two years, has he? You haven't known him longer than that, have you?

A   I have been there more than two years.

Q   Well, how long has Mr. Bryant been living there?

A   About two.

Q   And you say you live three miles north of Money?

A   Yes.

Q   Do you do business with Mr. Bryant?

A   No, Sir.

Q   Do you go to church with him?

A   I have been to church with him.

Q   How many times have you been to church with Mr. Bryant?

MR. BRELAND: We object to that Your Honor. That is not proper cross examination.

THE COURT: The objection is sustained.

MR. CHATHAM: That is all.

(WITNESS EXCUSED.)

* * * *

HAROLD TERRY,[7]

A witness introduced for and on behalf of the defendants, being first duly sworn, upon his oath testified as follows:

---

7. Harold E. Terry (1923–2013) "lived in Money, Leflore County, Mississippi, and was one of the character witnesses for [the defendants]. He served in Africa and Italy during World War II. [Around 1947] he rejoined the Army, where he helped train Korean War soldiers in Columbus, Georgia. He spent many years farming, but also worked in law enforcement, the insurance industry, and was an antique dealer. . . ." Anderson, "Who's Who in the Emmett Till Case."

DIRECT EXAMINATION BY
MR. KELLUM:

Q You are Mr. Harold Terry?

A That's right.

Q What age man are you, Sir?

A Thirty-two.

Q Where do you live, Mr. Terry?

A At Money.

Q How long have you lived at Money?

A Four years.

Q Do you know Mr. Roy Bryant?

A I do.

Q How long have you known Mr. Bryant?

A Since he has been there at Money.

Q Do you know how long he has been down there?

A About close to two years.

Q Do you know Mr. Roy Bryant's general reputation in the community in which he lives for peace and violence?

A I do.

Q Is that general reputation good or bad?

A It is good.

MR. KELLUM: Take the witness.

CROSS EXAMINATION BY
THE DISTRICT ATTORNEY:

Q Mr. Terry, what business are you in?

A I am a farmer.

Q And you say have lived down there in that community for about four years?

A Yes, Sir.

> **Q**   How far do you live from Money, and how far do you live from the store there?
>
> **A**   I live right in Money.
>
> **Q**   Do you do business with Mr. Bryant?
>
> **A**   No, Sir, I do not.
>
> **Q**   Do you know what his general reputation was for peace or violence before he came to Money?
>
> **A**   I didn't know him before he came to Money.
>
> **Q**   Therefore, you don't know what his reputation was for peace and violence before he came there, do you?
>
> **A**   No, Sir.
>
> **Q**   And since he has been there, what you know about him has been good?
>
> **A**   Yes, Sir.
>
> **Q**   Now you stated that his general reputation in the community for peace and violence was good. I want to ask you how many people you heard discuss Mr. Bryant's repuation [*sic*] during the past two years?
>
> **A**   I haven't heard Mr. Bryant discussed.
>
> **Q**   Then you haven't heard his reputation discussed?
>
> **A**   No, Sir.
>
> **Q**   Well, then, how do you know what his general reputation is?

MR. BRELAND: If the Court please, that is the best reputation a man can have, when nobody says nothing about him.

THE COURT: I think the question is proper, as to what he bases his previous statement on.

> **Q**   If you haven't heard his general reputation discussed by the people there in Money, during the past two years that he has lived there, then how do you know what his general reputation is?
>
> **A**   I haven't heard anything about Mr. Bryant.
>
> **Q**   Then you just stated what you think it is? Is that what you are stating now?

A   Yes, Sir.

Q   And that is just your opinion, is that right?

A   Yes, Sir.

Q   Who asked you to come here to testify today?

A   I volunteered to come up here.

Q   And you are in sympathy with Mr. Bryant, is that right, or is that wrong?

A   (The witness did not answer the question.)

Q   Why do you hesitate to answer, Mr. Terry?

A   (The witness did not answer the question.)

MR. CHATHAM: You can stand aside.

(WITNESS EXCUSED.)

* * * *

GROVER DUKE,[8]

A witness introduced for and on behalf of the defendants, being first duly sworn, upon his oath testified as follows:

DIRECT EXAMINATION BY
MR. KELLUM:

Q   You are Mr. Grover Duke?

A   Yes, Sir.

Q   What age man are you, Mr. Duke?

A   I am thirty years old.

Q   What business are you in?

A   Railroading.

Q   And where do you live?

A   Money, Mississippi.

---

8. Grover Duke (1924–1982) "lived in Money, Leflore County, Mississippi. . . . He worked for the railroad, lived across from the Bryant store in Money. . . ." Anderson, "Who's Who in the Emmett Till Case."

Q   How long have you lived in Money?

A   One year and a half.

Q   Do you know Mr. Roy Bryant?

A   Yes, Sir.

Q   How long have you known him?

A   Two years.

Q   Do you know Mr. Roy Bryant's general reputation there in the community in which he lives for peace and violence?

A   Yes, Sir.

Q   Is that reputation good or bad?

A   Good.

MR. KELLUM: Take the witness.

CROSS EXAMINATION BY THE DISTRICT ATTORNEY:

Q   Mr. Duke, what particular kind of work do you do on the railroad?

A   I am a section foreman.

Q   That is a good vocation. My father was one also, you see. You say you have lived in Money for a year and a half?

A   Yes, Sir.

Q   And you have known Mr. Bryant for two years?

A   Yes, Sir.

Q   Did you know him before he came to Money?

A   Yes, Sir.

Q   The year and a half that you have been there, you haven't heard of him being involved in any crime or anything like that?

A   No, Sir.

Q   And for that reason, you say his reputation for peace and violence is good?

A   Yes.

Q How many people have you heard discuss his reputation, Mr. Duke?

A I never heard it discussed one way or the other.

Q So actually you don't know just what his general reputation is in and around Money, you having been there for a year and a half, do you?

MR. BRELAND: If the Court please, we object to that. I think that is the best reputation a man can have, if he had never been talked about in his community where he lives.

THE COURT: I think you can ask him what he bases his statement on as to his general reputation.

Q Mr. Duke, since you have been in Money, and before that, I gather that you have formed a friendship with Mr. Bryant, is that right?

A Yes.

Q And as one friend to another, you would naturally come up here today to do what you can to help him out of his difficulty, if your testimony would help, isn't that right?

A Yes, Sir.

Q Did he ask you to come here and testify?

A No, Sir.

Q Who asked you to come up here and testify?

A I believe it was a brother-in-law of the defendant.

Q Mr. Bryant's brother-in-law?

A Yes, Sir.

Q And he asked you to come up here and testify for him?

A I volunteered to come.

Q And you are in sympathy with him, isn't that right?

A Yes, Sir.

MR. CHATHAM: That is all.

(WITNESS EXCUSED.)

* * * *

FRANKLIN SMITH,[9]

A witness introduced for and on behalf of the defendants, being first duly sworn, upon his oath testified as follows?

DIRECT EXAMINATION BY
MR. KELLUM:

Q   This is Mr. Franklin Smith?

A   Yes, Sir.

Q   Where do you live, Mr. Smith?

A   At Money.

Q   Money, Mississippi?

A   That's right.

Q   How long have you lived at Money?

A   About thirty years; since 1926.

Q   I believe Money is in Leflore County, is that right?

A   Yes, Sir.

Q   And the sheriff down there is Mr. George Smith?

A   Yes, Sir.

Q   I notice your name is Smith. Are you any relation to the Sheriff?

A   A cousin.

Q   Do you know Mr. Roy Bryant?

A   Yes, Sir.

Q   Where does he live?

A   At Money.

Q   Do you know Mr. Roy Bryant's general reputation in the community in which he lives for peace and violence?

A   Yes, Sir.

Q   Is that reputation good or bad?

A   It is good.

---

9. Franklin Smith (1918–?) lived in Money, Leflore County. Anderson, "Who's Who in the Emmett Till Case."

MR. KELLUM: Take the witness.

CROSS EXAMINATION BY
THE DISTRICT ATTORNEY:

Q   Mr. Smith, what do you do for a living?

A   My main occupation is farming, Sir. I have a little block of land. And I also have other sidelines.

Q   Mr. Smith, what would you say as to the general reputation of Mr. Roy Bryant in that community since August 28th, of this year?

MR. KELLUM: We object to that, Your Honor.

THE COURT: The objection is sustained.

Q   How long have you known Mr. Bryant, Mr. Smith?

A   About two years.

Q   And your statement here that he is a man of a good general reputation in the community is based on the knowledge that you gained about him during the two years that he has been there at Money, is that right?

A   Yes, Sir.

Q   Is he a member of the same church you are?

A   Yes, Sir.

Q   And you see him there regularly, do you?

A   Occasionally.

MR. CARLTON: We object to that, Your Honor.

THE COURT: The objection is sustained.

Q   Now during the time you have known him, you have formed a friendship with him, haven't you?

A   Yes, Sir.

Q   And on account of that friendship, you volunteered your services to come up here and help him out in any way that you could in this trial, is that right?

A   Yes, Sir.

Q And that is the reason you are up here?

A Yes, Sir.

Q And you are in sympathy with him and you want to do every-thing you can to help him, isn't that right?

A Yes, Sir.

MR. CHATHAM: That is all

(WITNESS EXCUSED.)

* * * *

MR. BRELAND: The defendants rest.

THE COURT: The defendants rest. What says the State?

MR. SMITH: If the Court please, we have nothing in rebuttal.

THE COURT: The State rests.

MR. BRELAND: The State having rested, and the defense having closed their case, the defendants J. W. Milam and Roy Bryant now move the Court to exclude all the evidence for and on behalf of the State of Mississippi, and to direct the jury to return a verdict of Not Guilty.

And now comes the defendant, J. W. Milam, and moves the Court to exclude all the evidence introduced for and on behalf of the State of Mississippi as against him, and to direct the jury to return a verdict of Not Guilty as to the defendant, Mr. J. W. Milam.

And now comes the defendant, Roy Bryant, and moves the Court to exclude all the evidence introduced for and on behalf of the State of Mississippi, and to direct the jury to return a verdict of Not Guilty as to him.

THE COURT: Those motions and each of them will be overruled. The Court will now stand at ease for about five or ten minutes.

PART II

Summary of
Closing Arguments

Summary of
Closing Arguments

As indicated by the fragmentary text of the trial transcript as set out below, the closing arguments of both the prosecution and the defense were never included in the transcript, though the names and order of the lawyers' presentations for the closing arguments were noted. Newspaper and magazine accounts from the time[1] did, however, make it possible to reconstruct the main arguments and provide an informed sense of what was presented in summation to the jury.

---

1. See, e.g., James Hicks, "Miss. DA Pleads in Vain for Lynching Conviction," *Houston Informer*, October 1, 1955, p. 1; Wakefield, "Justice in Summer," p. 285; "Defense Urges Acquittal; State Asserts Defendants Guilty of Cowardly Crime," *Laurel Leader-Call*, September 23, 1955, p. 1; James Featherston & W.C. Shoemaker, "Verdict Awarded in Till Trial," *Jackson Daily News*, September 23, 1955, p. 1; "District Attorney Opens State's Final Arguments in Sumner Trial; Jury May Return Verdict Today," *Daily Corinthian*, September 23, 1955, p. 1; *Commercial Appeal*, September 24, 1955, p. 2; Sam Johnson, "Jury Hears Defense and Prosecution Arguments as Testimony Ends in Kidnapping-Slaying Case," *Greenwood Commonwealth*, September 23, 1955, p. 1; "Till Case Defendants Freed by Jury on Third Round Because of Doubt Concerning Identification of Body," *Jackson-Clarion Ledger*, September 24, 1955, p. 1; John Herbers, "Not Guilty Verdict in Wolf Whistle Murder Trial," *Greenwood Morning Star*, September 24, 1955, p. 1; John M. Popham, "Mississippi Jury Acquits 2 Accused of Youth's Killing," *New York Times*, September 24, 1955, p. 1; John Brehl, "Smoked Fags during Trial Happily Light Up Stogies as Jury Says 'Not Guilty,'" *Toronto Star*, September 26, 1955; "D.A. Asserts Negro Slaying was a 'Cowardly Act' in Final Argument," *Wisconsin Rapids Tribune*, September 23, 1955, p. 1. See also Houck & Grindy, *Emmett Till*, p. 180 n. 61; Tyson, *The Blood of Emmett Till*, pp. 169–76; Anderson, *Emmett Till*, pp. 147–53; Metress, *The Lynching of Emmett Till*, pp. 99–111; Gorn, *Let the People See*, pp. 164–70, 332–33 n. 9.

"After a week of temperatures well into the nineties, the last day of the trial—the first day of autumn—began with thunderstorms and a heavy downpour at dawn. The rain brought no relief inside the courtroom, leaving it just as hot and more humid than ever."[2] The defense ended its arguments in the early morning, whereupon the court proceeded to closing arguments.

The text immediately below is a continuation of the trial transcript.

(At this point in the proceedings, 10:23 a.m., the Court took a recess until 10:38 a.m., this date, at which time the proceedings were resumed.)

(The District Attorney, Mr. Chatham, makes an opening argument to the jury, and also reads his instructions, approved by the Court, to the jury.)

(Mr. Henderson, one of the defense counsel, then reads his instructions, approved by the Court, to the jury.)[3]

(Mr. Carlton, another defense counsel, makes an argument on behalf of the defendants to the jury.)

(Mr. Kellum, another defense counsel, makes further argument on behalf of the defendants to the jury.)

(At this point in the proceedings, 11:55 a.m., the Court took a recess until 1:50 p.m., this date, at which time the proceedings were resumed.)

(Mr. Whitten, another defense counsel, makes the further and final argument on behalf of the defendants to the Court.)

(Mr. Smith, Special Assistant to the District Attorney, makes the closing argument for the State to the jury.)

---

2. Gorn, *Let the People See,* p. 162.

3. Some newspaper accounts indicated that Judge Swango read the instructions to the jury, which is the common practice. See Houck & Grindy, *Emmett Till,* pp. 105, 180 n. 62.

Chapter 9

THE STATE'S CLOSING ARGUMENTS, FIRST ROUND

"THE GUILTY FLEE WHERE NO MAN PURSUETH"

The testimony, limited as it was, came to an end, and the grand judicial finale was about to begin. As it did, "[t]here seemed to be a degree of tension in the courtroom as spectators and newsmen realized that the arguments to the jury would soon begin."[1] Before they did, however, and during a recess, "the court provided newsmen with copies of the instructions that would be handed the jury when it retired to make its decision."[2]

The Court allotted seventy minutes to each side for its closing arguments, all of which time both sides used. As the summations began, the "green plaster walls of the room had grown darker from the clouds of the rain that was [pouring down] outside."[3]

Summations began with Gerald Chatham presenting the prosecution's opening summation. This would be his swan song, for within a year Chatham would be dead—"he suffered from high blood pressure, heart trouble, and severe nosebleeds."[4] He must have sensed this

---

1. Dave Bready, "Sidelights at Sumner Trial," *Greenwood Commonwealth*, September 23, 1955, p. 1.

2. *Ibid.* No complete set of the jury instructions has ever been made public.

3. Dan Wakefield, "Justice in Sumner," *The Nation*, October 1, 1955, in Metress, *The Lynching of Emmett Till*, p. 122.

4. Anderson, *Emmett Till*, p. 73.

would be the end as he "told the jury that he had been District Attorney for 15 years and that he was retiring soon and thanked them for their courtesy."[5]

He spoke for nearly fifty minutes. "His style was dramatic, his voice deep and booming. . . . Sweating freely though he'd shed his coat, he pounded the table, pointed at the defendants, and waved his arms. Journalists expressed admiration for the enthusiasm of his oratory and the quality of his arguments."[6] As recounted by James Hicks, writing for the *Cleveland Call and Post*, by "every courtroom standard, the Mississippi-born district attorney made a great case for the dead colored youth."[7] While Chatham spoke, Bryant puffed on a cigar, Milam peered down at a newspaper, Juanita Milam seemed restless, and Carolyn Bryant appeared to be listening. "The jurors, however, were fixed on Chatham."[8] As Hicks perceived it, "one got the feeling that he was in a Baptist church and that Chatham was the Baptist preacher. For his numerous moments of brilliant oratory, he brought tears to the eyes not only of those seated at the colored press tables but to some of the white listeners as well."[9]

Though cameras were allowed in the courtroom, photographing was only permitted during recess periods. (Ernest Withers's iconic photo of Moses Wright pointing at Roy Bryant proved to be the lone exception—though prohibited, it then went unpunished.[10]) During Chatham's closing argument, "one reporter raised his camera but was

---

5. Murray Kempton, "2 Face Trial as 'Whistle' Kidnappers—Due to Post Bond and Go Home," *New York Post*, September 25, 1955, in Metress, *The Lynching of Emmett Till*, p. 109.

6. Gorn, *Let the People See*, p. 164. See also Anderson, *Emmett Till*, pp. 147–48; Metress, *The Lynching of Emmett Till*, pp. 99–104; Tyson, *The Blood of Emmett Till*, pp. 169–71.

7. James Hicks, "Called Lynch-Murder, 'Morally, Legally' Wrong," *Cleveland Call and Post*, October 1, 1955, in Metress, *The Lynching of Emmett Till*, p. 102.

8. Anderson, *Emmett Till*, p. 148.

9. Hicks, "Called Lynch-Murder, 'Morally, Legally'" Wrong," p. 102.

10. See Till-Mobley & Benson, *Death of Innocence*, p. 174. See also Geoff Bennett, Harry Zahn, & Juliet Fuisz, "The Double Life of Civil Rights Photographer Ernest Withers," PBS, July 31, 2022, https://www.pbs.org/video/ernie-s-secret-1659294040/ ("Withers was also an FBI informant funneling information to the bureau about the civil rights movement and its leaders.").

quickly spotted by Judge Swango, who, interrupting Chatham, ordered the erring photographer to leave the room."[11]

Recall that from the very outset Chatham never called for the death penalty "since," as he put it, "a substantial part of the state's evidence is circumstantial." And as a tactical matter, he noted that he was "not going to give the prospective jurors a chance to disqualify themselves because they don't believe in a death sentence." He maintained that position throughout, asking instead for a life imprisonment sentence.[12]

Finally, though the court reporter noted that Chatham read "his instructions, approved by the Court, to the jury," there does not appear to be any published record of that. The common practice is for the lawyers on both sides to draft proposed jury instructions and for the judge to thereafter review and approve them and then read them to the jury.

CHATHAM FOR THE PROSECUTION: MAIN CLOSING ARGUMENTS

1. *Premeditated Crimes—Kidnapping and Murder*: To demonstrate malice aforethought, Chatham spoke dramatically: "[T]he very first word of the state's testimony was dripping with the blood of Emmett Till. What were those words, gentlemen? They were, 'Preacher, preacher. I want that boy from Chicago—that boy that did the talking in Money,' they said. That wasn't an invitation to that card game [as] they claimed."[13] The crimes the defendants committed were neither done in a provoked moment nor the result of any reckless behavior. No, they were *calculated* crimes. By way of additional evidence of malicious minds, Chatham shouted, "[To] hide that dastardly, cowardly act, they tied barbed wire to his neck and a heavy gin fan and dumped him into the

---

11. Anderson, *Emmett Till*, p. 149.

12. Sam Johnson, "In Trial of White Men at Sumner: Selection of Jury Nearing Completion," *Greenwood Commonwealth* (AP), September 19, 1955, p. 9; "Mississippi Jurors Free Pair in Slaying of Vacationing Boy, 14," *Philadelphia Inquirer*, September 24, 1955, pp. 1, 9; "Two White Men on Trial for Murder of Youngster: Indication State Would Not Ask for Death Penalty," *Birmingham World*, September 20, 1955, p. 1.

13. Anderson, *Emmett Till*, pp. 148, 428 n. 106.

river for the turtles and fish."[14] This was evidence of a "depraved heart murder." Even if not, it certainly was evidence of premeditated kidnapping leading up to murder.

2. *Duty to Protect Violated, Murderous Punishment Inflicted*: Once Bryant and Milam abducted Till from Moses Wright's home, at the very least they had a duty to protect the minor. As Chatham put it, they were "absolutely morally and legally responsible for his protection." But they breached that duty with vicious abandon. If indeed Emmett deserved to be punished, the worst they ought to have done was something far less severe. Speaking as one "born and bred in the South" ("I'll live and die in the South"), he stated that "the very worst punishment that could have occurred or should have occurred, if they had any idea in their minds this boy did anything, would have been to take a razor strop, turn him over a barrel, and give him a little beating."[15] He added, "I've whipped my boy. You've whipped yours." And then to put things in context, he emphasized that "you deal with a child as a child—not as if he were a man."[16] But that is not what Bryant and Milam had done; rather, their gunpoint abduction was nothing short of a "command of a summary court-martial with the death penalty."[17]

The state's argument boiled down to this: while a man might severely punish another man for whistling at his wife, that kind of punishment should never be meted out to a boy. What was left unstated, of course, is what every white male Mississippi juror knew: this was not just a boy, but a *Negro* boy. Race changed everything. By that bigoted measure, there was no duty owed to protect and no punishment too severe to inflict. Perhaps that explains Chatham's refusal to make race an explicit part of the state's case.

---

14. *Ibid.*, p. 148, 428–29 n. 107; Johnson, "In Trial of White Men at Sumner," p. 1.
15. Gorn, *Let the People See*, pp. 165, 332–33 n. 9; Tyson, *The Blood of Emmett Till*, pp. 170, 253 n. 14.
16. Anderson, *Emmett Till*, pp. 148, 429 n. 108.
17. Gorn, *Let the People See*, pp. 164, 332–33 n. 9.

3. *The Defendants' Presence at the Scenes of the Crimes*: Recall that Moses Wright testified as to Bryant and then Milam's presence at his home, the site of the kidnapping. Moreover, "Willie Reed told you he saw Emmett Till that Sunday morning on the Milam place and that he told you he later saw J. W. Milam with the pistol in his hand and that Moses Wright saw him also with a pistol." To buttress his argument, Chatham added, "If Willie Reed had been lying, the five lawyers for the defense would have had fifty people up here to say he was not qualified to speak. . . . But did they do this? They did not. They couldn't do it because Willie was telling the truth. But the next time that anyone saw that little boy his feet were sticking up out of the river and he was dead."[18]

Here, the best Chatham could do was to draw an inference since no witness actually *saw* either of the defendants murder Till. If one thus looked at the *circumstances*—angry men coming in the night with guns and the man with a gun at the scene of the beating—one might reasonably infer that these two men were the killers. After all, they had motive, and witnesses placed one or both of them at the scenes of the crimes.

4. *Establishing the Corpus Delicti—Identifying the Murder Victim*: Contrary to the incriminating evidence set out in Chapter 2, and as discussed in Chapter 7 and elsewhere, the defense went to great lengths to attempt to prove, by Sheriff Strider and so-called "expert witnesses," that the body pulled from the Tallahatchie River was not that of Emmett Till. To rebut this, Chatham advanced three main arguments: (1) Recognition by a loved one, (2) Sheriff's Strider's conflicting pretrial actions and statements, and (3) the absurdity of the expert witnesses' testimony.

The first argument, familiarity, began with an embellished story about Chatham's young son's dog that had been missing for days. When the dog was found in a ravine, its body was badly decomposed. "That dog's body was rotting and the meat was falling off its bones," is how Chatham presented it to the jury. But "my little boy pointed to it and said, 'That's old Shep, Pa. That's

---

18. Anderson, *Emmett Till*, pp. 149, 429 n. 112; Tyson, *The Blood of Emmett Till*, p. 170.

old Shep. My boy didn't need an undertaker or a sheriff to identify his dog. And we don't need them here to identify Emmett
Till. All we need is someone who loved and cared for him."[19] That
point led all too naturally to his next one, a yet stronger one—
Emmett's mother. "If there was a left ear, one hairline," Chatham
emphasized, "then I say to you Mamie Bradley was God's given
witness to identify him."[20] Mamie Till-Bradley's identification of
her son, plus her husband's "L. T." ring on the finger, made it clear
that everyone who saw the body knew whose it was.

The next point in this line of argument concerned Sheriff
Strider's conflicting pretrial and trial statements. Sheriff Strider
had, after all, signed his name with "Till" on the death certificate
and then sent the body of that "little nigger boy in the river" to a
Black mortuary.[21]

5. *Willie Reed's Testimony*: This allowed the prosecution to high-
light four key points: (1) evidence that Reed saw a pickup truck
with white men in front and Black men in the bed of the truck,
(2) evidence that placed J. W. at the shed scene, (3) evidence that
Reed heard screams from the shed, and (4) evidence that the
same pickup truck drove away with the same group of men.
Though circumstantial and mainly (if not entirely) as to Milam's
guilt, such evidence pointed to criminal behavior.

6. *The Unreliability of So-Called "Expert" Witnesses' Testimony*:
"Everyone who has testified here has stated that this was the body
of a colored boy. When the sheriff was first told of the body, his
informer said, 'There's a little nigger boy in the river.'" And then
to drive the point home with a touch of sarcasm, Chatham added,
"Now we have this doctor [Luther Otken] come up here with all
his degrees and titles tell us that he could not tell whether it was

19. Gorn, *Let the People See*, pp. 166, 332–33 n. 9; Anderson, *Emmett Till*, pp. 148, 429
n. 109 (Chatham's son said that "his father exaggerated the story, but that it was the type
of anecdote, complete with embellishments, that good attorneys use in court."); Tyson,
The Blood of Emmett Till, pp. 170–71, 253 n. 15.

20. Hicks, "Called Lynch-Murder, 'Morally, Legally' Wrong," p. 103; Tyson, *The Blood
of Emmett Till*, pp. 171, 253 n. 15; Anderson, *Emmett Till*, pp. 148, 429 n. 109; Gorn, *Let the
People See*, pp. 166, 332–33 n. 9.

21. Anderson, *Emmett Till*, pp. 149, 429 n. 111.

a white boy or colored boy. . . . I tell you, the people of this state are wasting their money sending a man to school and educating him to be a doctor when he is not able to tell black from white; I don't want him writing any prescription for me."[22]

7. *The Morally Right and Southern Tradition Argument*: Closing arguments are not confined to legal arguments; they often include emotive arguments designed to arouse the jurors' sympathy. Thus it was that Chatham looked at the jurors and declared, "I am concerned with what is morally right or wrong." And then invoking southern traditions, he added, "To be concerned with anything else will be dangerous to the precepts and traditions of the South. If your verdict is influenced by anything except the evidence, you will endanger every custom and tradition we hold dear." To ignore such traditions and what is morally right, he told the court and jury, will have consequences: "The next time it may be you who will be sitting here crying."[23]

That ended the first round of the prosecution's summation. Robert Smith III would offer the rebuttal to the closing arguments made by the defense team. As for the third member of the prosecution's team, Hamilton Caldwell, he remained silent throughout the trial and closing arguments.

---

22. Metress, *The Lynching of Emmett Till*, p. 103; Gorn, *Let the People See*, pp. 165, 332–33 n. 9; Anderson, *Emmett Till*, pp. 149, 429 n. 111.

23. Gorn, *Let the People See*, pp. 166, 332–33 n. 9; Tyson, *The Blood of Emmett Till*, pp. 170, 253 n. 14; Metress, *The Lynching of Emmett Till*, p. 102.

Chapter 10

———

THE DEFENSE'S CLOSING ARGUMENTS "EVERY ANGLO-SAXON ONE OF YOU"

The defense team used three attorneys—Sidney Carlton, J. W. Kellum, and John Whitten—to present its main closing arguments. The court reporter noted that, at the outset of the defense's summation, "Mr. [Harvey] Henderson, one of the defense counsel, . . . [read] his instructions, approved by the Court, to the jury." Henderson, who otherwise said little during the trial, is reported to have opened the defense's summation with a brief comment admonishing the jurors that they must be "convinced beyond a reasonable doubt and moral certainty"[1] of each of the two defendants' guilt as to the charge of murder.

SUMMATION: THIRTEEN CLOSING ARGUMENTS BY THREE DEFENSE LAWYERS

SIDNEY CARLTON (*5 arguments*)

Sidney Carlton, clad in a dark suit, spoke next. Like Gerald Chatham, Carlton, the man who later became president of the Mississippi Bar Association, "was excited, and occasionally shouted,"[2] though his

———

1. Anderson, *Emmett Till*, pp. 149, 429 n. 114, citing James Featherston & W.C. Shoemaker, "Verdict Awarded in Till Trial," *Jackson Daily News*, September 23, 1955, pp. 1, 9.

2. Anderson, *Emmett Till*, pp. 149, 429 n. 115.

style was "less theatrical than Chatham's."[3] Even so, and as the trial had already borne out, at the right moment he could raise "his voice like the lash of a whip."[4] As he prepared to speak, Carlton "poured a paper cup of water from the green pitcher on the judge's desk."[5] He then proceeded to make five main arguments:

1. *No Evidence of Motive*: It was a strange twist. On the one hand, everyone knew why the defendants were being charged: the wolf whistle, and whatever else purportedly preceded it, prompted their ire. On the other hand, Carolyn Bryant's testimony (which strongly suggested Till was the "nigger man" offender) was offered outside the presence of the jury and then deemed inadmissible. Take that testimony out of the equation and, in Carlton's repetitive words, "Where's the motive? Where's the motive?" That explains, he stressed, why the prosecution spoke in "generalities[;] because the facts just don't bear out the guilt of these defendants."[6]

2. *No Link to the Defendants*: This argument was offered in tandem with the no motive argument. Again, if one excluded Carolyn Bryant's testimony, then the "only testimony that Emmett Till did anything with these defendants was Moses Wright's testimony that he heard the boy had done something." But if Moses Wright in fact knew that that boy was Emmett, Carlton added, "he would have gotten him out and whipped him himself." But he didn't. Thus, the inference was that since there was no link to Emmett Till, there could be no connection with the defendants. As Carlton put it, "The State did not link up the dead boy with the defendants."[7] To drive that point home, he made a bold move; he referenced evidence deemed to be inadmissible, namely, the "testimony by Bryant's wife did not implicate Till."[8]

---

3. Gorn, *Let the People See*, pp. 166, 332–33 n. 9.

4. Murray Kempton, "He Went All the Way," *New York Post*, September 22, 1955, p. 5.

5. Wakefield, "Justice in Sumner," p. 181.

6. Anderson, *Emmett Till*, pp. 149–50, 429 n. 115; Gorn, *Let the People See*, pp. 166, 332–33 n. 9.

7. Gorn, *Let the People See*, pp. 167, 332–33 n. 9.

8. Johnson, "Jury Hears Defense and Prosecution Arguments," p. 1.

3. *No Evil Intent*: One of the strongest arguments leveled against Roy Bryant was Moses Wright's testimony that Bryant had announced himself by name when he came to Wright's home late at night. In an attempt to counter that, Carlton argued that if Bryant had any malevolent intent, he never would have identified himself so openly. He turned to the jurors and asked, "How many Bryants are there in the state of Mississippi? Had any of you gone to Moses Wright's house with evil intent, would you have given your name? No one is that stupid; there's nothing reasonable about the state's case." And then with a rush of bravado, he added, "If that's identification, if that places these men at the scene, then none of us are safe."[9] By thus framing his argument, Carlton sought to transform one of the state's strongest arguments into a clever one for the defense. (Of course, Carlton knew otherwise. As Devery Anderson has noted, "In a deposition taken from Bryant on September 6, Carlton learned that his client 'did identify [him]self as Mr. Bryant when he went into the house.'"[10])

4. *Uncertainty as to Identity of Defendant*: This line of argument sought to either remove J. W. Milam from the scene of the kidnapping at Moses Wright's home or create doubt as to the possibility of identifying him as being there. Wright testified that it was dark and that the man he saw with Bryant was "big and bald." Surely, this was not sufficient to say beyond a reasonable doubt that this was J. W. Milam.[11]

5. *Uncertainty as to Identity of Corpse/No Scientific Evidence*: Carlton reminded the jurors that three witnesses (a medical doctor, an embalmer, and Sheriff Strider) had testified that the identity of the body was beyond recognition. But what of Mamie Till-Bradley's identification of her son? To that, Carlton had an answer, one that contested the trustworthiness of motherhood itself: "Sometimes mothers believe what they want to believe. I'm

9. *Ibid.*
10. Anderson, *Emmett Till*, pp. 150, 429 n. 117.
11. *Ibid.*, p. 150; Gorn, *Let the People See*, p. 167; Tyson, *The Blood of Emmett Till*, p. 171; and Metress, *The Lynching of Emmett Till*, p. 101.

sure Mamie Bradley thinks that the body was her son, but scientific facts show otherwise. We think we could have rested our case when the state rested. The state didn't prove anything."[12]

Sidney Carlton closed by referencing the great novelist Charles Dickens. The passage he quoted, with some revision, was from the final words of *A Tale of Two Cities*—words uttered by the novel's central character, barrister Sydney Carton. By putting Carton's words in Carlton's mouth, the savvy lawyer sought to make the jurors believe that, by acquitting the defendants, they were doing something noble: "May you feel, in the words of Charles Dickens, that 'tis a far, far better thing you do now than you have ever done."[13]

J. W. KELLUM *(4 arguments)*

In a 1979 video interview for *Eyes on the Prize*, Joseph W. Kellum opined that the trial had been a "fair" one and that there was a "lack of proof showing that the defendants were the criminal agent," so much so that "if there had been a conviction . . . [,] the Supreme Court of this state would have never let the conviction stand."[14] That opinion, championed nearly a quarter-century after the trial, informed how he began his four additional arguments following Carlton's summation.

1. *The Reasonable Doubt Argument*: First echoing and then amplifying what Harvey Henderson had said at the outset of the defense's summation, Kellum returned to the burden of proof ar-

---

12. Anderson, *Emmett Till*, pp. 151, 429 n. 119; Metress, *The Lynching of Emmett Till*, p. 110.

13. "Defense Lawyer Quotes Dickens in Final Plea," *Jackson State Times*, September 23, 1955; Anderson, *Emmett Till*, pp. 151, 429 n. 120; Kempton, "2 Face Trial as 'Whistle' Kidnappers," in Metress, *The Lynching of Emmett Till*, p. 110; Charles Dickens, ed. Richard Maxwell, *A Tale of Two Cities*, New York: Penguin (2003), p. 390 ("It is a far, far better thing that I do, than I have ever done; it is a far, far better rest that I go to than I have ever known.").

14. Interview with J. W. Kellum and Amzie Moore, conducted by Blackside Inc., August 29, 1979, for *Eyes on the Prize: America's Civil Rights Years (1954–1965)*, Washington University Libraries, Film and Media Archive, Henry Hampton Collection, http://repository.wustl.edu/downloads/9593tw90p.

gument: "We don't have to prove to you that it was not Till's body; we only have to raise a reasonable doubt."[15]

2. *The Time Discrepancy Argument*: Here Kellum repeated Dr. Otken's claim that the body discovered would have been in the river for eight to ten days, whereas Till had only been missing for three days. Assuming, hypothetically, that the body might be that of Emmett Till, the time discrepancy was too great to confirm that.[16] Of course, if that were true, Till would still be alive.

In the following two arguments, Kellum shifted conceptual gears. He moved from the legal to the rhetorical, from the rational to the parochial and then to the eternal:

3. *The Civics Argument—The Land of the Free*: This argument was designed to appeal to the jurors' southern-loving honor and pride–free from northern norms aimed at destroying the southern way of life. As "the custodians of American civilization," properly understood, they had to ensure that a guilty verdict not be rendered lest "freedom [be] lost forever." As a "peerage of democracy," it was their solemn duty to acquit the defendants. To provide yet more color to his arguments, he turned toward the jury and said, "I'll be waiting for you when you come out." "If your verdict is guilty," he added with dramatic emphasis, "if your verdict is guilty, I want you to tell me where is the land of the free and the home of the brave. I say to you, gentlemen, your forefathers will absolutely roll in their graves."[17] In other words, there was more, much more, at stake here than the niceties of the law; there was a *tradition* to be preserved—one in which Black people knew their place.

---

15. Gorn, *Let the People See*, pp. 167–68, 332–33 n. 9; Anderson, *Emmett Till*, pp. 151, 429 n. 121.

16. Gorn, *Let the People See*, pp. 168, 332–33 n. 9; Anderson, *Emmett Till*, pp. 151, 429 n. 122.

17. Anderson, *Emmett Till*, pp. 151, 429 n. 122; Tyson, *The Blood of Emmett Till*, p. 172.

4. *The Eternity Argument—The Summons to Cross the Great Divide*: With pride comes righteousness, and so Kellum turned to the eternal as a way of justifying the defense of his two clients charged with murdering a boy: "I want you to think of the future," is how he began. "When your summons comes to cross the Great Divide, and, as you enter your father's house—a home not made by hand but eternal in the heavens, you can look back to where your father's feet have trod and see your good record written in the sands of time. And when you go down to your lonely silent tomb to a sleep that knows no dreams, I want you to hold in the palm of your hand a record of service to God and your fellow man. And the only way you can do this is to turn these boys loose."[18] The intended impression was another variation on preserving the southern way, but this time shrouded in a more grandiose vernacular.

With those four arguments, Kellum returned to his seat. As noon neared (it was 11:55 a.m.), Judge Swango declared the court in recess for lunch until 1:50 p.m.

JOHN W. WHITTEN JR. *(4 arguments)*

At the time of the trial in 1955, John Whitten "was a young man with glasses and an empty face."[19] Clean-shaven and pale, he came to court "in a neatly pressed suit and a white shirt that defied perspiration. . . ."[20] That face and his role in the trial, especially his closing arguments for the defense, garnered considerable public attention, as did some of the things he said and did after the trial. When he died in February 2003 (he was eighty-three), the obituary in the *Greenwood Commonwealth* listed his life accomplishments: "[He] served as counsel for the Tallahatchie County Board of Supervisors for 50 years and to the Tallahatchie General Hospital for 44 years. He was also the attorney for

---

18. Kempton, "2 Face Trial as 'Whistle' Kidnappers," p. 110. The Kellum quote, as Kempton noted, was "stolen from the late Paul Johnson, who used to use it in his habitually losing campaigns for governor of the state. It is a blend of William Cullen Bryant and Robert Ingersoll." *Ibid.*, p. 111.

19. *Ibid.*, p. 108.

20. Wakefield, "Justice in Sumner," in Metress, *The Lynching of Emmett Till*, p. 123.

the Yazoo-Mississippi Levee Board for 20 years. He was a member of Sumner Presbyterian Church."[21] Though that paper had conducted extensive coverage of the Till trial, in the end Whitten's significant role in it went unmentioned in his obituary.

As revealed in the four arguments listed below, Whitten's summation was by far the most preposterous and the most openly racist.

1. *The Plot to Shame the South*: This claim was yet another attempt to a sway the jury that the real culprits in all of this were not the two defendants but a cadre of others hell bent on annihilating the southern way of life. It was a continuation of Kellum's argument but this time with even more bravado: "There are people in the United States who want to defy the customs of the South. . . . [They] would commit perhaps any crime known to man in order to widen the gap. These people are not all in Gary and Chicago; they are in Jackson and Vicksburg; and, if Moses Wright knows one, he didn't have to go far to find him. And they include some of the most astute students of psychology known anywhere. They include doctors and undertakers, and they have ready access to a corpse which could meet their purpose."[22]

   Though Whitten cleverly "avoided mentioning him by name, . . . the latter reference was to Dr. T.R.M. Howard, whose clinic in Mound Bayou could easily have provided a body,"[23] or so Whitten would have had the jury believe.

2. *The Evil Conspiracy and the Planted Ring*: Building on his claim that there were those plotting to shame the South, Whitten took his argument a giant step further: "They would not be above putting a rotting, stinking body in the river in the hope it would be identified as Emmett Till."[24] In other words, this evil plot was concocted "by organizations who would like to destroy the southern way of life." Here again, the implicit reference was to

---

21. "John Wallace Whitten Jr.," Obituary, *Greenwood Commonwealth*, February 19, 2003.

22. Kempton, "2 Face Trial as 'Whistle' Kidnappers," p. 108.

23. Anderson, *Emmett Till*, pp. 152, 430 n. 127. See also Beito & Beito, *T.R.M. Howard*, p. 134.

24. Johnson, "Jury Hears Defense and Prosecution Arguments," p. 1.

Dr. Howard and his circle of friends at the NAACP. He assured the jurors that it was "not as fantastic as it may seem."[25] (This unsubstantiated claim had been floated early on by Sheriff Strider in the days before the trial.[26])

As for the "L. T." ring found on the body (the one with the initials of Emmett's father on it), that, too, was planted by sinister agents hostile to the South. As reported by Dan Wakefield in his trial coverage for *The Nation*, "Mr. Whitten went on to declare he had an answer for the state's most convincing evidence—the ring of Emmett Till that was found on the body discovered in the Tallahatchie River. The body really wasn't Emmett Till, Whitten said, and the ring might have possibly been planted on it by the agents of a sinister group that is trying to destroy the social order of the South. . . ."[27] Here again, this argument was "only made in closing arguments. They didn't present any so-called evidence during the trial. They only allowed it in closing arguments, which didn't allow for any cross-examination on that point."[28]

Word of this purported conspiracy between Moses Wright and a sinister group may have found its way to the old sharecropper. "Just after Whitten finished, Moses Wright was observed in the sheriff's office, collecting his witness fee and preparing to leave. He didn't have to wait for the end of what he started." When asked if he was preparing to leave Mississippi, he replied, "I don't know. I got this country so scrounged down in me that I just don't know." With that, Moses Wright walked out of the courthouse.[29]

3. *The Disregard the Facts and Law Argument*: It was yet another bold move when Whitten, the lawyer, counseled the jury to disregard the law: "It is within your power to disregard all the facts,

25. Anderson, *Emmett Till*, pp. 152, 429 n. 124.

26. "Sheriff Says Body Found May Not Be Chicago Boy," *Richmond Times-Dispatch* (AP), September 3, 1955.

27. Wakefield, "Justice in Sumner," in Metress, *The Lynching of Emmett Till*, p. 123. See also Anderson, *Emmett Till*, pp. 152, 430 n. 126.

28. Kemper, interview with Devery Anderson, (23:00 through 23:55 minutes).

29. Kempton, "2 Face Trial as 'Whistle' Kidnappers," p. 111.

the evidence, and the law, and bring any decision you like based on any whim. There is no way anyone can punish you for any decision you make. The last time an attempt was made by a judge to punish a jury for refusing to follow his instructions was in England in the time of Charles II, and this was overruled. . . ."[30]

4. *The Anglo-Saxon Argument*: If the facts, evidence, and law were to be disregarded, the jurors were nonetheless encouraged to acquit the defendants if only to preserve the Anglo-Saxon racial tradition as it had long played out in their white world populated by Black people: "You are our hope and confidence to send these defendants back to their families happy. . . . [I have full confidence that] every last Anglo-Saxon one of you have [*sic*] the courage to free these men."[31]

With those words and arguments, John Whitten closed the case for the defense. In the years afterward he held steadfast and had no regrets. As for his role in the case, he was emphatic: "It didn't bother me at all. . . . If I went to the moral heart of every case that came to me, I'd starve to death. . . ."[32]

30. Tyson, *The Blood of Emmett Till*, pp. 173, 254 n. 26.

31. Kempton, "2 Face Trial as 'Whistle' Kidnappers," p. 108; Anderson, *Emmett Till*, pp. 152, 430 n. 128.

32. Hendrickson, *Sons of Mississippi*, pp. 10, 11.

Chapter 11

THE STATE'S CLOSING ARGUMENTS, SECOND ROUND
COUNTERING "FAR-FETCHED" CLAIMS

Robert B. Smith III, a marine captain in World War II and a former FBI agent, rose to give the last round of closing arguments for the State. Whatever remarks Smith might have prepared in advance, the vile untruths uttered by Whitten required a smack-down rebuttal. Since none of what Whitten had said about his various conspiracy theories had heretofore been entered into the trial record (and was therefore left immune from cross-examination), any refutation had to occur in the state's final round of closing arguments. And so Robert Smith set his sights on the closing arguments advanced by John Whitten.

1. *Outside Influence: A Pragmatic Perspective*: If there was anything that riled southerners, it was the condemnation of their way of life by self-righteous northerners. Smith agreed with Whitten that such outsiders were indeed trying to cast the South, and Mississippi in particular, in an evil light. "[T]here is no doubt that outside influences are trying to destroy our way of life," Smith declared. By his estimate, a not guilty verdict would only empower such outside forces in a spirited campaign against Mississippi. "If J. W. Milam and Roy Bryant are turned loose, it will serve the purpose of the very organizations that have come down here to stir up trouble. If you convict them, no one can use this to raise funds to fight us in our defense of southern traditions. . . .

305

[Moreover, o]nce we take the life, liberty, or pursuit of happiness from anyone, we will be put on the defensive and become vulnerable in trying to justify our stand."[1] Smith's take was a pragmatic one, the truth of which was buttressed by the national and international attention the savage murder had already received.

2. *Preserving the Rights of Everyone: A Patriotic Perspective*: It fell to Smith, on the one hand, to inspire the twelve white jurors to embrace what was best in their tradition while, on the other hand, encouraging them to reject what was worst in that same tradition. To that end, he spoke of the need for impartial justice duly sensitive to the rights of all citizens: "Gentlemen, we're on the defensive," is how he began. In other words, justice itself was being attacked here. "Only so long as we can preserve the rights of everyone—white or black—can we keep our way of life." That *our* meant safeguarding the rights of *all* people, no matter what the color of their skin. "Emmett Till down here in Mississippi was a citizen of the United States; he was entitled to his life and liberty."[2] Smith's take here was a patriotic one, the truth of which would take a long time to become self-evident. But in order to buttress that line of argument, Smith had to *remove* the question of race from the legal equation. It was highly ironic since the essence of the crimes committed turned on Emmett Till's race. To go there, however, Smith would surely have enraged the all-white jury. It was a sign of the times, a hallmark of the history of racism itself: when race was the motive for murder, it was erased from the record.

3. *Response to a Far-Fetched Claim*: Whitten's closing argument about outside groups "planting a dead body in the river and claim[ing] it was Emmett Till" and Moses Wright's part in such conspiracy, was, as Smith portrayed it, "the most far-fetched argument I've ever heard in a courtroom." After all, he added, Wright was "a good old country Negro, and you know he's not going to lie." As for Willie Reed's testimony, it took a lot of cour-

---

1. Anderson, *Emmett Till*, pp. 153, 430 n. 130; Gorn, *Let the People See*, pp. 169, 332 n. 8.

2. Kempton, "2 Face Trial as 'Whistle' Kidnappers," p. 108.

age to come into an almost all-white courtroom and accuse two white men of murder—"I don't know but what Willie Reed had more nerve than I have," said Smith.[3]

Thus did Smith end the arguments for the prosecution, and with that he returned to the prosecution's table.

* * * *

All the legal arguments had been made, all twenty-two witnesses had testified, and the State and defense teams had completed their summations. "Judge Swango had only brief instructions to the [jury] before excusing them, and also provided them a form upon which to write their verdict."[4] Before they were excused, however, the "13th alternate juror [Willie Havens] was dismissed . . . and 12 short-sleeved men, mostly farmers, entered a small room and began considering the case against"[5] the two defendants. It was about 2:35 p.m. when the large door to the jury room, "missing both its latch and lock, was closed shut. . . ."[6]

Once the jurors left the room, Mamie Till-Bradley turned to Congressman Charles Diggs of Michigan, a civil rights activist who had been with her throughout the trial, and said, "The jury has retired, and it's time for us to retire." He replied, "What, and miss the verdict?" She thought that this was "one verdict he might want to miss." As she recalled in her 2003 memoir, "If that jury came back with an acquittal, then white folks were going to know for sure they could get away with murder. It was going to be an open season on black folks and we were going to be the prime targets. I was not about to wait around for that."[7] With that, she left with Diggs, Willie Reed, and Dr. T.R.M. Howard, and moved through the thick crowds back to safety at Howard's place at Mound Bayou. She thus rendered her own verdict even before the jury rendered its.

---

3. Kempton, "2 Face Trial as 'Whistle' Kidnappers," pp. 108–09; Anderson, *Emmett Till*, p. 153; Gorn, *Let the People See*, pp. 168–69, 332 n. 8; Tyson, *The Blood of Emmett Till*, pp. 175, 254 n. 30.

4. Anderson, *Emmett Till*, pp. 153, 430 n. 132.

5. Sam Johnson, "District Attorney Not Concerned by Outside Agitation and Pressure," *Greenwood Commonwealth* (AP), September 23, 1955, p. 1.

6. Anderson, *Emmett Till*, p. 153.

7. Till-Mobley & Benson, *Death of Innocence*, p. 189.

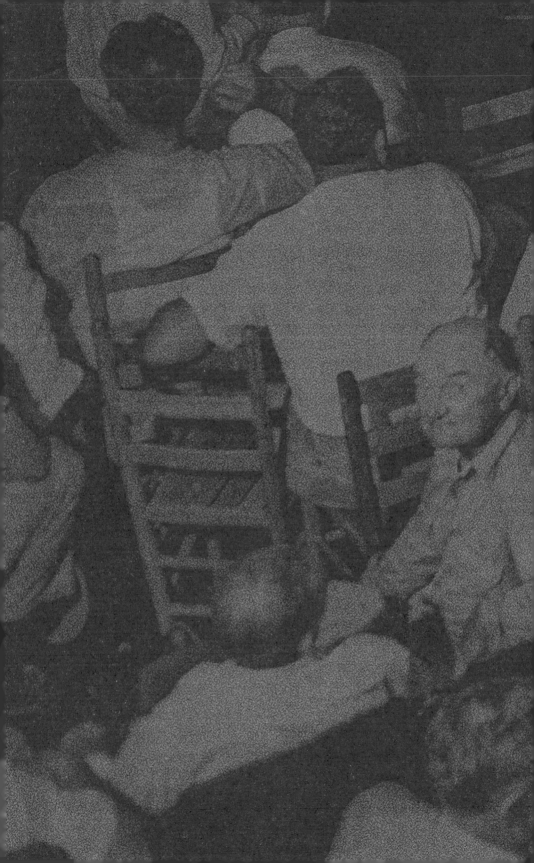

PART III

The Verdict

Chapter 12

THE PREDICTABLE
OUTCOME

"Mamie Bradley was not in the courtroom when the verdict was read. Having guessed what the outcome of the trial would be, she'd left Mississippi and was at a mass rally in Detroit on the day the verdict was announced. But by the next day, she had returned home to Chicago and checked into the Provident Hospital for what the [*Chicago*] *Defender* described as 'nervous fatigue.'"[1]

At this point, the text of the official transcript continues below:

(THE COURT then appointed Mr. [James] J. A. Shaw, Jr., as spokesman for the jury. Also, the Court excused Mr. Willie Havens, who had been selected as the one extra juror to hear this case, and he was discharged from further jury duty by the Court.)

(At 2:34 p.m., this date, the jury retired to the jury room for deliberation,[2] and at 3:42 p.m., this date, it was announced that the jury has reached a verdict, and at that time the jury returned to the courtroom, and the proceedings continued as follows:)

THE COURT: Have you gentlemen reached a verdict?

---

1. Michaeli, *The Defender*, pp. 331, 581 n. 31, citing "Till's Mother, Reed Collapse," *Chicago Defender*, October 8, 1955, p. 1.

2. "The jury had been secluded in the Delta Inn, a hotel about one hundred yards from the courthouse in Sumner. . . . It was 'rumored that every [juror] was contacted by a member of the Citizens Council to make sure he voted 'the right way.'" Whitaker, MA thesis, p. 154 (based on interviews with jurors).

MR. SHAW (The Spokesman for the jury [juror number 4]): Yes, Sir, we have.[3]

THE COURT: Mr. Clerk, will you read the verdict?

MR. COX, THE CLERK: [3:43 PM, CDT] "Not Guilty."[4]

THE COURT: I don't believe that is in accordance with a proper verdict that should be returned. That is not worded properly. Will you Gentlemen of the jury return to the jury room and bring in a correct verdict. You had a form to be used for that. But this is not a complete verdict.

(The jury then again retired to the jury room, and returned shortly thereafter to the courtroom, and the proceedings continued as follows:)

THE COURT: Have you gentlemen reached a complete verdict now? Has your verdict been made in accordance with the form that was given you?

MR. SHAW: Yes, Sir.[5]

THE COURT: Will you give the verdict to the clerk, please, Mr. Shaw. (A paper was handed to the clerk.)

Will you now read the verdict, Mr. Clerk.[6]

---

3. "A shout of celebration went up from the crowd, and the judge demanded quiet." Tyson, *The Blood of Emmett Till*, p. 179.

4. "The jury cast three ballots. According to one juror, all the ballots were alike—each "not guilty." Sheriff-elect Harry Dogan sent word to the jurors to wait a while before coming out—to make it "look good." It was hot. The jury sent out for Cokes. After one hour and seven minutes of 'deliberation,' the jury returned." As one juror put it, "If we hadn't stopped to drink pop, it wouldn't have taken that long." Whitaker, "A Case Study of Southern Justice," pp. 154–55, 211 (footnotes omitted). "The first tabulation had been nine for acquittal, three abstaining, the second ten for acquittal, two abstaining." The third ballot was unanimous. Whitfield, *A Death in the Delta*, p. 42. See also Brooks, Shin, & Jones, "Author of 1963 Thesis Investigation" ("three members of the jury required convincing by other jurors after first voting to convict Till's killers").

5. After the verdict was rendered, County prosecuting attorney James Hamilton Caldwell surmised, "The simple fact was that a Negro had insulted a white woman. Her husband and his relative would not be prosecuted for killing him." Whitaker, "A Case Study in Southern Justice," p. 211 (quote from Whitaker referencing Caldwell).

6. "The fresh cigars burning in their mouths and with their clan all around them, J. W. Milam and Roy Bryant . . . leaned back in their chairs and heard a 67-minute jury of their peers acquit them" of murder. Kempton, "2 Face Trial as 'Whistle' Kidnappers."

MR. COX: "We, the jury, find the defendants: Not Guilty."[7]

(At 3:50 p.m., this date, Court was adjourned.)[8]

(TRIAL COMPLETED.[9])

* * * *

CERTIFICATE OF COURT REPORTER

(STATE OF MISSISSIPPI)

(Certificate, TATE COUNTY)

I, **JAMES T. O'DAY**, specially appointed Official Court Reporter for the Seventeenth Judicial District of the State, do hereby certify that the above and forgoing pages of typewritten matter contain a true and correct copy of my shorthand notes, properly transcribed, as taken down by me during the trial in the case of:

STATE OF MISSISSIPPI VS.

J. W. MILAM and ROY BRYANT

Circuit Court, Second District of Tallahatchie County, State of Mississippi.

---

7. "Having been sternly warned by the judge to refrain from emotional outbursts when the verdict was returned, white onlookers quietly shook men's hands in congratulation while the blacks in the courtroom stood stunned." Michaeli, *The Defender*, p. 331. About the same time, "[Sheriff] Strider reached forward to congratulate" the defendants. Herbers & Rosen, *Deep South Dispatch*, p. 66.

After their murder trial, Milam and Bryant "were abandoned by all their supporters. . . . [T]he white folks of the Delta didn't appreciate having all that attention that Bryant and Milam had attracted down there." Till-Mobley & Benson, *Death of Innocence*, p. 261.

8. "Of the jurors polled, not a single one doubted that Milam and Bryant, or the Negroes supposedly with them, had killed Emmett Till." Whitaker, MA thesis, p. 155. See also Herbers & Rosen, *Deep South Dispatch*, p. 53 ("When I arrived in Money, not only was everyone in town talking about Till's disappearance, they also knew exactly who was responsible.").

9. "Willie Reed, having fled to Chicago after his testimony, collapsed after hearing the verdict and was being treated in . . . a South Side hospital." Michaeli, *The Defender*, pp. 331, 581 n. 31, citing *Chicago Defender*, "Till's Mother, Reed Collapse," p. 1.

September Term, 1955—As to the best of my ability. Same being a trial and hearing before the Honorable Curtis M. Swango, Jr., Circuit Judge, Seventeenth Judicial District of this State.

I further certify that the foregoing is a true and complete transcript of the record of proceedings as made during the trial of this cause.

IN TESTIMONY WHEREOF, I have hereunto set my hand and official signature, this 28th day of October, a.d. 1955.

/s/ James T. O'Day Official Court Reporter[10]

---

10. "In the United States and abroad, the trial and acquittal garnered much scrutiny and controversy. Defenders of the verdict, particularly in the white southern press, described the trial process as fair and the evidence as weak. Leading Mississippi newspapers strongly criticized the NAACP and its 'sympathizers' for their presence in Sumner, and blamed them for the worldwide condemnation of Mississippians and their justice system. On the other hand, the acquittal galvanized those who viewed it as both a failure of the American legal system and a pivotal event in race relations. The African American press, northern press organizations, and many other groups denounced the verdict and called for nationwide protests and boycotts." Margaret M. Russell, "Reopening the Emmett Till Case: Lessons and Challenges for Critical Race Practice," *Fordham Law Review*, vol. 73 (2005), p. 2101, at pp. 2120–21 (footnotes omitted).

PART IV

Tragedy on Trial

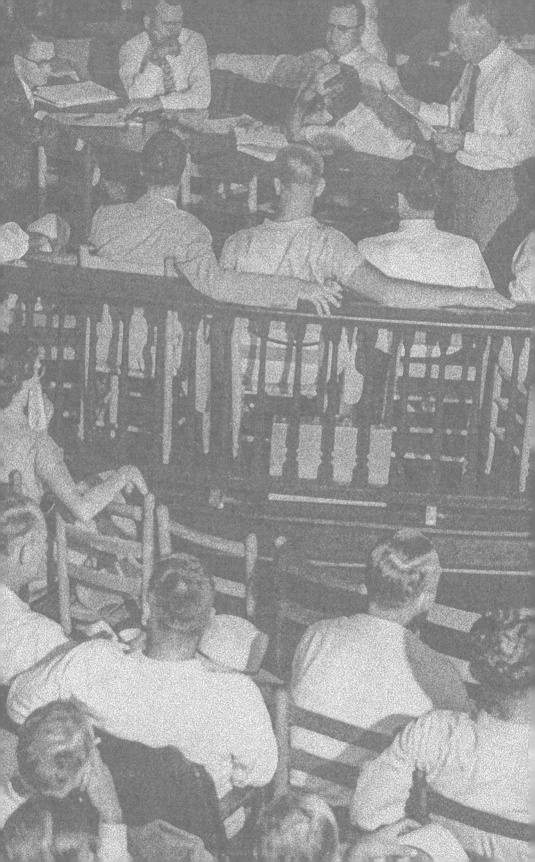

Chapter 13

THE "TICKING TIME BOMB"

Following the "not guilty" verdict, the poet Langston Hughes, writing on the *Chicago Defender's* editorial page, expressed in poignant verse what was in the hearts of people of conscience:

> *Oh, What Sorrow!*
> *Oh, What Pity!*
> *Oh, What Pain*
> *That Tears and Blood*
> *Should Mix Like Rain*
> *And Terror Come Again*
> *To Mississippi.*[1]

Of course, the matter was not over since the legal proceedings had not run their full and final course. Thus, the sorrow and pain to which Langston Hughes gave poetic intensity was not over.

* * * *

A time bomb is ticking away in my Mississippi.
—DR. T.R.M. HOWARD (1956)[2]

After the trial but while the defendants were on bail pending a grand jury hearing on the kidnapping charges against them, rumors of all kinds circulated. "The verdict gave rise to rumors that Till might still

---

1. Hughes, "Langston Hughes Wonders Why No Lynching Probes," p. 4.
2. Foreword by Dr. T.R.M. Howard, in Olive Arnold Adams, *Time Bomb: Mississippi Exposed and the Full Story of Emmett Till*, Mississippi Regional Council of Negro Leadership (1956), p. 6.

be alive. Sheriff H. C. Strider . . . said he heard Till was in Detroit but added 'as far as knowing anything definite, I don't know it.'"[3] Such unfounded rumors notwithstanding, at least two things were obvious:

1. the defendants were guilty of murder,[4] and
2. the jury would acquit both of them no matter what the evidence.[5]

Thus, what was really on trial, and what preordained the result in the case, was a way of life, a master-servant heritage. In this year after *Brown v. Board of Education*, there was enormous pushback against those forces that sought to change the southern way of life—namely, the long-held southern tradition of white supremacy and all its necessary infrastructure, such as segregation, Jim Crow laws, voting and jury-selection laws, and the protection of white women's "virtue."

Though not always explicit as to the evidence admitted into the record, what was otherwise apparent in the court of public opinion and doubtlessly in the minds of the jurors was the specter of sexual assault. The precipitating incident, the alleged touching and the whistle, occurred at the Bryant Grocery and Meat Market. Carolyn Bryant was purportedly a victim of sexual assault at the hands of a Black "man": the obvious reference was to Till, though the defense's legal strategy

---

3. "Bryant and Milam Released on $10,000 Bonds: Appearance Before Grand Jury November 7," *Greenwood Commonwealth*, September 30, 1955, p. 1.

4. "The trial was bizarre in [many] respects. At no time did the five defense attorneys even ask the brothers [privately] if they were guilty. 'My wife kept asking me if they did it,' said one attorney, 'and I didn't want to have to lie to her. I just told her I didn't know.'" Whitaker, "A Case Study in Southern Justice," p. 207.

5. The purported reason for the verdict as explained by one juror was that "generally everyone reached the conclusion that the body was not definitely identified." It was also stated that "[w]e had a picture of the body with us in the jury room, and it seemed to us the body was so badly decomposed it could not be identified." Tyson, *The Blood of Emmett Till*, pp. 180, 255 nn. 11, 13, citing Herbers, "Not Guilty Verdict in Wolf Whistle Murder Trial," p. 1, and *Chicago Tribune*, September 24, 1955. "Hugh Whitaker . . . returned half a dozen years later and interviewed nine of the twelve jurors. He found that not one had ever doubted that my Milam and Bryant had killed Emmett Till, and only one had entertained Sheriff Strider's suggestion that the corpse might not have been Till's. . . All of the jurors Whitaker interviewed agreed that the sole reason they had voted 'not guilty' was because a black boy had insulted a white woman, and therefore her kinsmen could not be blamed for killing him." Tyson, *The Blood of Emmett Till*, p. 180.

prevented her from mentioning his name lest she contradict her husband's pretrial statement that, when they brought Till to her, she said he was not the one and the boy was released. This was less a legal argument than it was one designed to further inflame the jury—thus, the reference to it in the defense's closing arguments. But more was needed. For, while Bryant and Milam had beaten the murder charges, they still had to face the *kidnapping* charges against them. To the extent that they had any defense on that count, if tried, they would have to argue that they went to Moses Wright's house where they *asked* Till to come with them to the market to be identified. Since the defendants were not tried for kidnapping, the defense team in the murder trial had to skirt around that issue.

* * * *

In that the kidnapping charges were still pending even after the murder verdict was rendered, Judge Swango announced that the prosecution had requested that the kidnapping charges be dropped *as far as Tallahatchie County was concerned*, since those charges fell within the jurisdiction of Leflore County, where the kidnapping occurred.[6]

In the confusion of it all, what went largely overlooked (save for what was said in the Black press) was the question of whether others had aided and abetted in the kidnapping and murder. At trial, Willie Reed testified there were *other* white men at the shed in addition to J. W. Milam—but who? Suspects included

1. Roy Bryant;
2. Leslie Milam (brother of J. W. and half-brother to Roy Bryant: in 1974 he confessed on his death bed that he was involved in the murder);
3. Edward Milam (J W.'s brother);
4. Melvin Campbell (J. W.'s brother-in-law—many years later Carolyn claimed that Melvin, not J. W., shot Emmett);

---

6. See Porteous, "Next: 2 Face Kidnap Charges," p. 1. "After Swango thanked the jury, defense counsel moved to dismiss the kidnapping charges on the grounds that jurisdiction rightly belonged to Leflore County. Prosecutors and the judge agreed, and Milam and Bryant were bound over to Sheriff Smith." Gorn, *Let the People See*, p. 174.

5. Elmer Kimball (J.W.'s good friend was at the kidnapping scene and probably at the murder scene);

6. Hubert Clark (another friend of J.W.'s who was probably at the murder scene).[7]

And what about the young Black men who worked for Milam and were in his pickup? Might they have held Emmett down in the back of the truck and cleaned up the murder scene? Suspects included

1. Henry Lee Loggins (who continued throughout his life to deny his presence at the crime scene);

2. Levi Collins;[8]

3. Willie Hubbard;[9] or

4. Otha Johnson[10] (who, just before dying in 2003, confessed to his son of his involvement).[11]

In the end, none of these men testified at trial. None was charged with kidnapping. Their links to the crimes surfaced mainly in the Black press and in interviews in later days.

---

7. Anderson, *Emmett Till*, p. 375.

8. James L. Hicks, "Reporter Tells It All," *Los Angeles Sentinel*, October 4, 1955, pp. 1–2. But see "Negroes Deny Any Knowledge of Slaying," *Greenwood Commonwealth* (AP), October 4, 1955, p. 8.

9. Joe Willie Hubbard (c. 1928–?) "was alleged by T.R.M. Howard to have been with J.W. Milam and Roy Bryant in the murder of Emmett Till. This claim was also put forth by two other writers who published investigative pieces on the murder in 1956. See Olive Arnold Adams in *Time Bomb: Mississippi Exposed and the Full Story of Emmett Till*, and Amos Dixon (pseudonym) in a series of articles in the *California Eagle* (although Adams uses the pseudonym 'Herbert' for Hubbard). Although Willie Reed and Henry Loggins recently recalled having once known Hubbard, no one knows what happened to him." Anderson, "Who's Who in the Emmett Till Case."

10. Otha Johnson Jr. (1934–2002) "was, according to his son, with Roy Bryant and J.W. Milam on the night they kidnapped and murdered Emmett Till, as stated in the FBI report of its 2004–2006 investigation. He may have been one of four black men seen by Willie Reed on the back of a truck on the morning of Till's murder." Anderson, "Who's Who in the Emmett Till Case."

11. See Beito & Beito, *T.R.M. Howard*, pp. 166–70.

Chapter 14

KIDNAPPING CHARGES
NEW GRAND JURY EMPANELED—
NO INDICTMENTS

There was no lack of evidence....
Somewhere along the line something went wrong—
and it was a shameful, evil wrong.

—Editorial, *Chicago Daily Sun-Times*[1]

After the defendants were acquitted of murder, "Milam and Bryant were turned over to Leflore County authorities and taken to Greenwood, Mississippi jail charged with kidnapping Emmett Till." County Judge Charles Pollard "will set bail" at a bond hearing.[2] At that brief hearing, Judge Pollard "read the court order stating that the men, having entered pleas of 'not guilty' to the kidnapping charges, 'and the court having heard and considered the evidence and being duly advised in the premises, is of the opinion that said defendants should be and they are hereby bound over to await the action of the grand jury of this county.' They were then released on bonds of $10,000 each [since kidnapping, unlike murder, was a bondable offense]. . . . On the day that Milam and Bryant were released from jail, the Criminal Division of the US Department of Justice quietly made a request for an investigation into the Till case, explained FBI assistant director Alex

---

1. Editorial, "Darkness in Mississippi," *Chicago Daily Sun-Times*, November 11, 1955, p. 37.
2. Kempton, "2 Face Trial as 'Whistle' Kidnappers."

Rosen, 'in order that we may be in a position to determine whether the Civil Rights Statute is involved.'"[3] The week-long or so investigation related to the question of whether Henry Lee Loggins and Levi Collins had been illegally seized and incarcerated by any local officials in order to prevent them from testifying in the Till trial. If so, that would constitute a violation of federal law (18 U.S.C. § 242[4]). After interviews with prosecutor Robert Smith, Sheriff Strider, and his deputy, and a highway patrol investigation, it was determined that there was insufficient evidence to conclude that Loggins and Collins had been wrongfully detained by local officials during the trial. With that, that investigation ended.[5]

Meanwhile, Moses Wright left his home and belongings and went to New York to start a new life.[6] Nonetheless, he "promised Sheriff George Smith that he would be back in Greenwood on November 7 when the Leflore County grand jury took up [the] kidnapping charges. . . . 'You won't even have to issue a subpoena for me,' Wright told Smith."[7]

---

3. "Bryant and Milam Released on $10,000 Bonds for Appearance Before Grand Jury," *Greenwood Commonwealth* September 30, 1955, p. 1; Helen Shearon, "Bryant and Milam Freed Under Bond," *Memphis Commercial Appeal* October 1, 1955, p. 1, and Anderson, *Emmett Till*, pp. 177–78 (re FBI investigation). See also "Bryant, Milam Released Under $10,000 Bond in Emmett Till Kidnapping," *Jackson Daily News*, September 30, 1955, p. 1 (noting bond had been paid by "wealthy planters"); Houck & Grindy, *Emmett Till*, p. 125 (noting that "[b]oth men were 'congratulated' upon release by none other than Sheriff George Smith").

4. "Whoever, under color of any law, statute, ordinance, regulation, or custom, willfully subjects any person in any State . . . to the deprivation of any rights, privileges, or immunities secured or protected by the Constitution or laws of the United States, or to different punishments, pains, or penalties, on account of such person being . . . by reason of his color, or race, than are prescribed for the punishment of citizens, shall be fined under this title or imprisoned not more than one year, or both. . . ." Note that this law applies only to government officials and not private persons such as Milam and Bryant.

5. Anderson, *Emmett Till*, p. 178. In 1962, "J. J. Breland, told graduate student Hugh Stephen Whitaker . . . that Collins and Loggins had [secretly] been kept in jail [in another county] during the trial" at the behest of Sheriff H. C. Strider. *Ibid.*, p. 379.

6. After the trial, Moses Wright left for Middle Island, New York, where he was to begin work at the Bair Lustgarten Farms and Nurseries. Paul Burton, "'Old Man Moses' Sells Out, He'll Move to New York," *Clarion-Ledger*, September 26, 1955, p. 1; Houck & Grindy, *Emmett Till*, p. 117.

7. Gorn, *Let The People See*, pp. 218, 346 n. 1.

On November 8, 1955, a Leflore County grand jury was empaneled to consider the kidnapping charges against the defendants. The matter, heard in closed court, was presented to the grand jury by Stanny Sanders[8] and John J. Fraser Jr., with no defense counsel present as is the norm. Circuit Judge Arthur Jordan presided.[9] The twenty-member, all-white male grand jury panel[10] heard testimony from four witnesses:

1. Moses Wright (2:20 p.m., approximately five minutes),

2. Willie Reed[11] (3:18 p.m., approximately twenty minutes)

3. Deputy Sheriff John Ed Cothran (3:34 p.m.)

4. Sheriff George Smith

5. Moses Wright recalled (4:03 p.m., approximately two minutes)

→ TOTAL GRAND JURY HEARING TIME: about three hours[12]

Neither Elizabeth Wright (who witnessed the kidnapping) nor the two boys who were with Emmett at the house that night testified (the latter were in Chicago).

---

8. Stanny Sanders (1919–1971) "of Indianola, Leflore County, was a district prosecutor who worked on the kidnapping case against J. W. Milam and Roy Bryant. He later served on the defense team during the 1964 murder trials of Byron De La Beckwith, accused killer of civil rights leader Medgar Evers. The library at Mississippi Delta Community College is named after him."

9. Anderson, *Emmett Till*, p. 240; Houck & Grindy, *Emmett Till*, p. 116.

10. The panel consisted of the following men: June Broadway (foreman), Charles W. King, John Herbert Burrett, George A. Richardson, G. H. Banks, Roy L. Kelly Jr., Mike J. Ballas, Dewey B. Watson, R. V. Howard, S. B. Taylor, J. V. Guess, Dexter Deaton, William B. Colvin, H. V. Carpenter, Frank W. Truitt, Frank Thach, U. S. Upchurch, David E. Nichols Jr., Donald M. Miller, and W. G. Somerville. "Grand Jury Is Selected Today," *Greenwood Commonwealth*, November 7, 1955, p. 1.

11. Dr. Howard arranged to relocate Reed to Chicago and afterward had him return to testify before the grand jury regarding the kidnapping charges. Thereafter, he left for Chicago. Gorn, *Let The People See*, pp. 196–97.

12. Anderson, *Emmett Till*, p. 205; Gorn, *Let The People See*, p. 220. Recall that "Bryant had admitted to the kidnapping when he was questioned by Leflore County Sheriff George Smith. Milam admitted to it when he was questioned by the Sheriff's deputy, John E. Cothran." Till-Mobley & Benson, *Death of Innocence*, p. 204.

WHAT WENT ON WITH
THE KIDNAPPING GRAND JURY

Did Emmett Till die in vain?
—Chicago Defender (1955)[13]

"They kept inferring that I just wanted to start trouble," Moses Wright said of the grand jury after the hearing. "Then they asked me a lot of questions about why I left Mississippi. I told them that J. W. Milam had threatened me, but they didn't believe me. I knew when I left the room they weren't going to do anything to those men."[14]

Willie Reed recounted "that the jury tried to confuse him by showing him several photos and told him to pick from them which ones were Emmett Till."[15]

On November 9, 1955, a spokesperson for the grand jury made a public announcement in front of the courthouse with press and television reporters capturing it all: "The Leflore County Mississippi grand jury in Greenwood adjourned just a short while ago and did not return an indictment in the Emmett Till kidnapping case."[16] With that the defendants beat both charges—no grand jury was ever empaneled again to consider whether they should be indicted for kidnapping. The constitutional doctrine of double jeopardy applies only when one has been *tried* for a crime. Since the defendants were never indicted and tried for kidnapping, another grand jury could have indicted them. Though another judge, at another time, could impanel a grand jury to consider indicting the defendants on kidnapping charges, that never occurred despite calls to do so.[17] Mamie Bradley was shocked: "I don't know what

---

13. "World Eyes Mississippi Grand Jury," *Chicago Defender*, November 12, 1955, p. 1.

14. Anderson, *Emmett Till*, p. 209.

15. *Ibid.*

16. Quoted in *Let the World See*, ABC docuseries, episode 2 (January 13, 2022) (newsreel footage); Sam Johnson, "Bryant and Milam Not Indicted for Kidnapping Emmett Louis Till," *Greenwood Commonwealth* (AP), November 9, 1955, p. 1; "Grand Jury Declines to Indict Bryant and Milam," *Greenwood Commonwealth*, November 9, 1955, p. 1; "End of Kidnapping Case," *Greenwood Commonwealth*, November 10, 1955, p. 1.

17. See Tell, *Confessional Crises and Cultural Politics*, pp. 73–74, 76.

to say. I don't see how they could fail to indict those men."[18] Moses Wright, then in Seattle speaking at an NAACP event, spoke frankly in summing up his sense of it all: "Mississippi hasn't got any law."[19]

The grand jury's conclusion was, to say the least, most strange and highly suspect. Recall that the first grand jury, in Tallahatchie County, concluded that there was ample evidence to indict Bryant and Milam for kidnapping. Add to that all the evidence amassed at the murder trial, which buttressed the guilt of the two defendants on this score. That abundance of evidence was confirmed by two witnesses who *saw* the kidnapping and by two sheriffs. Therefore, the Leflore grand jury was either already predetermined to exonerate Bryant and Milam or impermissibly swayed by then released news reports concerning the execution of Emmett's father for rape and murder while he served overseas in World War II.[20]

There was also Sheriff George Smith's most curious response to it all: "I've been in the business for 22 years and I know what you can get and what you can't get," he told reporters. And then he added, "I don't think . . . the Negroes wanted an indictment. They want something to hold up as an example of injustice to keep attacking us on." As Elliot Gorn has observed, "The charge was false and absurd. This hardly seemed the same man who acquitted himself very professionally throughout the initial investigation and murder trial. . . ."[21] Two years later, Smith told a *Jackson State Times* reporter, "I hate to even mention the case. . . . I don't ever want my name printed again in connection with the people involved in this case."[22]

Finally, though Chicago NAACP attorney William Henry Huff had early on threatened to sue the defendants (and Carolyn Bryant and

18. "2 Free in Till Kidnapping: Case Declared Closed," *Evening Star*, Washington, D.C., November 10, 1955, sect. A, p. 33.

19. "Jurors Refuse to Indict 2 as Till Kidnappers," *Chicago Tribune*, November 10, 1955, p. 2, quoted in Michaeli, *The Defender*, p. 332.

20. Anderson, *Emmett Till*, pp. 193–94, 383–84 nn. 36 & 37, p. 440 n. 116 (the headline in the *Jackson Daily News* read "Till's Dad Raped 2 Women, Murdered a Third in Italy").

21. Gorn, *Let The People See*, pp. 221–22, 347 n. 12.

22. Al Kuettner, "After Two Years, Few Talk About the Till Case," *Jackson State Times*, August 28, 1957, in Mississippi State Sovereignty Papers (filed November 17, 1958).

Leslie Milam) each for $100,000 in damages if they were acquitted,[23] nothing came of the threat, and understandably so given the state of things in Mississippi.[24] Then there was the question raised by NAACP executive secretary Roy Wilkins: "[S]ince Mississippi jurors have determined that Milam and Bryant did not kidnap and murder Till, who did commit the crimes?"[25] That question, the answer to which was evident to all, was left unaddressed by the law in 1955 and for all time thereafter.

---

23. George W. Brown, "Mrs. Bradley Plans Suits," *Pittsburg Courier*, October 22, 1955, p. 1.

24. "Speedy Trial Planned in Kidnap-Slaying Case," *Greenwood Commonwealth*, September 7, 1955, p. 1; Till-Mobley & Benson, *Death of Innocence*, p. 208 (the suit never came to pass owing to the belief that "it would be futile after the jury acquittal in Sumner and the grand jury decision [not to indict the defendants for kidnapping]. . . .").

25. "End of Kidnapping Case Where Leflore Concerned," *Greenwood Commonwealth*, November 10, 1955, p. 1.

PART V

Justice (Still) Delayed—
The Unending and Tortured Story of Emmett Till

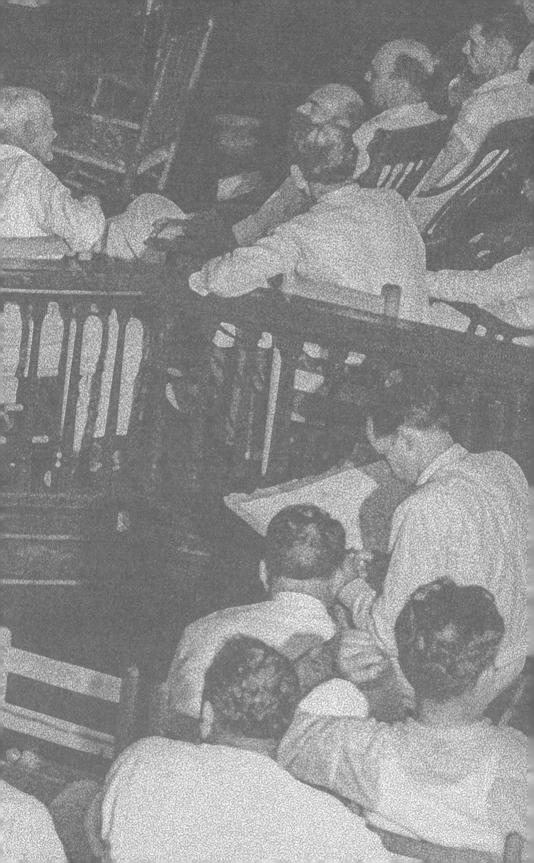

Chapter 15

THE "SHOCKING STORY" AND THE ART OF DECEPTION

His murder remained a case of injustice.

—KHALIL MUHAMMAD (2022)[1]

For all the untruths and half-truths in the trial transcript, it does provide some meaningful points of reference by which to judge what did or did not occur on the night Emmett Till was first kidnapped and thereafter murdered. If truth be known, and as stated earlier, everyone knew that Bryant and Milam were guilty as originally charged.[2] In that respect, though the defense, aided by Sheriff Strider, had blurred the truth beyond recognition, there was still enough evidence presented that the defendants *and others* were criminally culpable. But even that measure of truth would soon be tortured thanks to the devious actions of a freelance writer working in tandem with the lawyers for the defense. In the process, the truths of the trial succumbed to the revisionist accounts that would subsequently appear in the popular press. Incredibly, while those false accounts were being crafted, the wheels of law were still turning, as a grand jury in another county had to determine the defendants' guilt on charges of kidnapping. What that meant is that the revisionist accounts had to be presented in such a way and duly mindful of what had been offered into evidence at the trial so as not to incriminate the two defendants when it came to kidnapping. It

---

1. *Let the World See*, ABC docuseries, episode 3 (January 22, 2022).
2. "[F]ew whites in Sumner disputed [the] contention that J. W. Milam and Roy Bryant were guilty. But the locals invariably replied, 'The jury knows better than to do anything to them.'" Nichter, "'Did Emmett Till Die in Vain?,'" p. 43 n. 42.

was a tall task, but one that the defense team and the freelance writer executed with great cunning.

* * * *

Not long after the trial, a writer named William Bradford Huie wedged his way, with cash in hand, into the offices of John Whitten and J. J. Breland, two of the defense's attorneys. It was the start of a secret exploit designed to redefine the history of the Black boy whose badly brutalized body was fished out of the Tallahatchie River. That violation of the truth—perpetuated by Huie and a cadre of co-conspirators—stands as an enduring symbol of the varied evils of racial injustice in modern America.

The lead defense lawyers (Breland and Whitten) had a strong interest in having Huie write their story: "[B]ecause they were segregationists, [they] wanted Huie to write his article. Huie knew this." In an October 18, 1955, letter to newspaper editor Basil L. Walters, "he confided . . . that Breland and Whitten went along with his plan because they thought his story would help their segregationist cause: 'Publication of this story, with all its revolting details, is exactly what Breland's group in Mississippi *wants*.'"[3] The idea of white sovereignty over "Negroes," especially those who offended white women, was reason enough to conspire with Huie to manufacture a "shocking story" of the most brutal kind of bigotry.

On October 12, 1955, Huie wrote to Roy Wilkins, then president of the NAACP. He wanted the NAACP to fund a proposed book project on the murder of Emmett Till. He assured Wilkins that he had already lined things up with the defendants' lawyers and was certain he could get confessions. "[U]sing nothing but facts," he stressed, "I can dramatize the abduction, torture, and murder of that boy in a way that will be more explosive than *Uncle Tom's Cabin*—and a lot more honest."[4] Nothing, however, came of it.

At the time of Till's murder, Huie was a 45-year-old freelance writer, a man skilled in the art of making secret deals that generated sensa-

---

3. Tell, *Confessional Crises and Cultural Politics*, pp. 78, 193 n. 63.
4. Gorn, *Let the People See*, pp. 235–37, 351 nn. 3, 7.

tional headlines. His scheme, now known in the trade as "checkbook journalism," involved paying sources for information. Huie's records reveal that he "paid Milam and Bryant's lawyers an advance of $1,260 [and agreed to pay] 10 percent of the net profits of the story for arranging a secret rendezvous in which the killers could tell their story."[5]

Not long after the jury handed down its "not guilty" verdict, Dr. T.R.M. Howard traveled to the Dexter Avenue Baptist Church (where Martin Luther King Jr. and Rosa Parks were in the audience), among other places, to talk about the Till murder.[6] Meanwhile, William Bradford Huie was on a different mission. He left the Holiday Inn in Greenwood, Mississippi, en route to meet with the defense lawyers. He had an idea, a plan, as to how the entire Till murder might be framed. As described by Devery Anderson, Huie arrived at 8:00 a.m. but didn't leave until around 1:00 p.m. He came with promises of money for the acquitted defendants and their lawyers and others who spoke to him, albeit on his own terms.[7] "Following the secret interview, he returned to his room at the Holiday Inn and dashed off an exuberant letter to Daniel D. Mich, editorial director of *Look* magazine:

> I have just returned from Sumner where I spent an almost unbelievable day in Whitten's office—with Bryant and Milam. We have reached a verbal agreement on all points; and they have told me the story of the abduction and murder. This was really amazing, for it was the first time they have told this story of the abduction and murder. Not one of their lawyers

---

5. Dave Tell, "The 'Shocking Story' of Emmett Till and the Politics of Public Confession," *Quarterly Journal of Speech*, vol., 94, no. 2 (May 2008), pp. 156–78 n. 14, citing William Bradford Huie letter to Dan Mich, October 23, 1955, The William Charvat Collection of American Fiction, The Ohio State University Libraries. The 2006 FBI report stated that "Bryant and Milam were paid $1,500 each for the interview, with their attorneys receiving $1,000." Famous Trials, "The Emmett Till Case: The FBI Report," p. 86. See also Parker Jr. & Benson, *A Few Days Full of Trouble*, p. 121 ("Huie was paid $7,500 from *Look* for the first publication and another $5,000 for second rights. He also was paid $25,000 by United Artists for a screenplay that never was made into a movie. He paid Milam and Bryant a total of $3,000 and their lawyers, Breland and Whitten, a total of $1,260. The money reportedly paid to Milam and Bryant in 1955 amounts to a little more than and $29,000 in today's [2023] dollars.") (footnotes omitted).

6. Anderson, *Emmett Till*, pp. 217–18.

7. *Ibid.*, pp. 224–32.

had heard it. . . . Perhaps I am too close to appraise it—but I can't see how it can miss being one of the most sensational stories ever published.[8]

In an August 1979 interview for the documentary *Eyes on the Prize*, Huie declared:

> [W]e had this strange situation because we're meeting in the library of this law firm. Milam and Bryant are sitting on one side of the table, and John Whitten and I sitting on the other side of the table. Now they're . . . going to tell me the story of why and how they killed the boy. I'm not doing the questioning. Their own lawyer is doing the questioning. And he's never heard their story. Not once. He defended [them though] he didn't ask them to sit across there and tell that story to him before he defended them. [9]

Thereafter, Huie emphasized that he was going to verify everything, locales and all:

> He [Whitten] becomes more interested—as interested in the story as I am. I just sit there, and I tell them, I said, "Now I'm going to make notes. And then during the day, I'm going to do two things. I'm going to be roughing out this story, and I'm also going where you say you went and I'm going to find evidence. You say you found this gin fan that you hung around his neck in a certain place. I'm going over there and find—I look around and find where you got that gin fan." "Well, okay, you'll find it right there." And I did that.[10]

As the suspense built, Huie outlined some of the key legal points relating to his *portrayals* of Milam and Bryant rather than paying them for what they actually said to him:

---

8. Tell, *Confessional Crises and Cultural Politics*, p. 63.

9. Interview with William Bradford Huie, conducted by Blackside, Inc., August 1979, for *Eyes on the Prize: America's Civil Rights Years (1954–1965)*. Washington University Libraries, Film and Media Archive, Henry Hampton Collection: http://digital.wustl.edu/e/eop/eopweb/hui0015.1034.050williambradfordhuie.html. These transcripts contain material that did not appear in the final program.

10. *Ibid*.

And I said, "Now, at the end of five days we're going to work here. I'm coming here at night to see you during the day. I'm going to be writing and going around and verifying. At the end of five days, I'm going to have something roughed out, and you bring your wife in here, who's involved, and I want all three of you to initial every page and to tell me that that's true and to tell Mr. Whitten that that's true. And I'll have a lawyer here too by then. And then I'll pay you $4,000. And I have the right to portray you in a film as the murderers by name with live actors as the murderers and that's what I'm paying you for. I'm not paying you for telling me the story." And, um, so that's how, that's how we got it. We, uh, I then—no one knew—I didn't go there for any particular magazine.[11]

Yet the best evidence of Huie's true intent is not to be found in what he said in the 1979 interview quoted above but rather in the 1955 "Consent and Release" agreement, which he persuaded J. W. Milam to sign. Among other things, that release—presumably seen and approved by the editors of *Look*—contained the following declarations:

1. "I have also read and fully understand this general rough outline and notes which are to be the basis for the article or story which Mr. Huie proposes to write, which are attached hereto, initialed by me and hereby made a part of this Consent and Release."

2. "This [Consent and Release Agreement] includes the right to report any or all of the details of my private life and that of my family, and to describe me, my character, and actions in such a manner as Mr. Huie, in his sole judgment, believes to be accurate. *This includes the right to portray me as one of those persons who abducted and killed* the Negro, Emmett Till, and to portray me, through the use of live actors, in any and all dramatic adaptations of the work." (Emphasis added.)[12]

---

11. *Ibid.*

12. "Consent and Release" agreement, signed by J. W. Milam, in Ohio State University Huie Papers. This document, from the William Bradford Papers at Ohio State University, was kindly shared with me by Professor David Tell.

Notice that even *before* the grand jury met in November 1955, Milam had admitted in this signed document that he had consented to allow Huie to portray him as the one who "abducted" (kidnapped) Till. This portrayal, however, was not to be understood as a *confession*, as the following passage from the "Consent and Release" agreement makes clear:

> The foregoing consent is in no way to be regarded or considered as an *admission* by me, express or implied, that I am a killer or possessed any other reprehensible characteristics, criminal or otherwise, which Mr. Huie may attribute to me, but is merely intended, for the consideration herein expressed, to irrevocably waive any right of legal action which I . . . might have by reason of anything contained in the work . . . against Mr. Huie or against anyone else he authorizes to print, publish, dramatize, circulate, distribute . . . or otherwise adapt the work in whole or part. . . .[13]

In other words, Huie bargained for the right to *portray* Milam however he liked ("in his sole judgment"), provided he did not have Milam's *admitting* to being the killer. That is, the *Look* story could contain no actual admission or confession of guilt, though it could imply such by way of Huie's portrayal. It was a fine line, but Huie managed to work it out—with the blessings of the editors of *Look*. So fine was that line that after the *Look* article was published Milam told a reporter that he didn't "know a damn thing about it, and you can quote me on that. . . . I never saw anyone named William Bradford Huie that I know of. . . . I never made any statements like that to anyone." Bryant took a different tack: "It's false."[14] Even so, *Look*'s general counsel, John F. Harding, defended the accuracy of the story.[15] Of course, all such statements were made mindful of an agreement for cash ("$3,500 to be paid jointly to Roy Bryant, Carolyn Bryant, and myself") that was to be kept *secret*:

---

13. *Ibid.* (Emphasis added.)

14. In his book *Wolf Whistle*, on page thirty-eight, Huie quotes J. W. Milam: "I shot him then. Just one shot . . . with a soft-nosed bullet. I would have caught him between the eyes, but just as I fired he sorta ducked his head and the bullet caught him at the right ear."

15. Quoted in Houck & Grindy, *Emmett Till and the Mississippi Press*, p. 150.

This Consent and Release is also given upon the express condition that the existence of the instrument and the fact of my cooperation with Mr. Huie in writing the work *will not be revealed publicly* unless I, my wife, Juanita, or another member of my family, and/or Roy Bryant, his wife, Carolyn, or another member of Mr. Bryant's family and/or anyone acting on my, our, or their behalf, should institute legal action against Mr. Huie, or any printer, publisher, producer, circulator, distributor, exhibitor, advertiser or promoter of the work. . . .[16]

Huie had a theory he wanted to be endorsed: that the defendants, Roy Bryant (whose wife was at the center of the case) and J. W. Milam, only meant to whip Till for whistling at Bryant's wife, Carolyn. "But they went too far and in a drunken state killed him."[17] Would Huie's main sources do their part and confess? Maybe. After all, the defendants could describe their homicidal actions free of fear because double jeopardy prevented them from being retried for the killing. The lawyers wanted money and the defendants needed it—so Milam and Bryant would "confess" to killing Till and "reveal" how it happened, or so Huie's story was publicized to stoke interest in it.

Huie knew the journalism world. He had been a reporter for the *Birmingham Post* and later, in 1950, was an editor at *American Mercury* magazine. While there, he shrewdly pumped up its circulation. Now, five years later he was on his own with grander plans. He was angling to sell a big story to *Look*, if only he could get all his paid sources to come along for the sensational ride.

The convoluted lies began with Huie's 1956 *Look* magazine article[18] followed by another *Look* article in 1957.[19] Both were later collected, expanded, and embellished in his 1959 tell-all book, *Wolf Whistle*. Years later, Huie's handiwork wedged itself into the celebrated *Eyes on the Prize* documentary, which featured Huie narrating his account of the murders.

---

16. *Ibid.* (Emphasis added.)

17. Anderson, *Emmett Till*, p. 226.

18. William Bradford Huie, "The Shocking Story of Approved Killing in Mississippi," *Look*, January 24, 1956, p. 48.

19. William Bradford Huie, "What's Happened to the Emmett Till Killers?" *Look*, January 22, 1957, p. 64.

There were obstacles. Huie's tale had to veer in and out of the truth to avoid raising fresh problems for the defendants. Even though they were guilty beyond all doubt, Milam and Bryant had been acquitted of murder. But *kidnapping* was another matter. The problem for Milam and Bryant was that they were never tried for kidnapping, so they were still legally vulnerable to a kidnapping charge. And there were *other* players who took part in the crimes who could find themselves criminally culpable for aiding in the kidnapping and murder. Huie also needed to falsify information about various locations to avoid revealing evidence of crimes committed there by the defendants' friends or employees. The effect of Huie's handiwork "was so profound that it pushed aside any serious discussion of accomplices for decades to come."[20]

All of this maneuvering meant that Huie had to get signed waivers,[21] omit key facts, exclude key witnesses and accomplices, relocate the scenes of certain acts,[22] rewrite what Till said and did, and rework how the boy was murdered,[23] or risk getting people in legal trouble. He also had to weave his story so that it *appeared* that the defendants had confessed to crimes without expressly saying so.[24] "[T]echnically speaking," as Dave Tell has emphasized, the *Look* story "was simply a magazine article written in the third person with no direct admissions of guilt. Legally there were no grounds for treating it as a confession without the testimony of Huie,"[25] which he refused to do. And to be on the safe side, Huie passed a copy of the galley proofs over to defense lawyer

---

20. David T. Beito & Linda Royster Beito, "Why It's Unlikely the Emmett Till Murder Mystery Will Ever Be Solved," History News Network, April 26, 2004, http://hnn.us/articles/4853.html.

21. See Tell, *Confessional Crises and Cultural Politics*, pp. 64–65.

22. See Tell, *Remembering Emmett Till*, pp. 63, 64–73.

23. According to the 2006 FBI report, Milam's actual account of how he murdered Till differed from the one portrayed by Huie: "About killing Till: 'Well, we done whopped the son of a bitch, and I had backed out on killin' the mother fucker . . ' ' . . . and we gonna take him to the hospital. But we done whopped that son of a bitch. I mean, it was, the, carryin' him to the hospital wouldn't have done him no good (laughs).' 'Put his ass in the Tallahatchie River.'" Famous Trials, "The Emmett Till Case: The FBI Report," p. 92. In other words, Emmett was probably already dead by the time they took him to the river ("Believing Till was dead, they placed his body in the back of a pick-up truck and drove around trying to figure out what to do with the body."). *Ibid.*, p. 93.

24. See Tell, *Confessional Crises and Cultural Politics*, pp. 67–77.

25. *Ibid.*, p. 77.

John Whitten "for the attorney to look over,"[26] just to be sure that the defendants and their lawyers remained beyond the boundaries of the law. "In other words, under the watchful eye of their attorneys, the killers signed off on a *particular* version of Till's murder."[27] Huie, the two defendants, and their lawyers performed this duplicitous dance with great care, each mindful of his own self-interest.

* * * *

I'm just in the business of establishing truth whenever possible.
And I have to believe that the truth is good.

—WILLIAM BRADFORD HUIE[28]

There are a lot of things to contest in Huie's account.

—CHRISTOPHER METRESS[29]

On January 24, 1956, *Look* published Huie's article "The Shocking Story of Approved Killing in Mississippi."[30] The editors provided an enticing preface, noting, "In the long history of man's inhumanity to man, racial conflict has produced some of the most horrible examples of brutality. The recent slaying of Emmett Till in Mississippi is a case in point." Then the editors, possibly unaware they were hoodwinked by Huie, issued a baldly false statement: "The editors of *Look* are convinced that they are presenting here, for the first time, the real story of that killing—the story no jury heard and no newspaper reader saw." So read advertisements they placed in various newspapers, the ones that proclaimed to "reveal *the truth* about the Emmett Till killing . . . [along with] the brutal step-by-step *full account* of what happened that fateful night. . . . Don't miss the shocking story in *Look*. It will be magazine history the minute it hits the newsstands."[31] Indeed, it did make history,

---

26. Anderson, *Emmett Till*, p. 233.

27. Tell, *Confessional Crises and Cultural Politics*, p. 78 (emphasis added).

28. Quoted in "William Bradford Huie and His Story of the Murder of Emmett Till," video, Lights, Camera Alabama, 2015 (narrated by Christopher Metress), https://www.lightscameraalabama.com/bjXA2eqVRC.

29. *Ibid.*

30. The following week, Chicago's *Daily Defender* published Mamie Till-Mobley's "Spent Sheltered Life Under Mama," January 31, 1956, p. 4 (describing Emmett's early life and habits).

31. Tell, *Confessional Crises and Cultural Politics*, pp. 70–71.

but for many of the wrong reasons. Even so, readers rushed to read the sensational story. *Look* printed six million copies, and then the article was reprinted for eleven million *Reader's Digest* subscribers.[32]

The crafty Huie did not disclose his sources in the article, except when in the few instances he quoted Milam. He did not name names and was circumspect in identifying places. "[O]ne of its most conspicuous features is the range of characters who do not appear. Levi Collins, Henry Lee Loggins, Willie Hubbard, Willie Reed, Frank Young,[33] Mandy Bradley, Add Reed, Medgar Evers, James Hicks, Clark Porteous, and even T.R.M. Howard—by October of 1955, all of these were commonly cited names in the various stories of Emmett Till."[34] Huie was also sly in arranging a pre-publication leak to a journalist friend at an African American newspaper.[35] His plan: build advance interest in his "exposé" concerning "heretofore unrevealed" information about the murder. His hope: legitimize his account while his journalist friend had no idea he was being played. That said, a grinning J. W. Milam was somewhat pleased with Huie's crafty handiwork: "I will say one thing for the article. It was written from a Mississippi viewpoint."[36]

Then there was Huie's 1959 book, *Wolf Whistle*,[37] which was yet another expanded and twisted account of the Till murder story purportedly based on the defendants' alleged confessions.[38] The book pledged

---

32. Tyson, *The Blood of Emmett Till*, p. 196.

33. Frank Young (c. 1920–?) "was a field worker who volunteered names of accomplices of J. W. Milam and Roy Bryant in the kidnapping and murder of Emmett Till to Dr. T.R.M. Howard, as well as leads to possible witnesses. It was intended that he testify on behalf of the prosecution at the Milam–Bryant murder trial, but for whatever reason, he left the courthouse and did not testify." Anderson, "Who's Who in the Emmett Till Case." See also Beito & Beito, *T.R.M. Howard*, pp. 135–37, 140.

34. Tell, *Remembering Emmett Till*, p. 58. Tell also lists Huie's omission of Leslie Milam, "J. W.'s brother and Roy Bryant's half-brother," who just before he died in 1974 "confessed to a local minister . . . that he was involved in the murder of Emmett Till." *Ibid.*, citing Anderson, *Emmett Till*, p. 335.

35. See *ibid.*, pp. 244–45.

36. Houck & Grindy, *Emmett Till and the Mississippi Press*, p. 150.

37. William Bradford Huie, *Wolf Whistle and Other Stories*, New York: Signet Books/The New American Library (1959).

38. As to the alleged confessions of the two defendants, there were notable differences between what Huie wrote for his *Look* article and later for his book. See Sharon Monteith, "The Murder of Emmett Till in the Melodramatic Imagination: William Brad-

to tell "the startling truth behind the murder of the fourteen-year-old Negro boy Emmett Till." Its scandalous Signet cover screamed "true stories of desire, greed, and deception by a fearless reporter." The author would expose the "startling stories of warring human passions" that led to Till's murder. With suspenseful verve, he would reveal how in 1955 a "brash Negro boy from Chicago was murdered" for whistling at "a white woman and why his killers went unpunished."

Sometimes one can judge a book by its cover, not for the promises it makes but for the lies it tells. The claim of "truth stranger than fiction" left a clue as to how much of Huie's exposé was true. Answer: not much. In addition to the *Look* articles and the book *Wolf Whistle*, Huie set out to make a full-length film; he had arranged for a film company to "dramatize" the story.[39] But as Devery Anderson also noted, "the film never came to fruition and the reasons for that are unknown."[40]

* * * *

It has been said that the "murder of Emmett Till was one of the seminal moments in our nation's civil rights movement[,] and the failure to bring his murderers to justice remains a stain on America's record of reconciliation."[41] It has also been observed that Huie's version of the Till tragedy "assumed the status of the 'primary' account of Till's murder for a very long time."[42] But in light of Huie's significant fabrications, how do we remember the events that defined such decisive moments? And how, for that matter, can there ever be any reconciliation? To an-

---

ford Huie and Vin Packer in the 1950s," in *Emmett Till in Literary Memory and Imagination*, eds. Harriet Pollack & Christopher Metress, Baton Rouge: Louisiana State University Press (2008), p. 43.

39. "Huie intended to tell the Till story, yet again, in a motion picture contracted to RKO, a natural choice of Hollywood studios for this racial-legal thriller, clearly, hoping that a current event that had already aroused public interest could be translated into a provocative mix of Old South clichés and sensationalism, a natural exploitation film. . . . But the film option was shelved. . . ." Monteith, "The Murder of Emmett Till in the Melodramatic Imagination," p. 36.

40. "The script still sits unproduced in Huie's papers at Ohio State University." Anderson, *Emmett Till*, pp. 242–43.

41. Amita Nerurkar, "Lawmakers Want 1955 Mississippi Murder Reopened," CNN, April 13, 2004 (quoting U.S. Senator Chuck Schumer).

42. Monteith, "The Murder of Emmett Till in the Melodramatic Imagination," p. 40.

swer such questions is to ask yet others: What is the life of a lie? And if that lie lives long enough, can it ever be erased from the public mind? Indeed, disproving a lie can be more difficult than proving the truth.

As early as 1956, in an interview in the *Chicago Defender*, Mamie Till-Bradley railed against Huie's "lies about my child." And reporters for the *Defender, Tri-State Defender, California Eagle, Jet*, and other African American papers and magazines continued to hone in on the flaws and falsehoods in Huie's accounts. There was, for example, an investigative series of articles published in the Los Angeles-based *California Eagle* written by Amos Dixon (a pseudonym).[43] This series, corroborated by a booklet by Olive Arnold Adams titled *Time Bomb: Mississippi Exposed and the Full Story of Emmett Till*, prompted a delegation of the National Council of Negro Women to arrange a meeting with J. Edgar Hoover and his assistant "to find out why Collins and Loggins had never been interviewed by the Criminal Division. . . ."[44] Nothing came of it, however, and the matter was dropped. Despite such accounts and attempts, Huie's contrived reports too often shaped the American mindset.

In *Wolf Whistle*, Huie appeared to take the high road, noting that "humanity needs crusaders. . . . [It] also needs understanding. And truth . . . promotes understanding."[45] But the truth was no essential part of Huie's agenda. "Huie's telling of the Till story is the single most influential account of the lynching ever produced. It is also the most misleading," said Dave Tell, the principal investigator of The Emmett Till Memory Project[46] and author of *Remembering Emmett Till*. "Virtually every sentence is false, intended to line the pockets of, in descending order, Huie, the defense lawyers, and the murderers."[47]

*   *   *   *

43. See Amos Dixon (pseudonym), "Mrs. Bryant Didn't Even Hear Emmett Till Whistle," *California Eagle*, January 26, 1956, sect. A, p. 1; "Milam Master-Minded Emmett Till Killing," *California Eagle*, February 2, 1956, sect. A, p. 1; "Till Case: Torture and Murder," *California Eagle*, February 9, 1956, sect. A, p. 1; "Till Case: Torture and Murder," *California Eagle*, February 16, 1956, sect. A, p. 1; "South Wins Out in Till Lynching," *California Eagle,* February 23, 1956, sect. A, p. 12.

44. Anderson, *Emmett Till*, pp. 246–49.

45. Huie, *Wolf Whistle*, p. 46.

46. https://tillapp.emmett-till.org.

47. Author interview with Dave Tell, 2020.

Even before the trial and the Huie stories, the murder of Emmett Till made it painfully clear there was a compelling need for federal intervention when it came to lynching people of color. Three days after the murder, the editors of the *Chicago Defender* telegrammed the White House and informed President Eisenhower and his staff of the killing: "A Chicago boy, Emmett Louis Till, 14, was kidnapped and lynched in Mississippi this week, would you let us know if your office has plans to take any action with reference to this shocking act of lawlessness." A similar request from NAACP lawyer William Henry Huff called on the FBI to investigate the case,[48] though it went unanswered.[49]

Thereafter, a delegation from the NAACP—one that included Roy Wilkins, Thurgood Marshall, and Medgar Evers—met with Justice Department officials. The Department responded that it lacked jurisdiction to get involved in a state murder case.[50] Despite a subsequent plea from Mamie Till-Bradley,[51] the president[52] kept quiet as his administration puzzled over what to do. After the trial, Eisenhower "asked FBI director J. Edgar Hoover to present a classified briefing about race on March 9, 1956, for the cabinet meeting at which the Administration would decide whether to approve, modify, or cancel [Attorney General Herbert] Brownell's plans to ask Congress for a new civil rights bill. No legislation had passed since Reconstruction."[53] But Hoover nixed the idea. "The FBI would tell the White House the boy's mother was being used by the Communist Party, and should not get a response, not even

---

48. International News Service, "Investigation of Boy's Death Ordered by Mississippi Governor," *Atlanta Daily World*, September 2, 1955, p. 1.

49. Louis Lautier, "Official Is Cautious on Lynch-Murder Commitment," *Atlanta Daily World*, September 9, 1955, p. 1. See also Anderson, *Emmett Till*, pp. 177, 199–201, 253. See also, "Civil Rights: The Emmett Till Case," Dwight D. Eisenhower papers, National Archives: https://www.eisenhowerlibrary.gov/research/online-documents /civil-rights-emmett-till-case.

50. Till-Mobley & Benson, *Death of Innocence*, p. 154.

51. "Till's Mother Says Ike Ignored Pleas for Help," *Chicago Defender*, November 10, 1956, p. 10.

52. Ten years earlier, General Eisenhower signed the execution order for Louis Till (Emmett's father) after he had been convicted of murdering a woman and raping two other women. Till-Mobley & Benson, *Death of Innocence*, p. 202.

53. Taylor Branch, *Parting the Waters: America in the King Years: 1954–1963*, New York: Simon & Schuster (1988), p. 181.

a letter of condolence from Eisenhower."[54] Thereafter, on November 22, 1955, E. Frederic Morrow[55] sent a White House internal memo warning of the "dangerous situation that is now afflicting the country" in light of the Till murder and the acquittals of the two defendants. "I feel the time has come," he stressed, that it might be advisable for Governor Adams[56] or Vice President Nixon to invite to Washington a dozen prominent Negro leaders in the country and sit down and exchange views on this very dangerous problem." The time, however, had not come. So, too, was the case with the Senate Subcommittee on Civil Rights, which declined to hold an investigative hearing into Till's murder.[57]

The result was that even a year after the murder and after nationwide protests, no federal legislation emerged to deal with racially motivated crimes or lynchings; such matters and murders remained largely under state or local control. That meant the evil that took the life of Emmett Till and so many others like him persisted almost unchecked.

*   *   *   *

> [T]he emotional impact of the case made it a rallying
> cry for change.
> —DEVERY S. ANDERSON[58]

Whatever else might be said of the verdict in the murder trial, the grand jury's shocking refusal to indict on the charge of kidnapping, and Huie's subsequent altered accounts of the abduction and killing, one thing is certain: they all helped to keep the tragedy in the public mind *and* in the minds of lawmakers. It was against that backdrop, and the continued opposition to *Brown v. Board*, that Congress (by a vote of 286–126 in the House and 72–18 in the Senate) passed and the president signed the Civil Rights Act of 1957. This was the first federal civil rights law passed by Congress since the Civil Rights Act of 1875. Several members of Congress "discussed and debated the Till case on the

---

54. Booker & Booker, *Shocking the Conscience*, p. 58.

55. Morrow was a former NAACP field secretary and the first African American to hold an executive position at the White House.

56. Llewelyn Sherman Adams was White House chief of staff, 1953–1958.

57. See Till-Mobley & Benson, *Death of Innocence*, p. 201.

58. Anderson, *Emmett Till*, p. 344.

floor of Congress."[59] Among other things, the Act established the Commission on Civil Rights and the Civil Rights Division in the Department of Justice.

Of course, southern opposition, though unsuccessful, was fierce—aggressive enough to kill some provisions of the act as initially proposed. Among others, Mississippi Congressman Jamie Whitten (cousin of defense counsel John Whitten) railed against calls for the need for legislation in light of the verdict in the Till murder trial: "It is easy to second guess," he emphatically declared, "either a jury or judge when one does not know all the facts or even when the facts are known."[60] True to form, South Carolina Senator Strom Thurmond "made a last-minute attempt to kill the bill by initiating a filibuster . . . that lasted for twenty-four hours and eighteen minutes (still the longest filibuster in the history of the Senate). . . ."[61]

*　*　*　*

I'm not in the law enforcement business, I'm just in the
business of establishing truth whenever possible.

—WILLIAM BRADFORD HUIE[62]

Over the years, praise for Huie's reputation and his reporting on the Till murder came from many quarters. "I think anyone who is a historian of that period is very fortunate if they happen to come across a moment when William Bradford Huie is at work because then you really get a window into the human drama of the situation," is how Juan Williams judged him. "You're not just dealing with dry facts and sort of historical accounts of what happened and who went where and who

---

59. U.S. Congress, *Congressional Record*, 84th Congress, 2d Sess., 1957, CII, Part 7, p. 8644, 8705, 9194, 9211, 9189; Part 8, p. 10998; Part 10, pp. 13182, 13338, cited in Whitaker, "A Case Study of Southern Justice," p. 185. See also Whitfield, *A Death in the Delta*, pp. 82–83.

60. Quoted in Anderson, *Emmett Till*, p. 346.

61. *Ibid.*, p. 347.

62. "I'm in the Truth Business: William Bradford Huie," YouTube, produced by The University of Alabama, Center for Public Television and Radio (with a grant from the Alabama Humanities Foundation, a state program of the National Endowment for the Humanities), uploaded by Bookmark with Don Noble, https://www.youtube.com/watch?v=XfRkbblwL E (at 2:45–2:50 and 55:26–55:31 minutes).

said what," he added.[63] Thus, the man and his Till story became a part of the fourteen-part documentary *Eyes on the Prize: America's Civil Rights Movement* that aired on PBS and elsewhere in 1987. The series used archival footage, stills, and interviews to tell its compelling stories. The award-winning documentary made Emmett Till "part of the freedom struggle's origin story for a national audience [and] placed his name squarely in its pantheon of heroes . . . [It] moved him from private remembrance back into the public realm."[64] The newsreel footage from the time (replete with clips from the open-casket funeral in Chicago) could not help but alert viewers anew to the evils of racism.

It was ironic. In some disturbing respects, "*Eyes on the Prize* legitimized Huie's account. It even put an aged, white-haired Huie on the screen, and gave him the privilege of narrating Till's story for yet another generation."[65] That same year, Juan Williams released a companion book[66] by the identical name. Here, too, the book quoted the "famed" Huie, which meant that his take on it all not only survived but thrived. The creators, however, were unaware of the inaccuracies in his accounts, though they had some "nagging suspicion[s]"[67] Huie had played them, much as he had done decades earlier with the editors of *Look* (assuming, of course, they were also unaware of his true intent). In the end, he was establishing *his* truth "whenever possible."

* * * *

63. *Ibid.* (at 1:45–2:04 minutes).

64. Gorn, *Let the People See*, p. 272.

65. Tell, *Remembering Emmett Till*, pp. 67–68.

66. Juan Williams, *Eyes on the Prize: America's Civil Rights Years, 1954–1965*, New York: Viking Penguin (1987).

67. As the producer and cinematographer of *Eyes on the Prize* has written, "So early in the process . . . there was a nagging suspicion that Bill Huie's account of the murderers' version was not entirely trustworthy." Jon Else, *True South: Henry Hampton and* Eyes on the Prize, *the Landmark Television Series that Reaffirmed the Civil Rights Movement*, New York: Viking (2012), pp. 242, 243.

How long must we wait for the Federal Government to act?
—*Chicago Defender* (1955)[68]

THE FBI REPORT

Despite the emergence of much-needed federal legislation such as the Civil Rights Acts of 1960, 1964, and 1968, the truth of the Till murder remained hidden even after the passage of these and other laws. That truth did not really surface until 2006, two decades after Huie died in late November 1986. Thanks in different ways to the persistent, astute, and talented efforts of Alvin Sykes, Congressman Bobby Rush, Keith Beauchamp, and Stanley Nelson,[69] among others, a path[70] was found by which the FBI could open an investigation[71] in 2004 into the kidnapping and murder. When the FBI released its 2006 "Prospective Report," it invalidated, among other things, much in Huie's story. Its findings, done under the direction of FBI agent Dale Killinger[72] of Oxford, were based on numerous interviews and an autopsy of Till's exhumed body, the latter of which created something of a stir.[73]

All of this and more, much more, was set out in its Prospective Report of Investigation on the kidnapping, murder, and aftermath of the Till tragedy. That 2006 public report was but a small part of eight thousand pages of investigative materials. Save for some pages acquired under FOIA requests, the lion's share of those pages was not publicly re-

---

68. "What You Can Do About the Disgrace in Sumner," *Chicago Defender*, October 1, 1955, in Metress, *The Lynching of Emmett Till*, p. 127.

69. See Monroe Dodd, "Pursuit of Truth," Kansas City Public Library (2014) (online); Luke Nozicka, Cortlynn Stark, & Bill Lukitsch, "Alvin Sykes: Force of Nature in Fight for Justice," *Kansas City Star*, March 21, 2021; Terr Wagner, "America's Civil Rights Revolution: Three Documentaries About Emmett Till's Murder in Mississippi," *Historical Journal of Radio, Film and Television,* vol. 30., no. 2 (June 2010), p. 87 (one catalyst for the investigation were two then recent documentaries: Stanley Nelson's Peabody-winning *The Murder of Emmett Till* (PBS American Experience, 2003) and Keith Beauchamp's *The Untold Story of Emmett Till* (ThinkFilm, 2005)); "Chicago Rep. Bobby L. Rush Calls for Emmett Till Murder Investigation," *Jet* (March 8, 2004), p. 36.

70. Anderson, *Emmett Till*, pp. 300–302, 312–14.

71. *Ibid.*, pp. xxiii, 283, 313–17, 337, 343.

72. Agent Killinger spent a year-and-a-half investigating the case; it took another five months to write the report, which totaled 178 pages, along with voluminous additional pages of attachments.

73. See Anderson, *Emmett Till*, p. 323 (Jesse Jackson, Sr., opposed the exhumation).

leased. And even the FOIA-acquired pages, like all the rest, were heavily redacted and do not contain the names of informants.[74]

The prospective report and the FOIA materials obtained from the investigation did, however, provide important information relating to the trial transcript and likewise to the claims made by Will Bradford Huie in his *Look* magazine articles and his subsequent *Wolf Whistle* book.

According to the report, a "comparison of the *Look* magazine statements and the evidence reveals a number of inconsistencies or differences."[75] Those "inconsistencies" amounted to no fewer than ten significant falsehoods in Huie's accounts. Four related to the size of the murder party, which Huie said consisted of two people, probably to protect others. Six of the other falsehoods concerned the purported locales of the various crimes.[76] For example, contrary to what Huie reported and largely consistent with Willie Reed's trial testimony, there were four white men in the cab and three black men in the bed of J. W. Milam's pickup truck parked on the Shurden plantation. (Huie tried to dismiss Reed's account as mistaken identity.[77]) And as previously noted and again contrary to what Huie claimed, Milam and Bryant did *not* act alone; they had accomplices.

* * * *

Armed with the right facts one can change the way history is written and encourage a nation to reevaluate that history.

—KEITH A. BEAUCHAMP (2008)[78]

Though the FBI's prospective report had undermined much in the Huie accounts, those accounts lived on in so many quarters, both in popular culture and historical narratives. Once the dye of his falsehoods had been poured into the beaker of the public mind, it became almost impossible to remove. Huie's first *Look* article "created and per-

---

74. See Gorn, *Let the People See*, p. 363 n. 1.

75. Famous Trials, "The Emmett Till Case: The FBI Report," p. 8.

76. See Tell, *Remembering Emmett Till*, pp. 75–76, 156, 158–60; Anderson, *Emmett Till*, pp. 227–49.

77. See "Approved Killing in Mississippi," *Tri-State Defender*, January 14, 1956, p. 1.

78. Keith A. Beauchamp, Foreword, in Houck & Grindy, *Emmett Till*, p. ix.

petuated a false narrative that has unfortunately been given authoritative status."[79] His various fabrications became imprinted on the culture;
they shaped public perceptions of the Till murder and trial and propa-
gated a false narrative for decades. That *Look* article was "such a smash-
ing sensation that few noted just how much of it diverged from previous accounts, both by the Black press and Huie himself."[80] Its perceived
accuracy was so great that Representative Charles Diggs (an African
American who attended the trial) inserted it into the *Congressional Record*.[81] In 1988, nearly a quarter-century after the release of Huie's accounts, Stephen Whitfield observed that "[t]he chief account of Till's
murder remains the article [written by] William Bradford Huie"[82] and
the extended book account that followed it. Since then, thanks to the
FBI report and some scholarly commentaries, there has been some,
though not enough, change in how the Till tragedy is perceived. For
example, as late as 2010, Emmett's cousin, Simeon Wright, who was
with him that fateful day, felt compelled to declare that Huie had "fabricated" facts and conversations. In his book on the Till kidnapping
and murder, Wright quipped, "[I]f the truth was [Huie's] business
when he wrote, he should have been bankrupt."[83] By that measure, had
the law permitted defamation against the dead, Mamie Till-Mobley
might well have prevailed in her libel lawsuit against Huie.[84]

---

79. Anderson, *Emmett Till*, p. 244.

80. Beito & Beito, *T.R.M. Howard*, p. 166.

81. *Ibid.*, p. 167.

82. Whitfield, *A Death in the Delta*, p. 51.

83. Wright, *Simeon's Story*, p. 133.

84. See Till-Mobley & Benson, *Death of Innocence*, pp. 215–16 (defamation lawsuit
dismissed).

Epilogue

TILTING TOWARD TRUTH
A COVENANT WITH OUR PAST

In 1973, the courtroom where the murder trial took place was renovated, modernized, and sanitized in ways that left few traces of the chamber in which Judge Swango presided over the case of *State of Mississippi v. J. W. Milam and Roy Bryant*. In the course of those renovations, the cotton gin fan that had been stored in the courthouse basement was first discarded and then disappeared. Moreover, "Mississippi officials never retained the transcript of the murder trial in their files." Even back then, the apparent lone surviving copy of the transcript given by J. J. Breland to Hugh Steven Whitaker was destroyed in a "basement flood in the 1970s."[1] It was all a part of the erasure of the history surrounding the trial.[2] (Fortunately, as previously noted, a largely complete copy of the trial transcript resurfaced decades later.)

---

1. Anderson, *Emmett Till*, pp. 325, 338, 353.

2. Many years later, the courtroom was restored to its original appearance. *See* Tell, *Remembering Emmett Till*, pp. 101, 122–24, 134–35. See also Parker Jr. & Benson, *A Few Days Full of Trouble*, p. 66 ("During the month of April 2017, . . . North Marion High School students . . . traveled 13 hours and 865 miles from their hometown in Farmington, West Virginia. They came to the Delta to reenact the Emmett Till murder trial in the restored Tallahatchie County Courthouse in Sumner, Mississippi, where it all took place between September 19 and 23, 1955."). Today, Benjamin Saulsberry of the Emmett Till Interpretive Center gives tours of the courtroom and hosts talks about the trial. See also Stephanie Markham, "Kankakee 8th Graders Reenact Historic Till Murder Trial," *Daily Journal* (Kankakee, Ill.), Jan. 21, 2023. The trial was also reenacted in Chicago in 2023. See Blair Ingenthron, "Photos: First Look at Collaboraction Theatre Company's TRIAL IN THE DELTA: THE MURDER OF EMMETT TILL," Broadway World: Chicago, Feb. 11, 2023, https://www.broadwayworld.com/chicago/article/Photos-First-Look-at -Collaboraction-Theatre-Companys-TRIAL-IN-THE-DELTA-THE-MURDER-OF -EMMETT-TILL-20230211.

In 2007, state senator David Jordan proposed a resolution calling on Mississippi to apologize for the handling of the Emmett Till murder investigation and trial; his official request also called for "reconciliation in this matter." The proposed resolution was killed in committee.[3]

In June of that year, the United States Senate Judiciary Committee issued its report in connection with the Emmett Till Unsolved Civil Rights Crime Act.[4] In that report,[5] U.S. Senator Patrick Leahy (D-VT) declared, "The brutal murder of Emmett Till was one of the most infamous acts of racial violence in American history, yet his killers were never punished." In that regard, he added, "Mississippi comprises the most significant percentage of unsolved civil rights cases. . . ." Given that, it was deemed "imperative to bring murderers to justice, even if several years or decades have passed since these heinous crimes were committed. Doing so brings truth, closure, healing, and reconciliation to the affected families, friends, communities, and our nation as a whole. The goal of the legislation, he stressed, was to bring "the perpetrators of racially motivated murders to justice. . . ." Nonetheless, even a half-century after the Till murder, that goal had yet to be achieved in the case, either in a legal or merely symbolic way.

That same year, Joyce Chiles, the district attorney for Mississippi's Fourth Judicial District, presented evidence before a Leflore grand jury to reopen the Till investigation, this time by way of a manslaughter indictment against Carolyn Bryant Donham. After hearing the evidence, which included a PowerPoint presentation by FBI agent Dale Killinger, the nineteen-member biracial jury composed of men and women deliberated for slightly over an hour before returning a unanimous "no bill," which then closed yet another chapter in the Till legal proceedings.[6]

* * * *

3. Anderson, *Emmett Till*, p. 351.

4. The law was reauthorized in the Emmett Till Unsolved Civil Rights Crimes Reauthorization Act of 2016.

5. 110th Congress (1st session, June 22, 2007, report no. 110-88, calendar no. 211, report accompanying Senate Bill 535).

6. Anderson, *Emmett Till*, p. 340; Jerry Mitchell, "Fact, Fiction, of Till's Murder," *Jackson Clarion-Ledger*, February 18, 2007; Jerry Mitchell, "Grand Jury Issues No Indictments in Till Killing," *Jackson Clarion-Ledger*, February 27, 2007.

Though Carolyn Donham had an extraordinary ability to avoid criminal prosecution, she was unable to avoid being interviewed by the FBI. Claiming she had no "conscience to clear," time and again she offered next to nothing to assist them. Much the same held true for Juanita Milam, save for this statement: "Uh, the only way I can figure it is that she [Carolyn] did not want to take care of the store. She thought this wild story would make Roy take care of the store instead of leavin' her with the kids and the store. This is a female point of view."[7]

In late August 2020, the FBI closed its investigation of the murder of Emmett Till.[8] Then in December 2021, the FBI closed a re-investigation into the murder.[9] In its December 6, 2021, press release, the Department of Justice reported the following:

> Today, Assistant Attorney General Kristen Clarke, Acting U.S. Attorney Clay Joyner, District Attorney W. Dewayne Richardson, and career attorneys and employees from the Civil Rights Division and the FBI met with members of Till's family, including a family member who had been a witness to the events preceding Till's abduction and murder. The purpose of the meeting was to explain the reasons for closing the investigation and to give the family an opportunity to ask questions about the department's investigation and conclusions.
>
> The department conducted the investigation as part of its Cold Case Initiative and pursuant to the passage of the Emmett Till Unsolved Civil Rights Crime Act (Till Act). The Cold Case Initiative is a comprehensive effort to identify and investigate racially motivated murders committed decades ago. As in all federal cases, the department may only bring a case with laws that were enacted at the time of the crime and are still within the statute of limitations. However, under the

---

7. Gorn, *Let the People See*, pp. 284–85, 286, 365 n. 23 (quoting FBI report).

8. See Jerry Mitchell, "Justice Department Calls It Quits on Emmett Till Probe. No Charges," MCIR (Mississippi Center for Investigative Reporting), August 28, 2020, https://www.mississippicir.org/news/justice-department-calls-it-quits-on-emmett-till-probe-no-charges.

9. See "Federal Officials Close Cold Case Re-Investigation of Murder of Emmett Till," United States Department of Justice, December 6, 2021, https://www.justice.gov/opa/pr/federal-officials-close-cold-case-re-investigation-murder-emmett-till.

Till Act, the federal government is authorized to assist state and local jurisdictions with investigating and, where possible, prosecuting such crimes.[10]

Neither federal law nor newly released alleged facts could change the outcome:

Because there were no federal hate crime statutes at the time of Till's death, the case was not then opened for federal investigation. In 2004, the department opened an investigation into Till's murder as part of its Cold Case Initiative, but determined after a thorough review that it lacked jurisdiction to bring federal charges.

The department reopened the matter in 2017 after a professor [Timothy B. Tyson[11]] alleged in a book he had written that a white woman [Carolyn Bryant Donham], who was a witness to crucial events leading up to Till's abduction and murder, had recanted her previous accounts of those events. In response, the department and the FBI examined whether the woman had recanted and, if so, whether she had information that would allow the prosecution of any living person.[12]

Later in that press release, the DOJ further explained why it was unable to proceed criminally against Carolyn Bryant Donham:

The woman, however, when asked about the alleged recantation, denied to the FBI that she ever recanted her testimony and provided no information beyond what was uncovered during the previous federal investigation. Although lying to the FBI is a federal offense, there is insufficient evidence to prove beyond a reasonable doubt that she lied to the FBI when she denied having recanted to the professor. *There is insufficient evidence to prove that she ever told the professor that any part of her testimony was untrue.* Although the professor represented that he had recorded two interviews with

---

10. *Ibid.*
11. Tyson, *The Blood of Emmett Till.*
12. United States Department of Justice, "Federal Officials Close Cold Case."

her, he provided the FBI with only one recording, which did not contain any recantation. In addition, although an assistant transcribed the two recordings, neither transcript contained the alleged recantation. The professor also provided inconsistent explanations about whether the missing recording included the alleged recantation or whether, instead, the woman made the key admission before he began recording the interview.[13]

As to whether or not Donham had lied to federal or state officials, there was this:

> Even if the government could prove that she recanted her prior state court testimony, the federal government could not prosecute her for perjury for her 1955 testimony. Perjury in state court is not a federal offense. Moreover, the statute of limitations, a deadline for bringing a prosecution, expired in 1960 on any state perjury offense. Similarly, the five-year statute of limitations has expired on any claim that she lied to the FBI during the 2004 investigation. However, in closing this matter without prosecution, the government does not take the position that the state court testimony the woman gave in 1955 was truthful or accurate. There remains considerable doubt as to the credibility of her version of events, which is contradicted by others who were with Till at the time, including the account of a living witness.[14]

The 2021 DOJ press release closed with these words:

> The government's re-investigation found no new evidence suggesting that either the woman or any other living person was involved in Till's abduction and murder. Even if such evidence could be developed, no federal hate crime laws existed in 1955, and the statute of limitations has run on the only civil rights statutes that were in effect at that time. As such, even if

---

13. *Ibid.* (Emphasis added.) For an informative account and refutation of the Tyson claim, see Jerry Mitchell, "The Emmett Till lynching has seen more than its share of liars. Is Tim Tyson one of them?," *Mississippi Today* (Aug. 28, 2023).

14. United States Department of Justice, "Federal Officials Close Cold Case."

a living suspect could now be identified, a federal prosecution for Till's abduction and murder would not be possible. . . . [15]

Then in July 2022, after the discovery of the 1955 unserved warrant for Carolyn Bryant's arrest[16] and the unauthorized release of Bryant's memoir,[17] the "Mississippi attorney general's office told the Associated Press it did not plan to prosecute Donham. 'There's no new evidence to open the case back up,' said Michelle Williams, chief of staff for Attorney General Lynn Fitch."[18]

It was over. Carolyn Bryant Donham had escaped the law's long arm. As noted in Chapter 5, there was the cruel and absurd irony of what she wrote in her memoir, which was released in 2022 without her authorization: "No one was ever held responsible for Emmett Till's death. The people that were involved in the unjust and gruesome murder should have been held accountable, but they walked free."[19] The murderous fact, however, was that *all* of Emmett Till's assailants and their collaborators "walked free."

* * * *

Wheeler Parker, still alive in 2023, would be the last of the living witnesses to report on what happened back in August 1955. In a coauthored book[20] released that year, Reverend Parker (then 83) added his important contribution to the historical record. Among other things,

---

15. *Ibid.*

16. See Timothy Bella & DeNeen L. Brown, "Emmett Till's Family Calls for Woman's Arrest after Finding 1955 Warrant," *Washington Post*, June 30, 2022. See also Jerry Mitchell, "Here's the Proof against Carolyn Bryant Donham in the Emmett Till Case. Is It Enough to Convict Her?," MCIR, July 12, 2022, https://www.mississippicir.org/news/heres-the-proof-against-carolyn-bryant-donham-in-the-emmett-till-case-is-it-enough-to-convict-her. See also Chapter 5 note 1, *supra* (regarding federal lawsuit filed to compel sheriff to execute warrant).

17. DeNeen L. Brown, "In Unpublished Memoir, Emmett Till's Accuser Calls Herself 'A Victim,'" *Washington Post*, July 18, 2022. See also Kevin L. Clark, "Emmett Till's Family Says Carolyn Bryant Donham's Unpublished Memoir Is Full of Lies," *Essence*, July 19, 2022, https://www.essence.com/news/emmett-till-accuser-memoir-inaccurate/.

18. Brown, "In Unpublished Memoir."

19. Excerpted from "I Am More Than a Wolf Whistle" by Carolyn Bryant Donham (made public July 2022, though intended to be sealed in the Southern Historical Collection at the University of North Carolina at Chapel Hill until 2036).

20. Parker Jr. & Benson, *A Few Days Full of Trouble.*

Parker was highly critical of Huie's *Look* magazine account of the kidnapping and murder and how it has long been portrayed as "the authoritative Emmett Till source...."[21] That account, he stressed, received such wide, immediate, and long-term attention that few noticed "all the flaws, misrepresentations, and dehumanization in the story."[22] Huie's portrayal neither comported with the facts of the case nor even the defense's arguments as set forth in the trial record.[23] Hence, in "large measure, the Huie piece in *Look* was a work of fiction."[24] Worse still, as Parker emphasized, "[l]ike the murder trial itself, the Huie story indicted Milam and Bryant and then acquitted them."[25]

* * * *

> We must 'carry the weight of memory, regardless of how painful or difficult.'
>
> —LONNIE BUNCH (2021)[26]

> 'Keith, you must continuously tell Emmett's story until man's consciousness is risen; only then there will be justice for Emmett Till.'
>
> —MAMIE TILL-MOBLEY to
> Keith Beauchamp[27]

Why has the history of the Till tragedy been so tortured? Why has it been filled with so much erasure, disregard, failed attempts, and so many falsehoods leaving little breathing room for the truth? First, the law failed and then history failed. Again, why? Was it, in principle, because

---

21. *Ibid.*, p. 113.

22. *Ibid.*, p. 112.

23. See, e.g., *ibid.*, pp. 113–14.

24. *Ibid.*, p. 122.

25. *Ibid.*, p. 115.

26. "Video Clip: Lonnie Bunch Discusses the Legacy of Emmett Till," C-SPAN, Sept. 2, 2021, https://www.c-span.org/classroom/document/?18354. See also Lonnie Bunch, *A Fool's Errand: Creating the National Museum of African American History and Culture in the Age of Bush, Obama, and Trump*, Washington, D.C: Smithsonian Books (2019), p. 27 (discussing the "power and centrality of memory").

27. Keith Beauchamp, "From Emmett Till to Tyre Nichols, Another Wakeup Call to Take Action," Hollywood Reporter, Feb. 14, 2023, https://www.hollywoodreporter.com/news/general-news/tyre-nichols-emmett-till-justice-keith-beauchamp-guest-column-1235324497/.

of what Hermann Göring (then president of the Reichstag) had proclaimed: "The victor will always be the judge"?[28] There is a measure of truth there despite the source.

When a life ends, the unrecorded memories die with it. The evil of oppression and murder is twofold: first, it stops the life and thus ends the prospect of its future, and then it destroys the memorial record of what life had been lived and how it had been lived. The same holds true for a sect, town, or even a civilization. History is written by the oppressors, the victors, and those who have a vested interest in preserving their supremacy over others *and* over time.[29] Central to that control over how history is recorded is denial—the repudiation of any wrongdoing. Coupled with that repudiation is the glorification of history as recounted by the oppressors. In the process, the dead remain dead, as does the history of their suffering.

Recorded history has always been the province of those in power; those whose power first thrusts them into the historical limelight and then darkens the history of the powerless. Far too often, neither historians nor those who cling to their words appreciate the importance of reading between the lines to reveal what has been lost *because* of history. Ironically, too often history tethered to polished documents and power distorts and eradicates the actual history of civilizations, cultures, and human beings.

If the shocking fact of lynchings in Mississippi[30] signified anything, it suggested that the murder of Emmett Till was on track to vanish into oblivion. The past would remain in the past, or so it seemed.[31] Certainly, Sheriff Strider did his best from the outset to make the murder disappear. And he might have been successful except for five things:

28. Quoted in Joe Julius Heydecker & Johannes Leeb, *The Nuremberg Trial: A History of Nazi Germany as Revealed Through the Testimony at Nuremburg*, trans. R.A. Downie, Madison, WI: Greenwood Press (1975), p. 84.

29. See David S. Reynolds, "In the Shadow of Slavery," in *New York Review of Books*, February 24, 2022, pp. 23, 24–25 ("In 2018, . . . U.S. taxpayers spent at least $40 million to support Confederate monuments, including statues, museums, cemeteries, and heritage groups. The history of black people has never received that kind of recognition.").

30. *The Murder of Emmett Till*, documentary (noting some five hundred lynchings before the Till murder trial).

31. See Houck & Grindy, *Emmett Till and the Mississippi Press*, pp. 154, 155 ("for thirty years the [Emmett Till] story did not hold much interest for scholars, playwrights, poets, and especially politicians").

(1) the photographs David Jackson took of the corpse; (2) the circulation of those photos in African American magazines and newspapers; (3) Mamie Till-Mobley's courageous decision to have Emmett's body shipped to Chicago and then to have an open casket funeral; (4) the vital work of T. R. M. Howard and the support from the NAACP; and (5) the Black and mainstream press coverage of it all. As all of that happened, the history that would not have been recorded began to be noticed. During those pinpoints in time, history was not being dictated by the conquerors.

Even so, the force of history, understood as the sovereign prerogative of the powerful, has a way of putting history back on the track of the oppressors. While Roy Bryant and J. W. Milam had little power as individuals, their whiteness did give them domain over people of color. And *that* is what was at stake in the whole Till tragedy from the pretrial falsehoods to the post-trial fabrications. That unchecked and unquestioned power over the other was what history too often records and then perpetuates. The failure of the legal system—from the corruptive influences of the sheriff to the corrosive ploys of the defense lawyers to the contemptible verdict of the jury—is evidence of this. It was the system operating as it too often does. Neither the courage of Moses Wright nor the conviction of Gerald Chatham could change that.

* * * *

Emmett's death . . . was a worldwide awakening. . . .
—MAMIE TILL-MOBLEY (2003)[32]

Mamie Till-Mobley's words ring as true today as when they were first put on display at Emmett's funeral in 1955. And yet America needed to awaken anew, as evidenced by the killings of so many other victims of racism, people such as George Floyd, Rayshard Brooks, Sandra Bland, Breonna Taylor, and Trayvon Martin, to list but a few. Tragedy, after all, only pricks the conscience of those who have a conscience.

---

32. Till-Mobley & Benson, *Death of Innocence*, p. 259. For an informative account of Till-Mobley's legacy, see Brandon M. Erby, "With the Movie 'Till,' Mamie Till-Mobley's Quest to Educate the World About Her Son's Lynching Marches On," The Conversation, Oct. 14, 2022 ("A critical component of Till-Mobley's legacy is how she produced and circulated information about her son's life and death, inside and outside the classroom.").

In the shadow of Bob Dylan's "Blowin' in the Wind" ballad and Dr. King's "I Have a Dream" speech, Sam Cooke held out hope that "A Change Is Gonna Come." But hope—that antidote that saves us from despair—must be buttressed by truth, courage, and a certain resolve to rectify the wrongs of the past, as difficult as that obligation is. And it may be that the times are different. Yet even in changing times, needed measures such as the Emmett Till Antilynching Act[33] have too long lingered in lawmakers' drawers. In that regard, let us enter into the record, and reflect upon, the poignant and profound words of Michael Eric Dyson:

> By choosing to honor the memory of Emmett Till, we make a covenant with our past to own its pain as our responsibility and to forgive its failures only if the wisdom we derive from their doing is made a conscious part of our present pacts of racial peace. After all, the repression of uncomfortable memories of racial calamity and the avoidance of past racial injustice has become all too common and convenient. But the only way old and deep wounds are healed is to confront their existence, and acknowledge their power to inflict even more suffering and harm if they go unchecked.[34]

That is where history, at once honest and horrifying, comes into play. We recreate ourselves when we reconstruct what has been lost to time, what has been buried under falsehoods and obfuscation. Thus we should return to the transcript of *State of Mississippi v. J. W. Milam and Roy Bryant*, but with new eyes and a new mindset. After all, where you stand defines what you see.

Sadly, like so much in the history of race in America, parts of the Till tragedy continue to be shrouded in agonizing doubt. The causes are bigotry, fear, greed, and indifference but also an engrained systemic racism—laws and customs predicated on white supremacy. The defendants lied; the sheriff lied; the accomplices hid; the defense lawyers smothered the truth; the all-white male jury happily bought it; thereafter a second grand jury ignored self-evident facts and refused to indict

---

33. See Appendix below.

34. Michael Eric Dyson, "The Legacy of Emmett Till," *Chicago Tribune*, August 10, 1991.

Bryant and Milam for kidnapping; Huie repackaged and hawked his "truth" wrapped in lies; and Carolyn Bryant Donham tried to run out truth's clock. Everything thereafter echoed down the halls of history even as truth refused to be silenced.

In the end, tragedy took its toll and justice never received its fair measure. Thus did evil manifest itself. And yet something in the human heart simply cannot abide the malice that David Jackson first exposed and Mamie Till-Mobley thereafter courageously revealed to the world. Take heed!

Appendix

THE EMMETT TILL
ANTILYNCHING ACT

The United States needs an anti-lynching law.

—SIDNEY REDMOND (1955), civil rights attorney[1]

"Emmett's lynching shaped my understanding of racism at an early age and deeply affected Black Americans of my generation and those that followed,"[2] is how seventy-six-year-old Congressman Bobby L. Rush (D-IL) framed it sixty-seven years after the Till tragedy. That awareness helps to explain what he had previously told a reporter: "I cannot imagine our nation did not have any federal law against lynching when so many African Americans have been lynched."[3] In 2018, Senator Cory Booker (D-NJ) and then Senator Kamala Harris (D-CA) along with Senator Timothy Scott (R-SC) introduced the Justice for Victims of Lynching Act, which would make lynching a federal crime. Though the measure passed the Senate unanimously in late December 2018, the bill died because it was not passed by the House before the

---

1. "NAACP Urges Anti-lynching Law," *Greenwood Commonwealth* (AP), November 14, 1955, p. 1.

2. Christine Chung, "Congress Honors Emmett Till and His Mother With Gold Medal Vote," *New York Times* December 22, 2022, https://www.nytimes.com/2022/12/22/us/emmett-till-mamie-congressional-medal.html.

3. Debora Berry, "America Has a History of Lynching, but It's Not a Federal Crime. The House Just Voted to Change That," *USA Today*, February 26, 2020, https://www.usatoday.com/story/news/politics/2020/02/26/emmett-till-antilynching-act-house-vote-bill/4871041002/. Subsequently, Congressman Rush successfully introduced a bill in the House to honor Emmett and his mother with the Congressional Gold Medal. The measure also passed in the Senate. See Christine Chung, "Congress Honors Emmett Till."

115th Congress ended on January 3, 2019. The following year, the House passed the Emmett Till Antilynching Act (H.R. 35) by a 410–4 vote. Even so, the successful efforts in the House failed to galvanize the Senate. The *New York Times* reported, "As Congress prepare[d] to wade into a contentious debate over legislation to address police brutality and systemic racial bias, a long-simmering dispute in the Senate over a far less controversial bill that would for the first time explicitly make lynching a federal crime . . . burst into public view."[4] Thus, on June 4, 2020, while protests and civil unrest over the murder of George Floyd were raging nationwide, the Senate considered the matter. Senator Rand Paul (R-KY), however, prevented the measure from being passed when he asked for unanimous consent to pass the bill with the amendment he proposed.

"It would speak volumes for the racial pain and the hurt of generations," Senator Booker objected. Raising his voice, he continued, "I do not need my colleague, the Senator from Kentucky, to tell me about one lynching in this country. I've stood in the museum in Montgomery, Alabama, and watched African American families weeping at the stories of pregnant women lynched in this country and their babies ripped out of them while this body did nothing.'"[5]

Though in 2022 the United States Senate passed a bill to posthumously award the Congressional Gold Medal to Emmett Till and his mother,[6] as of that late date Sidney Redmond's 1955 plea for a national

4. Nicholas Fandos, "Frustration and Fury as Rand Paul Holds Up Anti-lynching Bill in Senate," *New York Times*, June 5, 2020, https://www.nytimes.com/2020/06/05/us /politics/rand-paul-anti-lynching-bill-senate.html.

5. Clare Foran & Lauren Fox, "Emotional Debate Erupts over Anti-lynching Legislation as Cory Booker and Kamala Harris Speak Out Against Rand Paul Amendment," CNN, June 4, 2020, https://www.cnn.com/2020/06/04/politics/anti-lynching-bill-fight -senate-floor-cory-booker-rand-paul/index.html; Ted Barrett & Clare Foran, "Rand Paul Holds Up Anti-lynching Legislation as He Seeks Changes to Bill," CNN, June 3, 2020, https://www.cnn.com/2020/06/03/politics/rand-paul-lynching-legislation/index.html.

6. "Senate Passes Bill to Honor Emmett Till and His Mother," Associated Press, January 12, 2022 ("Sens. Cory Booker, D-N.J., and Richard Burr, R-N.C., introduced the bill to honor Till and his mother with the highest civilian honor that Congress awards. The House version of the legislation is sponsored by Rep. Bobby Rush, D-Ill. He also has sponsored a bill to issue a commemorative postage stamp in honor of Mamie Till-Mobley.").

anti-lynching law remained just that, a plea that seemed destined to linger in the halls of injustice.[7]

Weeks later, however, H.R. 55 was brought to the House for a vote; it was yet another anti-lynching bill introduced by Congressman Rush. The bill, named after Emmett Till, was approved by a 422–3 vote. Three Republicans (Andrew Clyde of Georgia, Thomas Massie of Kentucky, and Chip Roy of Texas) voted against the anti-lynching bill. For Representative Rush it was an occasion for hope: "The House today has sent a resounding message that our nation is finally reckoning with one of the darkest and most horrific periods of our history and that we are morally and legally committed to changing course," he said.[8] Then in early March 2022, the Senate unanimously passed the measure.[9] Congressman Rush saw it as a long overdue action: "Lynching has been a longstanding and uniquely American weapon of racial terror," he said. "Today, we correct this historic and abhorrent injustice."[10] After President Biden signed the bill on March 29, 2022,[11] Senator Booker commented, "[The Act] will not reverse the fear and suffering that

7. Ja'han Jones, "A Medal Is Nice, but Congress Should Honor Emmett Till by Passing Anti-lynching Law," MSNBC, January 12, 2022, https://www.msnbc.com/the-reidout /reidout-blog/emmett-till-medal-congressional-gold-medal-rcna11928. At the state level, in 2021, a bill (§ 145.984) titled the "Emmett Louis Till Victims Recovery Program" was introduced in the house of the Minnesota legislature (sub. 3: "The commissioner shall establish the Emmett Louis Till Victims Recovery Program to address the health and wellness needs of victims of a government-sponsored equal protection violation and the victims' families and heirs by confronting historical trauma that families experience through government-sponsored equal protection violations."). As of March 2022, the bill had not been enacted into law. See Minnesota HF2586, TrackBill, https://trackbill.com /bill/minnesota-house-file-2586-emmett-louis-till-victims-recovery-program-estalished /2107983/.

8. Emily Cochrane, "House Passes Bill to Make Lynching a Hate Crime," *New York Times*, February 28, 2022, https://www.nytimes.com/2022/02/28/us/politics/house-lynch ing-hate-crime.html.

9. Felicia Sonmez, "Senate Unanimously Passes Anti-lynching Bill After Century of Failure," *Washington Post*, March 7, 2022, https://www.washingtonpost.com/politics/2022 /03/07/senate-unanimously-passes-anti-lynching-bill-after-century-failure/.

10. "Rep. Bobby Rush's Emmett Till Antilynching Act Passes U.S. Senate Unanimously," Press Release, March 7, 2022, https://chicagocrusader.com/rep-bobby-rushs -emmett-till-antilynching-act-passes-u-s-senate-unanimously/.

11. See NBC News, "President Biden Signs Emmett Till Anti-lynching Act Into Law," YouTube, March 29, 2022, https://www.youtube.com/watch?v=IYmUmrzj0rE. See also "Remarks by President Biden at Signing of H.R. 55, the 'Emmett Till Antilynching Act,'" The White House, March 29, 2022, https://www.whitehouse.gov/briefing-room/speeches

Black communities endured during those years as this shameful instrument of terror was wielded by white supremacists to intimidate and oppress. But signing the Emmett Till Antilynching Act into law is a necessary step that signals our nation is willing to confront the darkness of its past to move towards a brighter future."[12] The text of the Act is set out below.

To amend section 249 of title 18, United States Code, to specify lynching as a hate crime act.

Be it enacted by the Senate and House of Representatives of the United States of America in Congress assembled,

SECTION 1. SHORT TITLE.

This Act may be cited as the "Emmett Till Antilynching Act."

SEC. 2. LYNCHING; OTHER CONSPIRACIES.

Section 249(a) of title 18, United States Code, is amended by adding at the end the following:

(5) LYNCHING.—Whoever conspires to commit any offense under paragraph (1), (2), or (3)[13] shall, if death or serious bodily injury (as

---

-remarks/2022/03/29/remarks-by-president-biden-at-signing-of-h-r-55-the-emmett-till-antilynching-act/.

12. Senator Cory Booker, Press Release, "Booker Statement on Signing of Emmett Till Antilynching Act into Law," March 29, 2022.

13. 18 U.S.C. §249—Hate crime acts provides in relevant part:

"(a) **In General.—**

(1) **Offenses involving actual or perceived race, color, religion, or national origin.**—Whoever, whether or not acting under color of law, willfully causes bodily injury to any person or, through the use of fire, a firearm, a dangerous weapon, or an explosive or incendiary device, attempts to cause bodily injury to any person, because of the actual or perceived race, color, religion, or national origin of any person—. . . .

(b) (i) death results from the offense; or

(ii) the offense includes kidnapping or an attempt to kidnap, aggravated sexual abuse or an attempt to commit aggravated sexual abuse, or an attempt to kill. . ."

Only Section (a)(1), applies to *race* and hate crimes related to race. In that regard its provisions apply to private persons and governmental agents as well as to crimes committed within a state or those committed interstate. The reason for this expanded cover-

defined in section 2246 of this title) results from the offense, be imprisoned for not more than 30 years, fined in accordance with this title, or both.

(6) OTHER CONSPIRACIES.—Whoever conspires[14] to commit any offense under paragraph (1), (2), or (3) shall, if death or serious bodily injury (as defined in section 2246 of this title) results from the offense, or if the offense includes kidnapping or an attempt to kidnap, aggravated sexual abuse or an attempt to commit aggravated sexual abuse, or an attempt to kill, be imprisoned for not more than 30 years, fined in accordance with this title, or both.

SEC. 3. DETERMINATION OF
BUDGETARY EFFECTS.

The budgetary effects of this Act, for the purpose of complying with the Statutory Pay-As-You-Go Act of 2010, shall be determined by reference to the latest statement titled "Budgetary Effects of PAYGO Legislation" for this Act, submitted for printing in the Congressional Record by the Chairman of the House Budget Committee, provided that such statement has been submitted prior to the vote on passage.

---

age stems from Congress's authority to implement the Thirteenth Amendment, which abolished slavery and seeks to eradicate the "badges and incidents of slavery." Thus, §249(a)(1) would apply to facts such as those in the Till kidnapping and murder case. Subsection (3) also applies to race hate crimes committed in a maritime context.

Finally, "the statute evidences a preference for state prosecution. Federal prosecution requires Justice Department certification that either (a) no state has jurisdiction over the offense; (b) the state where the offense occurred has requested federal prosecution; (c) state criminal proceedings have left the federal interest in eradicating hate crime violence unvindicated; or (d) federal prosecution is 'in the public interest and necessary to secure substantial justice.'" CRS Reports & Analysis, "When Are Violent Crimes Federal Hate Crimes?," June 14, 2016.

14. The new "hate crime" law amends the Matthew Shepard and James Byrd Jr. Hate Crimes Prevention Act of 2009 and prior federal hate crime laws to define lynching as also involving any conspiracy to commit any hate crime that results in death or serious bodily injury. The felony offense includes an enhanced penalty of thirty years and a "kidnapping or an attempt to kidnap" provision if a death results.

ABOUT THE AUTHOR

Ronald Collins is a retired law professor who last taught at the University of Washington Law School, where he was the Harold S. Shefelman Scholar.

After graduating from law school, Collins served as a law clerk to Oregon Supreme Court Justice Hans A. Linde and thereafter as a Supreme Court fellow under Chief Justice Warren Burger. Before teaching law for some three decades, he worked for the Legal Aid Foundation of Los Angeles and the Legal Aid Society of Orange County.

Collins is the author or coauthor of some twelve books and numerous scholarly articles that have appeared in journals such as the *Harvard* and *Stanford Law Reviews* and the *Supreme Court Review.* He is on the editorial board of SCOTUSblog and serves as editor of the weekly blog *First Amendment News* as well as the editor of the online journal *Attention.* He is also co-chair of the History Book Festival and the First Amendment Salons and was selected to be the first Distinguished Lecturer of the Lewes Public Library in Delaware.

Two of his previous books (with David Skover) told the story of a famed comedian and a celebrated poet through the lens of the law: *The Trials of Lenny Bruce: The Fall and Rise of an American Icon* (Sourcebooks, 2002) and *The People v. Ferlinghetti: The Fight to Publish Allen Ginsberg's Howl* (Rowman & Littlefield, 2019).

On the thirtieth anniversary of the Till murder and trial, he published an op-ed in the *Baltimore Sun* (September 23, 1985) titled "Emmett Till: Memories of a Time of Shame." Years later, on November 28,

2005, Collins conducted a public interview, at the Newseum in Washington, D.C., with Robert L. Carter (1917–2012), the lawyer who succeeded Thurgood Marshall as the general counsel of the NAACP and later served as a federal judge. Since then, he has three times taught a class titled "The Emmett Till Story Told Through the Lens of the Law."

He lives with his wife, Susan A. Cohen, in Lewes, Delaware.

ACKNOWLEDGMENTS

"Trial transcripts don't sell!"

That mantra (echoed by agents and editors alike) nearly torpedoed this project. With their eyes fixed on profit in the commercial market, they were indifferent to the historical importance of the trial transcript in the Emmett Till murder case and the need to elaborate on it, replete with additions, corrections, and refutations. And then there was the matter of the post-trial *Look* magazine story and how it had falsely reconfigured history in the service of profit and prominence. Here, too, commercial concerns triumphed over historical importance.

The result of it all was that many doors were closed many times.

There was, however, life after the fainthearted backed away. Fortunately, someone with backbone stepped forward and affirmed with conviction, "Why not? Of course! We'd be honored to publish this book; it needs to be out there." So spoke my publisher and friend KEITH SIPE—a humble man who has devoted his distinguished career to publishing books about law and life. So, to Keith, and LINDA LACY, too, I raise my glass in their honor. The work they do speaks volumes about the amazing people they are. Thanks also to RYLAND BOWMAN and JENNIFER NUZZI for their invaluable editorial assistance and to JENNIFER HILL for typesetting the text of the manuscript.

CONGRESSMAN BOBBY RUSH found his way into my life (thanks to Jamie Raskin) and then graced this book with the relentless and animated spirit of those who suffered and struggled to give life-affirming meaning to racial justice. It is a fitting tribute to the legacy of Emmett and his mother that Reverend Rush should lend his name and words to this project.

And a heartfelt thank you to CONGRESSMAN JAMIE RASKIN for being such a mensch and for his genuine and generous commitment to this project even when his service to the Republic was greatly needed and later when his health was in jeopardy.

I owe a debt of immense gratitude to DEVERY ANDERSON and DAVE TELL—two of the very best Till scholars—whose learned works guided me at countless turns. And both Devery and Dave kindly offered informed feedback on my manuscript. Their scholarship and assistance proved vital to my project.

ALEX LUBERTOZZI is a great guy and a true friend. He has been with me for the publishing ride for some two decades, both as an editor and as a book cover designer. His work always makes mine look better. Alex: May we have yet more rides together!

I also want to recognize REBECCA LOWE of the Lewes Public Library for making it possible for me to teach a class on the Till murder trial—teaching that class disciplined my thinking in ways that greatly helped shape my ideas for this book.

ELIZABETH GRIFFITH and ANN COMPTON parachuted in late in the day and offered important assistance. They were the gateway to Secretary Lonnie Bunch's contribution to this book. Their willingness to lend a helping hand is but one sign of the kind of resolute and caring women they are.

LONNIE BUNCH's help and inspiration proved vital in the closing days. He immediately realized the historical importance of the trial record and the need to explain it. In so many ways, Lonnie has committed himself to shining a true and illuminating light on the Till story and on others like it.

Special thanks also go out to DAVID HADDOCK for his important and thoughtful contributions to this project.

Though I had written about the Till murder decades ago, my renewed interest in the case began in earnest when I visited the Mississippi courthouse where the trial occurred. That visit was the result of a Distant Horizons civil rights tour my wife and I took, a marvelously informative series of events organized by its president JANET MOORE.

Once again, LINDA HOPKINS helped me stay on course even when I was unsure of just what that course was and whether I could ever successfully travel down it.

As always, there is SUSAN A. COHEN who has given so much of her life to allow me to live mine. Her help, bathed in love, humbles me since it is a debt that can never be fully repaid—still, I will try until the end of my days to repay it.

Finally, there is DYLAN COLLINS (our son) who lovingly and expertly acted as my digital publicist in ways entirely consistent with his own real-life commitment to racial justice.

INDEX